# GENDER DIFFERENCES
# AND THE MAKING OF
# LITURGICAL HISTORY

Mapping uncharted territory in the study of liturgy's past, this book offers a history to contemporary questions around gender and liturgical life. Teresa Berger looks at liturgy's past through the lens of gender history, understood as attending not only to the historically prominent binary of "men" and "women" but to all gender identities, including inter-sexed persons, ascetic virgins, eunuchs, and priestly men.

Demonstrating what a gender-attentive inquiry is able to achieve, Berger explores both traditional fundamentals such as liturgical space and eucharistic practice and also new ways of studying the past, for example by asking about the developing link between liturgical presiding and priestly masculinity. Drawing on historical case studies and focusing particularly on the early centuries of Christian worship, this book ultimately aims at the present by lifting a veil on liturgy's past to allow for a richly diverse notion of gender differences as these continue to shape liturgical life.

# LITURGY, WORSHIP AND SOCIETY

## SERIES EDITORS

*Dave Leal, Brasenose College, Oxford, UK*
*Bryan Spinks, Yale Divinity School, USA*
*Paul Bradshaw, University of Notre Dame, UK and USA*
*Phillip Tovey, Ripon College Cuddesdon, UK*
*Teresa Berger, Yale Divinity School, USA*

The Ashgate *Liturgy, Worship and Society* series forms an important 'library' on liturgical theory at a time of great change in the liturgy and much debate concerning traditional and new forms of worship, suitability and use of places of worship, and wider issues concerning interaction of liturgy, worship and contemporary society. Offering a thorough grounding in the historical and theological foundations of liturgy, this series explores and challenges many key issues of worship and liturgical theology, currently in hot debate within academe and within Christian churches worldwide – issues central to the future of the liturgy, to public and private worship, and set to make a significant impact on changing patterns of worship and the place of the church in contemporary society.

Other titles in the series:

*The Theory and Practice of Extended Communion*
Phillip Tovey

*Liturgical Space*
*Christian Worship and Church Buildings in Western Europe 1500–2000*
Nigel Yates

*First Communion*
*Ritual, Church and Popular Religious Identity*
Peter McGrail

*Early and Medieval Rituals and Theologies of Baptism*
*From the New Testament to the Council of Trent*
Bryan D. Spinks

*Reformation and Modern Rituals and Theologies of Baptism*
*From Luther to Contemporary Practices*
Bryan D. Spinks

# Gender Differences and the Making of Liturgical History

## Lifting a Veil on Liturgy's Past

TERESA BERGER
*Yale Institute of Sacred Music and Yale Divinity School, USA*

ASHGATE

© Teresa Berger 2011

Published by
Ashgate Publishing Limited
Wey Court East
Union Road
Farnham
Surrey, GU9 7PT
England

Ashgate Publishing Company
Suite 420
101 Cherry Street
Burlington
VT 05401-4405
USA

www.ashgate.com

**British Library Cataloguing in Publication Data**
Berger, Teresa.
  Gender differences and the making of liturgical history: lifting a veil on liturgy's past.
  – (Liturgy, worship and society) 1. Liturgics–Sociological aspects. 2. Sex differences–Religious aspects–Christianity–History of doctrines. 3. Women in public worship–History. 4. Christian transgender people–History.
  I. Title II. Series
  264'.00866–dc22

**Library of Congress Cataloging-in-Publication Data**
Berger, Teresa.
  Gender differences and the making of liturgical history: lifting a veil on liturgy's past/ Teresa Berger.
    p. cm.—(Liturgy, worship, and society series) Includes bibliographical references (p.) and index.
  ISBN 978-1-4094-2699-8 (hardcover : alk. paper) — ISBN 978-1-4094-2698-1 (pbk.:alk. paper) — ISBN 978-1-4094-2700-1 (ebook) 1. Liturgics. 2. Sex differences. 3. Women in Christianity. I. Title.
  BV178.B46 2011
  264.0082—dc22

2011010440

ISBN 9781409426998 (hbk)
ISBN 9781409426981 (pbk)
ISBN 9781409427001 (ebk)

MIX
Paper from
responsible sources
FSC
www.fsc.org    FSC® C018575

Printed and bound in Great Britain by the
MPG Books Group, UK

For my father

Dr. Erwin Maria Ludwig Berger

(April 11, 1907 – July 14, 1971)


*in paradisum deducant te angeli*

# Contents

# List of Abbreviations

ANF     The Ante-Nicene Fathers. 10 vols. Grand Rapids, MI: Eerdmans, 1978
CCSL    Corpus Christianorum, series latina. Turnhout: Brepols, 1954–
JSNT    Journal for the Study of the New Testament
NPNF    The Nicene and Post-Nicene Fathers, 2 series. Grand Rapids, MI: Eerdmans, 1978
PG      Patrologia graeca. Ed. J.-P. Migne. 162 vols. Paris:  Migne, 1857–86
PL      Patrologia latina. Ed. J.-P. Migne. 221 vols. Paris: Migne, 1844–64
SBL     Society of Biblical Literature

# Acknowledgments

Grateful acknowledgment is made to the following for permission to quote or use copyrighted material:

Brepols Publishers, for excerpts from *The Didascalia Apostolorum: An English Version*, edited and translated by Alistair Stewart-Sykes, Studia Traditionis Theologiae 1 (Turnhout: Brepols, 2009). © 2009, Brepols Publishers n.v., Turnhout, Belgium.

Oxford University Press, for excerpts from *The Ecclesiastical History of the English People*, by the Venerable Bede, edited and translated by Bertram Colgrave and R.A.B. Mynors (Oxford: Clarendon Press, 1991). © Oxford University Press, Oxford, England, UK.

The Catholic University of America Press, Washington, DC, for excerpts from Clement of Alexandria, *Christ the Educator*, translated by Simon P. Wood, Fathers of the Church 23 (New York: Fathers of the Church, Inc., 1954). © The Catholic University of America Press, Washington, DC, USA.

*Annali di studi religiosi*, for use of my essay "Liturgical History as Gender History—Why Not?," (11 [2010]: 1–18) in Chapter 1 of the present book. © *Annali di studi religiosi*, Centro per le scienze religiose, Trento, Italy.

# Preface

This book is an inquiry into the writing of liturgical history: what we think we know, what we can know, and what, at this point in time, we ought to know, given the insights that have emerged with the interpretive tools of gender history. Gender history, I hasten to emphasize, is understood throughout this book as attending to all gendering processes, not only the historically prominent binary of "men" and "women" but also to such gender identities as, for example, intersexed persons, ascetic virgins, eunuchs, and priestly men.

The subtitle of the book, *Lifting a Veil on Liturgy's Past*, might at first glance evoke concealed femininity only.[1] In reality, lifting a veil points to much richer possibilities. For one, the actual gender identity concealed behind a veil is open to surprises. A story told by Caesarius of Heisterbach about a monk who, disguised as a woman, joined a community of nuns illustrates the point.[2] Moreover, veils conceal not only faces but also other parts of the body. In some medieval paintings, for example, a veil functions like a fig leaf, to cover sites of sexed embodiment.[3] Lifting a veil, in short, is intriguingly open with regard to the particular gender identity lying behind the veil.[4] Last but not least, veils were part of the materiality of liturgy: veils covered women's heads during worship, and the faces of both men and women in prebaptismal exorcisms;[5] veils shielded the sanctuary and the altar;

---

[1]    For a historical overview of women and practices of veiling, see the study by Rosine A. Lambin, *Le voile des femmes. Un inventaire historique, social et psychologique*, Studia religiosa Helvetica, Series altera 3 (Bern: Peter Lang, 1999). In contemporary politics the struggle over the wearing of facial veils in public pitches some secular states against traditional Muslim women's practice.

[2]    For more on this see Jacqueline Murray, "Masculinizing Religious Life: Sexual Prowess, the Battle for Chastity and Monastic Identity," in *Holiness and Masculinity in the Middle Ages*, ed. P. H. Cullum and Katherine J. Lewis (Toronto: University of Toronto Press, 2005), 24–42.

[3]    A beautiful example is the delicate veil that covers the genitals of the infant Christ in "The Virgin of Humility" (ca. 1440) by Battista di Biagio Sanguigni, in the (private) Richard L. Feigen Collection. A reproduction of the painting can be found in the exhibition catalogue *Italian Paintings from the Richard L. Feigen Collection*, ed. Laurence Kanter and John Marciari (New Haven: Yale University Press, 2010), 87. I am deeply grateful to Richard L. Feigen for allowing me to use a detail of this painting for the cover of the present book.

[4]    Not that any gender identity will ever fully be disclosed by merely lifting a veil—gender is far too complex to be so easily discerned. The recent controversy over the gender identity of the South African athlete Caster Semenya illustrates this.

[5]    The latter seems to have been the case at least in fourth-century Jerusalem; see Cyril of Jerusalem, *Procatechesis* 9; English translation, together with the Greek text, in *St. Cyril*

guarded eucharistic vessels; marked changes in status, especially for brides and consecrated virgins; and became relics, as was the case with the Veil of the Virgin, revered in Constantinople, and the veil of Saint Elizabeth of Thuringia, worn after her death by her aunt, Saint Hedwig of Silesia, and upon Hedwig's death revered as a double relic.[6] In all of these liturgical practices, gender mattered: men did not cover their heads at prayer, monks did not "take the veil," and passing through a veil to the altar and touching sacred vessels was not open to just anybody. The image of lifting a veil, then, allows for a richly diverse notion of gender differences—which is what is needed when inquiring into liturgy's past.

The core of the present inquiry is a set of historical case studies that together form the center of the book. Highlighting four distinct topics, these case studies seek to demonstrate what a gender-attentive liturgical historiography entails and achieves. The case studies concentrate on the formative early centuries of liturgical history to display how gender differences shaped liturgical life from the very beginning.

Part I lays the methodological groundwork for those case studies by establishing the fundamental working presuppositions of the book. Among these is the core conviction that gender differences mattered profoundly in past liturgical life and practice, even if conventional liturgical history writing did not possess the interpretive tools to render visible this fundamental marker of liturgy's past convincingly. To substantiate this claim I trace the development of historical inquiry in the field of liturgical studies and argue that, with gender-analytical tools now available, a fresh look at the writing of liturgical history is imperative (Chapter 1). The subsequent chapter highlights the development of gender history and its key interpretive strategies, with a focus on their bearing on liturgical historiography (Chapter 2).

With these methodological chapters in place, Part II presents four case studies to demonstrate what a gender-attentive liturgical historiography entails. These open with two chapters on traditional fundamentals of liturgical historiography, one dedicated to liturgical space (Chapter 3) and one to eucharistic practice (Chapter 4). Both chapters attend to these fundamentals by inquiring into the presence of (always) gendered bodies, practices, and metaphors. The following two case studies move beyond conventional fundamentals of liturgical history writing to imagine alternative ways of studying liturgy's past, based on foregrounding questions of gender in worship. The first of these chapters inquires into gender

---

*of Jerusalem's Lectures on the Christian Sacraments*, ed. F. L. Cross (reprint: Crestwood, NY: St Vladimir's Seminary Press, 1986), 45.

⁶    Jonathan Goodall's entry "Veil" in *The New Westminster Dictionary of Liturgy & Worship*, ed. Paul Bradshaw (Louisville, KY: Westminster John Knox Press, 2002), 463–4, offers an overview, yet without any mention of the fact that women were supposed to come to worship wearing a veil (see e.g., 1 Cor 11:5f; Tertullian, *De Virginibus Velandis* 1; 11; *Didascalia Apostolorum* 3.26; *Apostolic Tradition* 18.5, et al.). Neither does Goodall acknowledge liturgical rituals that include veilings, such as the veiling of a bride, and the veiling of virgins.

differences as they shaped liturgical presence and participation by highlighting liturgical impediments based on bodily flows, especially menstruation and nocturnal emissions, sexual relations, and childbirth (Chapter 5). The subsequent chapter traces the emerging link between liturgical presiding and priestly masculinity, taking into account the concomitant questioning regarding liturgical leadership by other gender identities, among them women, eunuchs, and "incontinent" men (Chapter 6).

I hope that these historical case studies, in all their particularity, present a path to a deeper scholarly engagement with the manifold ways in which gender shaped liturgy's past. That said, the historical inquiry presented in Part II entails more than a simple study of liturgy's past with the interpretive tools of gender history, as crucial as I consider this task to be for liturgical scholarship today. The historiographic work in this book ultimately gestures toward a theological argument, namely about liturgical history as this history grounds authorizing claims to the past. The key question is this: what happens with authorizing claims to liturgy's past when a new liturgical historiography reconfigures the contours of this past? The question itself is not new; in recent years it has surfaced, for example, in relation to revisionist scholarship on the early centuries of Christian worship, and especially to the so-called *Apostolic Tradition*.[7] Yet the question has never been asked with regard to a revisionist history of liturgy based on the interpretive tools of gender history. The reason for this is simple. No history of liturgy to date has taken gender-interpretive tools as an integral part of its own historiographic inquiry. *Gender Differences and the Making of Liturgical History* is such an inquiry.

I attend to this inquiry's consequences for theological appeals to liturgical tradition in the third part of the book. This part comes in the form of an extended concluding chapter (Chapter 7). The task here is three-fold. First, I highlight the consequences, for liturgical historiography, of the findings of the previous chapters. Second, I attend to the theological question underlying the historiographic work of this book, namely: what happens to authorizing claims to the past when historical knowledge comes to be reconfigured in gender-attentive ways? Finally, I turn to contemporary discussions around gender and liturgy in order to ask: what happens to the many ways in which liturgy continues to be shaped by gender when these are seen as having a history— that is, when contemporary realities come to be seen as part of a long history of Christian worship that has never been devoid of gender processes which are basic, potent, and troubling ingredients of all liturgical life and practice?

With this glimpse of the book's main frame, I want to acknowledge at the outset that *Gender Differences and the Making of Liturgical History* is, for the most part, an inquiry into the Catholic tradition, both in the book's material contours and

---

[7]   This church order, assumed to reflect early third-century liturgical life in Rome, authorized some of the key liturgical reforms after the Second Vatican Council. What happens when the text's date, place of origin, and authorship (and together with them a certain degree of authority) suddenly appear much less certain?

in its key theological concern.[8] My hope is that even with this particular focus the book may inform the liturgical historiography of other ecclesial traditions. Arguably, the early centuries of Christian worship, on which much of my inquiry focuses, are of shared importance for almost all ecclesial communities. Moreover, by seeking to display a different story of a particular part of liturgy's past, the book ultimately aims at the present, where gender continues to shape liturgical life across denominational lines, even if in quite different configurations and struggles.

At the beginning of every chapter, I tell a story from the past that introduces the subject-matter of the chapter. This story-telling is quite intentional. I am convinced that history at heart is "a set of stories we tell," as Rowan Williams has put it.[9] In telling stories of liturgy's past, as this past was shaped by gender, I offer alternative materials to the more traditional canon of sources in liturgical historiography. I also seek to (re-)embed historical sources about liturgical practice in the stories of lived life to which these sources belong. Finally, the stories that open each chapter allow me to offer fleeting glimpses of periods in liturgical history that are not otherwise highlighted in the book.

Before I turn to the opening story of Chapter 1, another story demands to be told. This is the story of my profound gratitude to all those without whose encouragement, assistance, generosity, curiosity, expertise, and friendship this book would not have seen the light of day.

I am deeply grateful, first of all, to both the Yale Institute of Sacred Music and Yale Divinity School where the long-dormant vision behind *Gender Differences and the Making of Liturgical History* finally came to life. This was possible not least because of a generous set of research leaves. A heartfelt *Danke!* to Martin Jean, Director of the Yale Institute of Sacred Music, for his keen support of my work, and in particular for one day telling me he could not wait to see all my ideas in print; although I still felt unprepared, I sat down the next day to sketch the plan of this book. The Dean's Office of Yale Divinity School, in the person of Dean Harold W. Attridge and the amazing Grace (Pauls) by which he lives, has been a source of wisdom, wit, and encouragement throughout the writing of this book.

Several research assistants ably supported my work, and I gratefully acknowledge them here. Above all, I owe a million thanks to John Leinenweber, ISM Research Assistant, who edited, reedited, proofread, and indexed this book. I simply could not have completed this work without John's editorial skills and patient, unfailing labor. *Gratias tibi ago, Ioanne.* Ann R. Phelps, Mary K. Farag, and Sarah K. Johnson have been my student research assistants at Yale, and I am grateful for all their work.

---

[8]   I wish to acknowledge here that the image of a veil is not an innocent one (no image ever is). In the Christian tradition, as part of the reception history of 2 Cor 3:12–18, the Synagogue came to be depicted as blind and veiled, while her Christian counterpart, the Ecclesia, stood unveiled, her eyes wide open, seeing and knowing.

[9]   Rowan Williams, *Why Study the Past? The Quest for the Historical Church*, Sarum Theological Lectures (London: Darton, Longman and Todd, 2005), 1.

I thank a number of scholarly societies and institutions that invited me to give papers on the subject-matter of this book. Among them are the American Theological Society at its Annual Meeting in Princeton in 2007; the Theological Faculty of the University of Graz, Austria, in 2008; Duke Divinity School in 2009; the Center for Religious Studies at the Fondazione Bruno Kessler in Trento, Italy, where I was able to convene, with my colleague and friend Antonio Autiero, an interdisciplinary research seminar on "Gender, Ritual, and Liturgical Traditions" in December of 2009; and the University of Notre Dame's Department of Theology in 2010.

Several libraries and archives have provided invaluable support. First and foremost, I owe a depth of gratitude to the superb Yale University Library system, and especially to the staff of the Yale Divinity School Library and of the Beinecke Rare Book and Manuscript Library. I also thank the Burns Library at Boston College, the Universitäts- und Landesbibliothek Darmstadt, and the Erzbischöfliche Diözesan- und Dombibliothek Köln, for letting me study some of their unique materials.

I am profoundly grateful to those who generously gave their time to read, offer criticism, and discuss with me parts of this book. A special thanks to Lorna Collingridge who read and commented on the chapters as I wrote them and sustained me with her friendship throughout. Bryan Spinks, my colleague in liturgical studies at Yale who has so enriched my work with his own scholarly expertise, generously read and offered observations on chapters in progress. Others to whom I am grateful for conversation, feedback, inspiration, and expert advice include Paul Bradshaw, Stephen Davis, Mary Farag, Margot Fassler, Mary McClintock Fulkerson, Bert Groen, Bruce Gordon, Peter Hawkins, Mark Jordan, Vasileios Marinis, Byron Stuhlman, Robert Taft, Kathy Tanner, and Adela Yarbro Collins.

It has been a true delight to work with Ashgate, a new publisher for me. My heartfelt thanks to Sarah Lloyd, Ashgate's Religion and Theology publisher, to Ann Allen, Editorial Manager, to Bethan Dixon, Assistant Desk Editor, and to my colleagues on the editorial board of the series Liturgy, Worship and Society, for enthusiastically welcoming this book.

Finally, I owe oceans of gratitude to Peter Ludwig Berger and to M.K.G. for flourishing in their own ways while I wrote this book, and for thereby diverting, delighting, and sustaining me.

I dedicate this book to my father, Dr. Erwin Maria Ludwig Berger, *in memoriam*. In the years I knew him, he kept his distance from liturgical life. Yet he would have welcomed and loved this book—simply because it bears my name.

Teresa Maria Berger
Memorial of Saint Catherine of Siena, *doctor ecclesiae*
New Haven, Connecticut
April 29, 2011

# PART I
# Gendering Liturgy's Past:
# The Trouble, the Task, and the Tools

Part I of *Gender Differences and the Making of Liturgical History* lays the methodological groundwork for the case studies in Part II by establishing the fundamental working presuppositions of the book. Among these is the core conviction that gender differences mattered profoundly in past liturgical life and practice, even if conventional liturgical history writing did not possess the interpretive tools to render visible this fundamental marker of liturgy's past convincingly. To substantiate my claim, I trace the development of historical inquiry in the field of liturgical studies, and argue that, with the gender-analytical tools now available, a fresh look at the writing of liturgical history is imperative (Chapter 1). The following chapter highlights the development of gender history and its key interpretive strategies, with a focus on their bearing on liturgical historiography (Chapter 2).

# Chapter 1

# Gender History in
# Liturgy's Past—Why Not?

It was the year A.D. 1114. A church in Menat, Auvergne, opened its doors to an aging itinerant preacher, Robert of Arbrissel. Robert, who had founded the mixed monastery of Fontevraud, was on a journey together with ascetic companions, both male and female. The people of Menat warned Robert that *females* were forbidden to enter the church, explaining that a saint, revered in the region for centuries, had barred women from this house of God. A woman who defied this tradition would surely die. Robert of Arbrissel responded promptly. He entered the church, together with the women around him. In vain did the doorkeepers of the sanctuary invoke the local saint to intervene.

Inside the church, Robert began to preach. He justified his defiance of the centuries-old tradition of Menat by insisting: "do not continue in vain such foolish prayers! Know instead that the saints are not the enemies of the brides of Jesus Christ."[1] Robert went on to argue his point from the biblical precedent of a woman boldly approaching Christ ("the blessed sinful woman who kissed the feet of the Redeemer"), and from eucharistic practice: "If a woman takes and eats the body and blood of Jesus Christ, think what folly it is to believe that she may not enter a church!"[2] Robert's argument had the desired effect: the church in Menat, so his biographer tells us, was never again closed to women.

In the story of the church in Menat and of the brave women around Robert of Arbrissel who risked their lives by entering the sanctuary, liturgical practice, gender, and tradition form a complex and contested web of relationships. The story of the church in Menat allows us to introduce a crucial set of distinctions that underlie the scholarly inquiry that follows.

---

[1]   A critical edition of the hagiographic texts about Robert of Arbrissel is now available: *The Two Lives of Robert of Arbrissel, Founder of Fontevraud: Legends, Writings, and Testimonies*, ed. Jacques Dalarun et al., Disciplina Monastica 4 (Turnhout, Belgium: Brepols, 2006), here 295. Jacques Dalarun, the editor of the volume and a specialist on the life of Robert of Arbrissel, considers the story of Menat trustworthy, see p. 111, n. 302.

[2]   *The Two Lives of Robert of Arbrissel*, 295.

## Liturgy's Past: History, Historiography, Tradition

For the scholarly argument that constitutes this book, it is imperative to differentiate between four distinct, albeit intricately related, categories of historical analysis. Since in much of the literature these four categories appear muddled, I begin by parsing them here. Historical analysis starts with the past itself, that is, the "things that happen to have happened."[3] For liturgical life this means the liturgies, processions, holy day rituals, fasts, feasts, and liturgical devotions that Christians have engaged in from the earliest beginnings until now.[4] In the story of the church in Menat, this historical level would be the very moment in A.D. 1114 when Robert of Arbrissel arrived at the doorway, discovered that his female companions were barred from entering, defied the ban by walking into the sanctuary together with the women, and then justified their daring entry in a sermon. It is essential to acknowledge that this moment, like all worship life of the past, simply is no more. We have no direct access to this past. None of us can slip back into Menat's church to observe the women walking past the local doorkeepers into the sanctuary, just as surely as none of us can join an early Christian house-church at worship, take part in a medieval Corpus Christi procession, or be present at the funeral of Blessed Pope John XXIII. Our only access to these past liturgical practices is a mediated one, as indeed is every perception of reality, past and present. What we perceive as real is shaped by how we perceive and know in the first place. Mediated access to the past happens through a wide range of primary sources, among them liturgical texts, hagiographic or autobiographical accounts, imperial edicts, gravestone inscriptions, vestments, images, and musical scores. As crucially important as these sources are, none of them grants direct access to the past. Like all mediations, these too are "troubled" [Jon L. Berquist]. The story about the church of Menat tells its tale in textual representation, in a traditional historiographic format, centered on a male, named figure and his daring acts, while the truly daring women around Robert remain nameless, unnumbered, and dependent on the master narrative [he "led" them in].

With this distinction between the past itself, and witnesses to the past, we have already identified a second category of historical analysis, namely the sources for any knowledge of the past. These sources (including autobiographical materials, with their semblance of immediacy[5]) are shaped by those who created them, with their particular lenses and blindspots, as well as by those who authorized

---

[3]   Rowan Williams, *Why Study the Past? The Quest for the Historical Church,* Sarum Theological Lectures (London: Darton, Longman and Todd, 2005), 1.

[4]   A more detailed argument for an expansive understanding of the subject-matter of liturgical historiography is provided in what follows.

[5]   For autobiographical writings as a source for liturgical historiography see the important book by Friedrich Lurz, *Erlebte Liturgie. Autobiographische Schriften als liturgiewissenschaftliche Quellen*, Ästhetik Theologie Liturgik 28 (Münster: LIT Verlag, 2003).

their creation and/or transmission. Our knowledge of these authors and their contexts is never exhaustive. We cannot know all we need to know about them, especially when the texts are pre-modern. The story about the church in Menat illustrates this complexity. Its textual source has come down to us in a sixteenth-century Middle French translation, derived from a medieval Latin original.[6] The author of the original text in all likelihood was Prior Andreas of Fontevraud, a contemporary and follower of Robert of Arbrissel.[7] Prior Andreas's story may, at first sight, appear to be written with a traditional androcentric focus: the daring male at the center, unnamed women around him. Yet as a whole this particular *vita* of Robert of Arbrissel highlights Robert's women-identified actions in ways that an earlier *vita* had not. Only the *vita* of Prior Andreas tells the story of Robert's act of defiance at the church of Menat. This *vita* had been commissioned by the abbess appointed by Robert himself to rule the mixed monastery of Fontevraud, Petronilla of Chemillé. Abbess Petronilla had decided to complement the earlier *vita* she had also commissioned, written by a local bishop who had downplayed Robert's pronounced women-centered actions.[8] In short, the politics of gender are, in more ways than one, at the heart of the transmission of the story of Robert of Arbrissel at the church of Menat. As the sources for the life of Robert of Arbrissel show, troubles with the mediation of the past through textual representation are multiple. Such representation never maps neatly onto reality, especially not in hagiography. Hagiographic texts are not transcripts. To complicate matters when it comes to the particular *vitae* of Robert of Arbrissel, we have parts of the original two texts in translation only; the original texts are lost.

Further, and more general difficulties with the mediation of the past through textual representations include the (gender-specific) filtering of texts; the politics of documentation (also gendered) that made these texts, rather than others, available; and, finally, the narrator of the past and his or her patron in writing, neither of whom are gender-neutral either. Thus, it is no coincidence that we have no description of what happened in the church of Menat when Robert of Arbrissel arrived there from a woman who was present, nor from one of Menat's townsfolk. Historically, far fewer texts exist written by women than by men; and elite males have left far more writings than the "millions of men who were only men."[9] Because of Robert of Arbrissel's appointment of an abbess to oversee the mixed monastery of Fontevraud, however, a woman authorized Prior Andreas to write his *vita* of the founder. Whatever the specifics of this particular case, on the whole our materials for reconstructing the history of worship are gendered in their very basis, and this gendering is asymmetrical in a number of ways.

---

[6]   See *The Two Lives of Robert of Arbrissel*, 17.

[7]   Ibid., 17.

[8]   Ibid., 17. These included syneisactic practices.

[9]   The term is Thelma Fenster's, see her "Why Men?," in *Medieval Masculinities: Regarding Men in the Middle Ages*, ed. Clare A. Lees et al., Medieval Cultures 7 (Minneapolis: University of Minnesota Press, 1994), IX–XIII, here X.

A third category in the writing of liturgy's past—and one shaped by the asymmetries inherent in the second category—is historical research and the kind of historiography it produces. Especially if this historiographic knowledge production is gender-oblivious it will duplicate uncritically the gender asymmetries inherent in its sources. Such uncritical mirroring becomes especially pronounced if the one who produces such historical knowledge, on the basis of a set canon of sources and of received categories of analysis, remains oblivious to the role gender has played in transmitting some sources and not others. To go back to the story of Robert of Arbrissel in Menat: It took the development of gender analysis to set historians wondering about the women who accompanied Robert of Abrissel on his journeys, about the tradition of men and women cohabiting in ascetic renunciation, and about why we know so little of this form of life apart from negative stereotypes. Furthermore, it took sustained scholarly inquisitiveness about the exclusion of women from the sanctuary at Menat to unravel the complicated evidence for this centuries-old tradition, and more than textual analysis to render intelligible how the townsfolk of Menat gathered for worship. In particular, the witness of material culture played an important role here, namely the analysis of an architectural peculiarity in the form of an enormous entryway to the Menat sanctuary, which explained how local women may have "attended" church without in fact entering it.[10]

A last category in the writing of liturgy's past is concerned with authorizing claims to the past. In the life of the church this is the level of theological recourse to tradition. For the story about the church of Menat, such recourse becomes visible in conflicting claims to liturgical tradition at the moment when the gendering of this sacred space is questioned and contested. The villagers of Menat invoke an authorizing past in the form of an order from a local saint. Robert of Arbrissel counters with an alternative notion of sanctity ["saints are not the enemies of the brides of Jesus Christ"] and appeals to biblical precedent and to eucharistic practice to ground his defiance of Menat's tradition of excluding women from the sanctuary. To put my point more generally, traditioning happens when elements of the liturgical past take on an authorizing role for the present. In the Roman Catholic Church at least, such authorizing moves, when rendered decisively, are not made primarily by historians and scholars, but by the *magisterium*, the teaching authority of the church. This *magisterium* clearly is not gender neutral by any means, since it is tied to episcopal ordination, reserved to men. This fourth level is thus constituted more forcefully by gender than any of the other levels outlined here, since priestly ordination requires a particular gender identity, namely maleness.

So much for four distinct though interrelated categories of historical analysis. With these distinctions in place, my primary question in the chapters that follow is this: what consequences are there for liturgical history writing when gender

---

[10]   Jacques Dalarun has described this in his "Ève, Marie ou Madeleine? La dignité du corps féminin (VIe–XIIe siècles)," in *"Dieu changea de sexe, pour ainsi dire." La religion faite femme (XIe–XVe siècle)*, Vita regularis 37 (Berlin: LIT Verlag, 2008), 3–21.

is not only a fundamental marker of worship life in the past but also a crucial element in the formation of the sources for the study of the past, and by that very fact an ingredient in every narrative of the past? And what consequences are there for liturgical tradition when gender continues to play such a fundamental role in constituting authorizing claims to the past? And, finally, what happens in liturgical traditioning when this power of gender is not only asymmetrical but also unacknowledged?

Of the four categories of historical analysis identified above—the past of liturgical practices, the documentation of this past, the historiography of the past, and authorizing claims to this past—intervention and reconfiguration are not possible on every level, nor do they take the same shape for each level. On the first level, that of the past of liturgical practices, no intervention or reconfiguration is possible. The "pastness of the past"[11] simply puts it out of our hands, irrevocably so. On the second level, that of the witnesses to this past, historians confront a number of basic limitations and imbalances in documentation that also cannot be undone. This holds true even as new sources continue to be unearthed, the canon of sources expands, and witnesses to the past continue to be identified,[12] read, and interpreted afresh.[13] Fundamental imbalances in the sources remain. We will in all likelihood never have more than a dozen texts written by women during the first thousand years of Christian history. We will not suddenly be able to read, in the words of eunuchs or male serfs, how they practiced their faith and how they worshiped. We will not find many written sources revealing how priests in rural areas negotiated liturgical life and the practice of gender in their parishes. The contours of the record and the politics of documentation, as themselves a part of what happens to have happened, are out of our hands no less than the past to which they witness.

On the third level, namely the study and writing of history through analysis of the witnesses to the past, intervention and reconfiguration not only become possible but are intrinsic to its very existence. The writing of history—the making and remaking of a historical narrative—is after all the proper task of this level.

---

[11] The term is Janet Coleman's, see her *Ancient and Medieval Memories: Studies in the Reconstruction of the Past* (New York: Cambridge University Press, 1992), 285 and passim.

[12] This includes the possibility of questioning the assumed maleness of an anonymous author, such as that of the writer of the ninth-century *Vita Liutbirgae*. For more, see *Anchoress and Abbess in Ninth-Century Saxony: The* Lives *of Liutbirga of Wendhausen and Hathumoda of Gandersheim*, trans. with an introduction by Frederick S. Paxton, Medieval Texts in Translation (Washington, DC: Catholic University of America Press, 2009), 17–19.

[13] An intriguing example of a fresh, alternative reading of well known sources is Eamon Duffy's *Marking the Hours: English People and Their Prayers, 1240–1570* (New Haven: Yale University Press, 2006), in which Duffy concentrates on writings in the margins, fly-leaves, and blank spaces of Books of Hours, in order to understand the individual prayers of these books.

Here, the intervention of *Gender Differences and the Making of Liturgical History* finds its focus, even if its historiographic work gestures toward a fourth level, namely that of authorizing claims to the past, in the sense of liturgical tradition. The last two levels, the narrating of the past and authorizing claims to that past, are intimately connected. This connection is apparent not least when it comes to the occlusion of gender in a history of worship. But the gendered nature of liturgy's past is not the only matter where theological recourse to liturgical tradition is based on a problematic historiography. As Paul Bradshaw has wryly remarked, most liturgical theology rests either on "bad history" or on "no history at all."[14] The "no history" which is the concern of the present book is one that occludes gender as a fundamental marker of liturgy's past. A closer look at the workings of such liturgical historiography is in order here, so as to identify more precisely both the trouble and the task of lifting this veil on liturgy's past.

**The Traditional Writing of Liturgy's Past: Gender-Challenged**

In what follows, I map the development of the writing of liturgical history, so as to shed light on the ways in which gender has come to be written out of the historical record in the first place. In much of liturgical historiography, after all, facts are narrated as if gender was irrelevant in past liturgies. There is little recognition in such historiography that what comes to be configured as "fact" (and as a fact worth narrating) is always theory-specific.[15] If history "is driven by the historian's questions"[16] then the answers provided are not only shaped but also constrained by the questions the historian asks of the past. There is nothing "relativistic" about such an acknowledgment. It merely recognizes that history writing always takes place within particular cultural contexts, and that these contexts raise specific questions, while disregarding others, for the historian's interrogation of the past. The story of Robert of Arbrissel and his women companions who entered the church in Menat is a case in point. So is *Gender Differences and the Making of Liturgical History*. The story of the church in Menat would at best have been a marginal footnote in a traditional liturgical historiography, since this story involves neither a key rite (such as the Eucharist), nor a key ecclesial center (such as Cluny, Saint-Denis, or Chartres), nor a key figure (such as Gregory the Great or Abbot Suger). Similarly, the present book's focus on gender and liturgy's past—for which the story of the church in Menat serves as an introduction—would have been inconceivable a

---

[14]   See his "Difficulties in Doing Liturgical Theology," *Pacifica* 11 (1998): 181–94, here 193. Gender oblivion, however, is not at all what Bradshaw had in mind in his critique.

[15]   This concise formulation is Linda McDowell's; see her *Gender, Identity and Place: Understanding Feminist Geographies* (Minneapolis: University of Minnesota Press, 1999), 227.

[16]   Elizabeth A. Clark, *History, Theory, Text: Historians and the Linguistic Turn* (Cambridge, MA: Harvard University Press, 2004), 156.

century ago (and in all likelihood will be theorized quite differently a hundred years from now).

Liturgical historiography in the past, for all its skills and insights, was largely oblivious to gender as a fundamental marker of cultural formations, and thus presented seemingly non-gendered liturgical facts. The reasons for the *continuing* occlusion of gender in liturgical historiography—in contradistinction to some other contemporary disciplines, such as biblical studies or medieval history, in which gender analysis has contributed substantially to the field—are connected to the development of liturgical studies as a discipline, its scholarly practitioners, their construal of their subject-matter, and the conversation partners they privilege. A look back at the development of the discipline will substantiate this claim.

## The Making of Liturgical Studies

A history of the scholarly discipline of liturgical studies has yet to be written,[17] even as histories of worship continue to multiply. What is clear about the emergence of liturgical studies as a scholarly discipline is its roots in early modernity and its place within the development of the modern research university, with its particular practices and tools. This is not to say that no critical reflection on liturgical practice existed earlier, nor any scholarly engagement with liturgical texts and sources, nor analyses of liturgy's past. On the contrary, these kinds of critical-reflective engagements with liturgical practice and an authorizing past are as old as the first Christian gatherings for worship. One might argue, in fact, that there simply is no non-reflected and unmediated practice to be had, in liturgy as everywhere else. Thus, New Testament texts stand among the earliest witnesses to a critical engagement with practices of worship and with their history. Paul's appeal to the tradition he received and is handing on (παρέδωκα) regarding the celebration of the Lord's Supper (1 Cor 11:23) and his vision of how to practice spiritual gifts in worship (1 Cor 14) are cases in point. What is distinct, then, in the emergence of liturgical studies as a scholarly discipline in the late eighteenth and early nineteenth centuries is not the fact that liturgy becomes an object of critical analysis for the very first time, but rather the point at which liturgical studies takes shape within the broader emergence of modern knowledge production, with its particular forms of academic protocol. These modern protocols of knowledge production (objective, evidence-driven) shape liturgical scholarship even when it is not practiced at research universities but in older, ecclesial contexts, for example by a Benedictine monk-scholar or an Anglican parson-scholar.

---

[17] An excellent brief sketch, focused on the German-speaking context, is provided in Albert Gerhards and Benedikt Kranemann, *Einführung in die Liturgiewissenschaft*, Einführung Theologie (Darmstadt: Wissenschaftliche Buchgesellschaft, 2006), 25–42.

*"Liturgics": Born of a Woman?*

The late-eighteenth century witnessed the first appearance of "liturgics" in a German-speaking university setting, initially as a sub-field of pastoral theology.[18] If this initial appearance, during state-ordered reforms of the university-based theological curriculum, represents the birth of liturgics as a modern scholarly discipline, then we owe this birth to a powerful woman, Empress Maria Theresia of Austria (1717–80). The emergence of "liturgics" (*Liturgik*) as part of the establishment of a new discipline, pastoral theology, decreed for all Austrian universities by the Empress in 1777, was part of a larger set of Catholic Enlightenment reforms, designed to draw on the practice of religion for practical, moral, and pedagogical purposes.[19] Not surprisingly, the term "liturgy" as an overarching category for a pluriformity of ecclesial ritual actions to be studied in "liturgics" now comes to the forefront,[20] establishing not only a particular disciplinary shape but also distinct boundaries for the emerging scholarly field. This development was supported, within Roman Catholicism, by the fact that the sixteenth-century Tridentine liturgical reforms had strengthened the impression that proper liturgy was only worship authorized by the highest ecclesial authority, i.e, Rome. With "liturgy" increasingly meaning the official, prescribed, written texts of the church's ritual life, other liturgical expressions come to be relegated to the margins of scholarly inquiry.[21] In tandem with this strict bounding of the field, categories such as "popular piety" and, later, "para-liturgies" emerge to denote the manifold ritual practices now increasingly written out of the scholarly construal of "liturgy" proper. It is important to recognize here that categories of analysis, as they emerge at particular moments in time, are never analytically neutral, but always shaped by the world-views of their designers. Not surprisingly, today it is precisely scholars of "pre-modern," especially medieval, life, who criticize this narrow, "modern" disciplinary boundary of liturgical studies as deeply problematic and inadequate.[22] With regard to my own guiding interests in *Gender Differences*

---

[18]   See Franz Kohlschein, "Zur Geschichte der Liturgiewissenschaft im katholischen deutschsprachigen Bereich," in *Liturgiewissenschaft—Studien zur Wissenschaftsgeschichte*, ed. Franz Kohlschein and Peter Wünsche, Liturgiewissenschaftliche Quellen und Forschungen 78 (Münster: Aschendorff, 1996), 1–72, here 9–12. Kohlschein notes that the term "liturgics" surfaces in Protestant writings at about the same time.

[19]   Ibid., 9–12.

[20]   The term "liturgy" as an overarching term does not emerge in the West until the sixteenth century; see Pierre-Marie Gy, *La Liturgie dans l'histoire* (Paris: Editions Saint-Paul, 1990), 177–84.

[21]   Cf. Arnold Angenendt, *Liturgik und Historik. Gab es eine organische Liturgie-Entwicklung?* Quaestiones Disputatae 189 (Freiburg i.B.: Herder, 2001), 142.

[22]   See, for example, C. Clifford Flanigan et al., "Liturgy as Social Performance: Expanding the Definitions," in *The Liturgy of the Medieval Church*, ed. Thomas J. Heffernan and E. Ann Matter (Kalamazoo, MI: Medieval Institute Publications, 2001),

*and the Making of Liturgical History*, I note that the emerging focus on official, prescribed, written texts also bore within it a weakening of the visibility of gender in liturgical practice, since it is not in prescribed texts that gender's workings are most visible when it comes to worship.

*(Gendered) Sites and Texts*

With the emergence of modern forms of knowledge production, liturgical studies moved elsewhere than, say, the occasional reflections in New Testament epistles, the postbaptismal catecheses of the early church, the medieval allegorical interpretations of liturgy, the theological arguments born out of contestations and reformations in liturgical life, and the rubricism of post-Tridentine liturgical catechesis. The location of liturgical studies as a scholarly field of inquiry came in growing measure to be the academy. This does not mean that liturgical studies were no longer anchored in ecclesial, and more specifically, monastic contexts. Indeed, liturgical studies continued to thrive there well into the twentieth century. Two of the key twentieth-century books of liturgical historiography originated in lectures given to monastic communities: Anton Baumstark's *Liturgie comparée* and Gregory Dix's *The Shape of the Liturgy.* At the same time, the more the discipline of liturgical studies grew into an academic field in its own right, the less influence the ecclesial and monastic sites of liturgical scholarship seemed to carry.

Empress Maria Theresia notwithstanding, the academy in which liturgical studies ultimately found a home was established as a specifically gender-constrained terrain of scholarly inquiry. The knowing subject was male, even if the scientific claim to lack of bias hid this gender-specific scholarly agency.[23] Women did not enter the world of higher education in substantial numbers until well into the twentieth century; for the theological disciplines, liturgical studies included, this entry took place only in the second half of the century. Earlier sites of liturgical scholarship, such as female convents, which had produced, for example, the eucharistic reflections of Hildegard of Bingen, were lost or devalued much earlier, namely with the emergence of the medieval universities.[24]

---

695–714, and Gerd Althoff, "The Variability of Rituals in the Middle Ages," in *Medieval Concepts of the Past: Ritual, Memory, Historiography,* ed. Gerd Althoff et al., Publications of the German Historical Institute (New York: Cambridge University Press, 2002), 71–87. I note here, however, that Josef Andreas Jungmann, preeminent scholar of liturgical history in the twentieth century, had himself already called for a broadening of the understanding of what counts as liturgy; see an early essay of his, repeatedly reprinted, "Was ist Liturgie?," *Zeitschrift für Katholische Liturgie* 55 (1931): 83–102.

[23]  For more on these developments, especially in relation to the field of history, see Bonnie G. Smith, *The Gender of History: Men, Women, and Historical Practice* (Cambridge, MA: Harvard University Press, 1998).

[24]  Hans-Joachim Schmidt, "Geschichte und Prophetie: Rezeption der Texte Hildegards von Bingen im 13. Jahrhundert," in *Hildegard von Bingen in ihrem historischen Umfeld,*

The field of liturgical studies as it took shape in early modernity initially concentrated its scholarly work on the study and editing of ancient liturgical texts and their interpreters. An example can be found in the work of the Maurists, French Benedictine monks of the Congregation of Saint-Maur, who in the seventeenth century began a remarkable series of editions of manuscripts, many of these liturgically relevant. Similarly, the Bollandists, a group of Belgian Jesuits, started their massive series of saints' lives, the *Acta Sanctorum,* in the seventeenth century. The volumes were published in the order of feast days in the liturgical calendar. In the nineteenth century, the (re-)founded Benedictine Abbey of Solesmes rose to prominence not only because of its abbot, Prosper Guéranger, but also through the publication of the *Dictionnaire d'archéologie chrétienne et de liturgie,* edited by the monk-scholars Fernand Cabrol (1855–1937) and Henri Leclercq (1869–1945).[25] Drawing on these various collections of texts, historians of liturgy began to engage questions of origin and development using the historiographic tools of their time, especially philological analyses of primary texts. In England, the nineteenth-century Anglo-Catholic movement generated sustained interest in "liturgiology" (John Mason Neale) and produced editions of primary texts as well as historical inquiries into liturgical developments.[26]

*Liturgical Studies in the Long Twentieth Century*

With the beginning of the twentieth century, a number of distinct emphases emerged within liturgical historiography, all following standard historical, exegetical, and philological approaches of their time. The most important of these emphases bear highlighting here because they have continued to shape, in various ways, the

ed. Alfred Haverkamp (Mainz: Verlag Philipp von Zabern, 2000), 489–517, has shown how within decades after her death Hildegard came to be read extremely narrowly, as an oracle who predicted the future. Schmidt argues that one reason for this narrow reception of Hildegard's vast corpus is the shift in knowledge production from monastic communities to universities.

[25]    The entry "woman" is revealing not only in its sketch of the historical development but also in its wide-ranging, detailed, and quite nuanced reading of the sources, see Henri Leclercq, "Femme," in *Dictionnaire d'archéologie chrétienne et de liturgie* 5,1 (Paris: Letouzey et Ané, 1922), 1300–1353.

[26]    Examples of editions of liturgical texts are John Mason Neale's publication of parts of Durandus's *Rationale Divinorum Officiorum* in English translation (*The Symbolism of Churches and Church Ornaments* [Leeds: T. W. Green, 1843]), and John Henry Newman's *Hymni ecclesiae e Brevario Parisiensi* (Oxford: Parker, 1838). The best-known example of an historical inquiry is William Palmer's learned *Origines Liturgicae, or, Antiquities of the English Ritual* (Oxford: At the University Press, 1836). For more on the place of liturgy in the Anglo-Catholic movement, see Teresa Berger, *Liturgie—Spiegel der Kirche. Eine systematisch-theologische Analyse des liturgischen Gedankenguts im Traktarianismus,* Forschungen zur Systematischen und Ökumenischen Theologie 52 (Göttingen: Vandenhoeck and Ruprecht, 1986).

development of the field over the past hundred years. The first emphasis might be described as the in-depth analysis of the historical development of a particular rite. The overarching objective here was an explanation of how a particular rite came to have its present form. A preeminent exponent of this form of liturgical historiography was Josef Andreas Jungmann, S.J. (1889–1975), best known for his magisterial *Missarum Solemnia*, first published in 1948. The German sub-title describes the intention of this historiography well: *Eine genetische Erklärung der römischen Messe*. Jungmann sought to offer a narrative of the "genetic" development of the Roman Mass. Giving the then-known form of the Mass, this history had a clear and present purpose, namely the demonstration that the Mass had developed not only with continuities but also much change. At a point in time when the Roman Mass still seemed irreproachable, such historicizing underwrote a progressive project, ultimately that of liturgical reform.[27] At the same time, Jungmann was obviously working with the historical tools of his time. The material basis of his analysis was almost exclusively liturgical texts, which he interpreted with the exegetical tools of his time, especially philological ones. Gender analysis was not a tool available to Jungmann; neither does gender analysis produce its clearest results when applied to liturgical texts alone.

It is no surprise, then, that in the one thousand pages of *The Mass of the Roman Rite* women appear just over ten times, and only in passages that narrate women's liturgical presence as problematic, marginal, or, simply, absent. Neither do men who were "only men" make much of an appearance in this liturgical historiography, nor are priests seen as having a gendered particularity of their own. Gender history would later reveal such (seemingly) ungendered histories of the liturgy as quite particular representations of the past. These histories were event-centered institutional chronicles and histories of male elites and their textual productions. Such history writing "naturally" by-passed liturgical sites not shaped according to the accepted scholarly paradigm. In this way it projected on the object studied what its own interpretive strategies and investigative procedures required: a narrative of liturgy's past seemingly untouched by gender.

The fact that these interpretive strategies functioned with only limited success already points to the importance of gendering processes in liturgy's past. One can, after all, not really write a history of the Eucharist without at some point confronting the fact that gender is inscribed into its very celebration, if only through specifications as to the gender of the presider. Indeed, as some studies had already shown (without that being their point), the historical narrative of the liturgy was profoundly shaped by gender differences and symbolic meanings associated with femininity and masculinity. Adolph Franz (1842–1916) and his seminal work

---

[27] For more on this point, see Rudolf Pacik, "Josef Andreas Jungmann: Liturgiegeschichtliche Forschung als Mittel religiöser Reform," *Liturgisches Jahrbuch* 43 (1993): 62–84.

on medieval benedictions is a case in point.[28] Since Franz was clear that ecclesial benedictions did not happen only in church but were a part of everyday religious life, he could not but include liturgical blessings used by the faithful. Thus, for example, Franz cites a blessing with a mandrake, for which an actual text is found in Hildegard of Bingen's *Physica*.[29] This blessing, "modeled on the example of a liturgical prayer," with an invocation, anamnesis, and epiclesis, was to be used by the faithful in their homes to relieve sadness.[30] For Adolph Franz, these and similar practices of blessing were a part of what liturgical historiography had to cover. In a similar vein, Peter Browe, S.J. (1876–1949), in his sustained research into medieval eucharistic practices, attended to the breadth of ritualizing that surrounded the basic act of celebrating Mass, from the reception of *viaticum* to eucharistic visions to magic practices involving hosts. As with the work of Franz, gender as a factor in liturgical life thus broadly conceived is readily apparent throughout Browe's work.[31] An example is his study of the frequency of eucharistic reception among saintly women and men in the Middle Ages.[32] At the very outset Browe confronts the gender-specific unevenness of his sources, noting that while we have some information about women's reception of communion, we know hardly anything about the eucharistic reception of men who were "only men." The hagiographic literature that was Browe's main source of information about the frequency of eucharistic reception (as opposed to legislation about such frequency) is gender-assymetric: most of the saintly men whose lives were recorded became priests, and were thus noted for presiding at Mass, a road not open to women.[33]

I note in passing that Browe (whose disciplinary home was moral theology) also wrote a book on "medieval sexual ethics," whose focus really was on gender-specific liturgical taboos and pollutions.[34] In 1936, Browe published his research

---

[28]   Adolph Franz, *Die kirchlichen Benediktionen im Mittelalter*, 2 vols. (Freiburg i.B.: Herder, 1909; reprint Graz: Akademische Druck- und Verlagsanstalt, 1960). It took exactly a hundred years for Franz's subject-matter to be treated again in a scholarly volume: see Derek A. Rivard's recent *Blessing the World: Ritual and Lay Piety in Medieval Religion* (Washington, DC: The Catholic University of America Press, 2009).

[29]   Franz, *Die kirchlichen Benediktionen im Mittelalter*, 1:420f. In the footnote Franz misidentifies the place of this blessing in Hildegard's *Physica*; it is found in book 1:56, not book 2:56.

[30]   Ibid., 1:420. Translation mine.

[31]   Peter Browe's disparate studies on the Eucharist have now been edited in one volume, *Die Eucharistie im Mittelalter. Liturgiehistorische Forschungen in kulturwissenschaftlicher Absicht*, ed. Hubertus Lutterbach and Thomas Flammer, Vergessene Theologen 1 (Münster: LIT Verlag, 2003).

[32]   Peter Browe, "Die Kommunion der Heiligen im Mittelalter," in *Die Eucharistie im Mittelalter*, 199–209, here 199f.

[33]   Browe does acknowledge the existence of female clerics in earlier centuries, ibid., 119, see n. 46.

[34]   Peter Browe, *Beiträge zur Sexualethik des Mittelalters*, Breslauer Studien zur historischen Theologie 23 (Breslau: Verlag Müller and Seiffert, 1932).

on the history of castration—only at first sight a seemingly arcane subject. Browe's history had a contemporary purpose. He notes in the introduction recent legislation both in Nazi Germany and in North America (!) that allowed for the sterilization of certain parts of the population.[35] Browe's work in this regard is a stark reminder of how the historians' questions of the past are shaped, for better and for worse, by their own times.

What the examples of Adolph Franz and Peter Browe show is that traditional liturgical historiographies can attest the power of gender—even if that is not their intention—when the subject-matter "liturgy" is conceived broadly, with attention to a wide range of liturgical practices. Gender and genre, in other words, are not unrelated in historiography.[36] In traditional liturgical historiography as a whole, however, with its particular construal of what counted as "liturgy," gender is marginal in the subject deemed central to the history of worship: the development of rites, texts, and institutions. Moreover, where gender does surface, traditional liturgical history presents it to be natural, essential, and binary—as did most history writing at the time.

With their broad interest in liturgical practices, Franz and Browe stand at the beginning of a second trend in twentieth-century scholarship in liturgical studies, the turn to cultural analysis. Franz himself suggested that this was to be his focus.[37] Granted that the understanding of culture changed fundamentally in the twentieth century, a "cultural" approach to liturgical history remained somewhat on the margins until cultural studies irrupted as a vibrant field of scholarly inquiry in the second half of the twentieth century. A mid-century expression of a cultural history of liturgy is found in the work of Anton Ludwig Mayer (1891–1982) who sought to elucidate, in liturgical developments and changes, the impact of larger cultural trends. Mayer's focus was on elite intellectual history, however. Somewhat later conversation partners for historians of liturgy are provided by the French Annales school, especially as it begins to focus on "mentalité" (Arnold Angenendt is a case in point), and, most recently, by historians in conversation with cultural studies.[38]

A different emphasis in early twentieth-century liturgical historiography emerges with the work of Anton Baumstark (1872–1948) and his program of

---

[35] Peter Browe, *Die Geschichte der Entmannung. Eine religions- und rechtsgeschichtliche Studie*, Breslauer Studien zur historischen Theologie Neue Folge 1 (Breslau: Verlag Müller & Seiffert, 1936), 1.

[36] See Elizabeth A. Clark, "Women, Gender, and the Study of Christian History," *Church History* 70/3 (2001): 395–426, here 411.

[37] Franz, *Die kirchlichen Benediktionen im Mittelalter*, 1:VI.

[38] Miri Rubin's work on Corpus Christi and Robert Orsi's work on women's devotion to St. Jude are two examples of this approach; see also C. Clifford Flanigan et al., "Liturgy as Social Performance: Expanding the Definitions," in *The Liturgy of the Medieval Church*, ed. Thomas J. Heffernan and E. Ann Matter (Kalamazoo, MI: Medieval Institute Publications, 2001), 695–714.

*liturgie comparée*, comparative liturgical historiography.[39] To a greater degree than Jungmann, Baumstark sought to elucidate liturgical development by comparative analysis across ritual families, East and West. In this, he worked with a strong philological emphasis, and at the same time a keen interest in questions of methodology. One chapter in his *Comparative Liturgy* seeks to describe "The Laws of Liturgical Evolution."[40] As others have noted, the influence of contemporary developments in evolutionary biology, especially the work of Charles Darwin, is noticeable here, not only in Baumstark's basic model of historical development, but also in the theorizing of liturgical development by those who followed him.[41] One might think of this historiographic model as liturgical evolutionism. The influence of evolutionary models and language remains quite pronounced, for example when liturgical development comes to be described in terms of a "selective evolution," with "the weaker variants of the species" dying out as "the fittist" survive.[42] Conceiving liturgical history in linear or evolutionist terms has had an effect of almost naturalizing power: a historical narrative is imagined whose unfolding requires the identification of individual elements that become stepping stones for later progress.

Gregory Dix (1901–52), especially in his *The Shape of the Liturgy*, took yet a different approach. First published in 1945, this book exerted tremendous influence on liturgical scholarship, especially in the English-speaking world. Dix's basic methodological strategy was to move beyond a narrow focus on texts to an analysis of ritual structures, and it was here—in a common shape—that he thought to find the earliest expression of (eucharistic) worship.

The liturgical scholarship described so far is, for the most part, that of the first half of the twentieth century. Before I turn to the second half of the twentieth

---

[39]    *Liturgie comparée* was the title of a series of lectures Baumstark first gave in Chevetogne in 1932, then published as a series of articles, and, finally, in 1939 in book form. The English edition by F. L. Cross, *Comparative Liturgy*, is a translation of the third edition of the French book as revised by Bernard Botte (Westminster, MD: The Newman Press, 1958).

[40]    Baumstark, *Comparative Liturgy*, ch. 2. For the reception history of Baumstark's work, see *Comparative Liturgy Fifty Years after Anton Baumstark (1872–1948)*, ed. Robert F. Taft and Gabriele Winkler, Orientalia Christiana Analecta 265 (Rome: Pontificio Istituto Orientale, 2001).

[41]    See Fritz West, *The Comparative Liturgy of Anton Baumstark*, Alcuin Club and Group for Renewal of Worship Joint Liturgical Studies 31 (Bramcote: Grove Books, 1995). See also Paul F. Bradshaw, *The Search for the Origins of Christian Worship: Sources and Methods for the Study of Early Liturgy*, 2d ed. (New York: Oxford University Press, 2002), 9. I disagree with West and Bradshaw on their neat distinction between nature and culture, as if what we conceive of as "nature" were a natural given and not socially constructed.

[42]    The example is from Robert F. Taft, "How Liturgies Grow: The Evolution of the Byzantine Divine Liturgy," now included in his *Beyond East and West: Problems in Liturgical Understanding*, 2d ed. (Rome: Edizioni Orientalia Christiana, Pontifical Oriental Institute, 2001), 203f.

century, I note the obvious, namely that liturgical historiography has always moved in tandem with broader developments, not only in historiography but also in intellectual and cultural trends. Any historical sketch of the discipline of liturgical historiography needs to attend carefully to this fact and render it visible as an integral part of all history writing rather than as accidental, or as, in and of itself, problematic. That said, it is time to turn to the developments in historiography that so vibrantly mark the second half of the twentieth century and the beginnings of the twenty-first.

## Contesting Conventional Histories

In the second half of the twentieth century, the field of history as a scholarly discipline becomes a vibrant, changing, and contested terrain. This development and the attendant reconfigurations of the historian's tasks and tools are many. Newer developments and shifts in the field of history include the many variants of social history, whether the French Annales school, Marxist history, or local histories. What all these have in common is a critical analysis of conventional historiography as one constrained by a narrow focus on a particular set of sites (elite institutions, usually political or ecclesial), a small number of historic agents ("hegemonic males"), and, dependent on them, a host of historiographic presuppositions and occlusions that neatly follow.

Liturgical studies has not remained untouched by the critical developments in historiography, albeit seeking to develop the strengths of earlier approaches while mingling them with newer approaches. Four methodological consequences deserve mention here. The first concerns a broadening of the material object of historical analysis. Liturgy's past is no longer understood as accessible primarily through the study of liturgical texts. Instead, there has been a deepened appreciation of liturgy as a multi-textured practice, in which not only words but also space, images, acoustics, material culture, bodies, voices, and instruments play a role. Writing a history of worship thus involves the study of practices rather than an analysis of liturgical texts only. Second, liturgical texts themselves have come to be read afresh, as a form of "living literature"[43] with a quite complicated relationship to the past they embody. A rubric, for example, seeks to enjoin a specific liturgical action, yet the mere existence of a rubric does not mean that the action itself took place. Third, there has been a move beyond the (at heart: modern) bounded-ness of the term "liturgy" to an older, more comprehensive understanding of liturgical practice that includes not only the key sacramental rites, but ecclesial rituals more broadly, among them processions, blessings, domestic liturgical practices, and feasts and fasts as these shape everyday life. Lastly, the *context* of worship, that is its situated-ness in the material realities of lived life including particular cultural,

---

[43]   See Bradshaw, *Search for the Origins*, 5.

geographic and geopolitical givens, has increasingly come to the fore in liturgical scholarship.

None of these shifts happened as a development in liturgical studies alone. On the contrary, these developments are related to and indeed fueled by wide-ranging shifts in intellectual knowledge production, especially by the twentieth-century anthropological and linguistic turns. For liturgical studies in the second half of the twentieth century this meant a definite broadening of scholarly tools of analysis. Fields and subfields from within the social sciences—such as cultural anthropology, semiotics, sociology, performance theory, ritual studies, and ethnography—began to supplement the more traditional ancillary disciplines of liturgical studies. The pluriformity of methods for the study of liturgy—and the way in which these methods construct the object of their inquiry—mirrors the expansion of methods of inquiry in other scholarly disciplines. In contemporary liturgical studies, diachronic textual analysis, analyses of ritual actions, questions about meaning (theological, anthropological, cultural), and contextual analysis, to name but the dominant approaches, all cohabit.

Overall, liturgical studies in the past decades has moved to the social sciences as a new conversation partner. This holds true not only in the contemporary pastoral side of liturgical studies but also for its historical analyses. Two recent histories of worship in fact self-identify as social histories: Martin Stringer's *A Sociological History of Christian Worship* and Frank Senn's *The People's Work: A Social History of the Liturgy*.[44] Neither of these two studies employs gender as a category of historical analysis, although both seek to attend to women as liturgical agents. Tellingly, "men" as the relational "other" of women remain mostly invisible, as does the category gender itself.

The linguistic turn in historiography, with its focus on the textual representation of the past as our main access to what happens to have happened, has not had a strong impact on the writing of liturgical history. That said, even the historiography of Christian worship cannot but be shaped by broader intellectual trends, postmodern formations included. An example may be found in the work of Paul F. Bradshaw, who, in a range of scholarly publications spanning the last 30 years, has rewritten the history of the early centuries of Christian worship as we knew it. His methodological principles, seemingly generated simply by a fresh, careful rereading of the sources themselves, nevertheless bear the stamp of their time, in this case a telling affinity to postmodern theories of knowledge. Leaving behind both previous certainties and a sense of a historiographic master narrative, Bradshaw, in the preface to the 2002 edition of his *The Search for the Origins of Christian Worship*, emphasizes his conviction that "we know much, much less

---

[44] Martin D. Stringer, *A Sociological History of Christian Worship* (New York: Cambridge University Press, 2005); Frank C. Senn, *The People's Work: A Social History of the Liturgy* (Minneapolis: Fortress Press, 2006). Robert Taft's work has also increasingly drawn on the interpretive strategies of social history, see for example his *Through Their Own Eyes: Liturgy as the Byzantines Saw It* (Berkeley, CA: InterOrthodox Press, 2006).

about the liturgical practices of the first three centuries of Christianity than we once thought that we did."[45] In the book's introductory methodological chapter (substantially rewritten from the first edition of a decade earlier), Bradshaw outlines the development of his own interpretative strategies, essentially mapping, in conversation with earlier approaches, his move away from a narrative of neatly linear development toward an acknowledgment of the starkly fragmentary and disparate nature of the extant evidence, and its radically local character. Bradshaw stresses the need for a "hermeneutic of suspicion"[46] *vis-à-vis* what earliest liturgical sources might claim for themselves (their apostolic origin being the most obvious example) and highlights the silences, absences, and aporias the historian encounters in these sources. He cautions against the assumption that texts simply mean what they purport to say, and instead encourages historians of liturgy to ask what might have engendered something being said in the first place and what function the text might have had. An example is Bradshaw's interpretive stance *vis-à-vis* liturgical injunctions. He sees the latter as pointing to an existing yet contested practice rather than to an absence. With such methodological principles, Bradshaw finds himself in the midst of what drives postmodern historical analyses: an emphasis on fragmentariness, the mediations of textual representations, discontinuity, and difference. Such a reading of Bradshaw's methodological principles does not— at least in my understanding of the workings of liturgical historiography—in any way negate his findings and re-readings of the origins of Christian worship. Rather, such a reading simply suggests how these findings are produced under the conditions of the author's own times.

## Women: Beginning to Make Liturgical History Gender-Attentive

Given these various engagements with newer developments in the field of history, what about gender analysis as a conversation partner for liturgical historiography? The answer to this question will depend in part on how one understands the field of gender analysis in the first place. An interest in women's voices and feminist theory as these emerged in the early 1970s has certainly found a place in liturgical studies, even if most prominently in its pastoral side. The literature there has grown to be quite substantial.[47] The impact of women's history and feminist historiography on the writing of liturgical history, however, is much less pronounced.

---

[45]   Bradshaw, *Search for the Origins*, X.

[46]   The term, adopted from Paul Ricoeur's interpretation of Marx, Nietzsche, and Freud as "masters of suspicion" (*Freud and Philosophy: An Essay on Interpretation* [New Haven: Yale University Press, 1970], 33), became central to feminist interrogations of traditional historiography and the knowledge it had produced.

[47]   In *Women's Ways of Worship*, 109–43, I sketch in more detail the engagement with women's issues in liturgical practice.

It would be a mistake to think that women begin to make liturgical history merely with the 1960s, just as it would be wrong to claim that critical reflection on liturgy emerges with modernity. Such misconceptions can only be maintained by limiting the critical engagement with liturgy to the practice of professional academic research. As I have indicated above, reflections on and critical engagement with worship are as old as the first Christian gatherings, and those included women. About these women's engagement with worship we can know very little; throughout the following centuries, however, we do get glimpses of women's engagement with and reflection on liturgical practice, from Egeria's travelogue to the Holy Land in the late fourth century to the ninth-century Frankish noblewoman Dhuoda's written advice to her son on the recitation of the psalms; from Hildegard of Bingen and Teresa of Avila's rich reflections on liturgy to the work of Josephine Mayer in the 1930s [!] on women deacons in the early church.

The emergence of women's voices in liturgical studies in the second half of the twentieth century has to be seen within this larger trajectory. What is new in this more recent emergence is the fact that women, who had begun to enter the academy in sustained numbers with the twentieth century, now also gained access to the scholarly discipline of liturgical studies. The first doctorate in liturgical studies at a Roman Catholic faculty, at least in Europe, came in 1965, when Irmgard Pahl defended her dissertation at the University of Munich. The point here is a broader one than, simply, the entry of female bodies into a field of scholarly inquiry traditionally linked with priestly ordination and/or a religious vocation. This entry meant access to a particular material practice, with its own scholarly protocols and possibilities, including sustained access to important libraries, academic networks, employment opportunities, and professional status and voice. The beginnings of liturgical scholarship in conversation with women's history and feminist theory lie here.

A sustained expression in print of this conversation appeared in 1990 in a volume titled *Liturgie und Frauenfrage*.[48] Roughly half of the essays were dedicated to historical inquiries. The thematic range was broad indeed, from an essay on the Holy Spirit as mother in Syriac and Armenian sources (Gabriele Winkler) to a discussion of gender roles in sixteenth-century Lutheran worship (Karl-Heinrich Bieritz), and Catherine Winkworth as a translator of hymns (Geoffrey Wainwright). The approach in this volume was basically one of "adding women" to the traditional history of worship, which had largely left them invisible. *Liturgie und Frauenfrage* was soon followed by two monographs that analyzed in detail two very different moments in liturgical history using the interpretive lenses of women's history.

---

[48]   Teresa Berger and Albert Gerhards, eds., *Liturgie und Frauenfrage. Ein Beitrag zur Frauenforschung aus liturgiewissenschaftlicher Sicht*, Pietas Liturgica 7 (St. Ottilien: EOS-Verlag, 1990). As far as earlier studies are concerned, I note Marjorie Procter-Smith's *Women in Shaker Community and Worship: A Feminist Analysis of the Uses of Religious Symbolism* (Lewiston, NY: E. Mellen Press, 1985); and *In Her Own Rite: Constructing Feminist Liturgical Tradition* (Nashville, TN: Abingdon Press, 1990).

Gisela Muschiol, in her magisterial study *Famula Dei* (1994), examined the liturgical lives of women's communities in Romano-Merovingian Gaul. Muschiol showed that the center of daily life in these communities was a liturgy the women themselves shaped and celebrated under the liturgical presidency of their abbess, including the practice of hearing confessions, and absolving.[49] The women thus exercised a considerable measure of control over their own liturgical lives. My *Liturgie und Frauenseele* (1993) focused on the early twentieth-century Liturgical Movement; the study asked about the presence of women in this movement, as well as the role of feminine images in the movement's theology of liturgy.[50] Not in the field of liturgical studies proper, yet with profound relevance for an analysis of women's liturgical practices, was the study by Robert Orsi, *Thank You, St. Jude* (1996), which focused on the prayers and practices of American Catholic women devoted to the patron saint of hopeless causes.[51] Orsi used ethnographic research to read women's prayer practices as ways of negotiating particular cultural shifts in their lives.

*Women's Ways of Worship*, published in 1999, sought to introduce gender analysis to the study of liturgy's past and to bridge the growing rift, in liturgical historiography, between the conventional historical narrative and the ever-growing study of women's history. The book sketched three basic moments in the history of women at worship, in terms of methodological presuppositions and also in terms of material reconstruction. The subtitle of the book, *Gender Analysis and Liturgical History*, already laid claim to the broader field of gender studies, while the book's focus remained on one particular aspect of gender identity, namely "women." Gender theory did make its force felt in how the category "woman" was understood: not as a stable marker of identity, but as fundamentally unstable, always shifting, and profoundly shaped by other markers of difference such as status, ethnicity and race, age, geographic location, etc. With this interpretive focus, the book attempted to intervene critically in the scholarly writing of liturgical history, a field that—except for the individual studies just highlighted—had remained largely untouched by the scholarly work in women's history.[52] Yet looking at *Women's Ways of Worship* 12 years later, it is clear that the book was not able sufficiently to pursue the always relational character of its key category, "women."

---

[49]  See Gisela Muschiol, *Famula Dei. Zur Liturgie in merowingischen Frauenklöstern*, Beiträge zur Geschichte des alten Mönchtums und des Benediktinerordens 41 (Münster: Aschendorff, 1994).

[50]  Teresa Berger, *"Liturgie und Frauenseele." Die Liturgische Bewegung aus der Sicht der Frauenforschung*, Praktische Theologie Heute 10 (Stuttgart: Kohlhammer Verlag, 1993).

[51]  Robert A. Orsi, *Thank You, St. Jude: Women's Devotion to the Patron Saint of Hopeless Causes* (New Haven: Yale University Press, 1996).

[52]  J. Frank Henderson's work on primary documents related to women and worship in the Middle Ages is a wonderful exception, see his website: http://www.jfrankhenderson. com/womenandworship.htm.

Similarly, the book did not attend to genders other than those constructed within the traditional binary of masculinity and femininity.

I now come to the shift that lies at the heart of *Gender Differences and the Making of Liturgical History*, namely that from women's history to gender history. Before I map this shift in some detail, one last publication needs to be mentioned, which remained largely unmarked by that shift: Susan White's *A History of Women in Christian Worship*. White seeks to shed light on such important topics as places of women's worship, women of influence, forms of women's liturgical piety, churchgoing on Sunday, the household as a ritual site, and the liturgical arts.[53] Yet the author continues to draw on categories of women's history (especially women's "experience") that had already come to be criticized as problematic because not historically accessible, at least not in any immediate way.[54]

In the dozen years since the publication of *Women's Ways of Worship*, gender theory has forcefully expanded, and now comprises a broad range of diverse and complex scholarly projects. Today, gender history has convincingly moved beyond attending simply to "women" and thereby leaving a host of other gendered identities, including "men," unmarked. The following chapter traces this crucial development in more detail, in order to render visible what it might mean to make gender history an integral part of the ongoing work of writing the history of liturgy's past.

Before I turn to this task, I wish to return to the year A.D. 1114 and the church in Menat. When the women around Robert of Arbrissel risked their lives by entering this sanctuary, they did not introduce gender into this liturgical space for the first time. Gender had marked liturgical life in Menat as long as gendered bodies had gathered there for worship, whether male (clerical and lay) bodies alone or women together with lay men. What Robert of Arbrissel and his female companions did that day was to render visible, to question, and to contest the gender-specific ground rules of this sanctuary, which by A.D. 1114 had become a saintly tradition, set in stone. In so doing, they created space for a different future. *Gender Differences and the Making of Liturgical History* seeks to follow in their footsteps.

---

[53]  Susan J. White, *A History of Women in Christian Worship* (Cleveland: The Pilgrim Press, 2003). Despite the title, the focus lies on post-Reformation, English-speaking, literate, North Atlantic Protestants.

[54]  White's book also contains a number of descriptions of women's liturgical practices that would apply just as well to lay men, something that remains unacknowledged because the category gender is not sufficiently theorized. In a number of cases, White reads texts by women as simply providing historical facts, thus sidestepping an analysis of textual representation and mediation. Thus, for example, Saint Veronica ends up in a subchapter on "dead women" when that she ever lived in the first place is questionable.

# Chapter 2
# From Women to Gender Differences in Liturgy's Past

In a treatise written toward the end of the fourth century, John Chrysostom (+407) laments something he has witnessed in the liturgical assembly, namely that virgins who cohabit with men in sexual renunciation are met at the church door by their ascetic partners and then guided by them into the sanctuary. Chrysostom writes, accusingly: "In church they [the ascetic men] bring unspeakable disgrace upon themselves ... The men receive the women at the door, strutting [σοβοῦσι] as if they had been transformed into eunuchs, and when everyone is looking, they guide them in with enormous pride. Nor do they slink away, but go so far as to glory in their performance. Even at the most awesome hours of the mysteries, they are much occupied with waiting on the virgins' pleasure, providing many of the spectators with an occasion for offense."[1]

Granted that Chrysostom employs gender stereotypes in this text (e.g., the eunuch as impotent, servile, and pretentious, all in one) as well as the language of theatrical shows ("performance," "spectators"),[2] the glimpse of lived liturgy in the midst of this literary representation nevertheless is intriguing. It tells us that ascetic men accompanied the virgins with whom they cohabited to their particular place in the sanctuary; this was part of the gathering of an assembly for worship, and also noticeable. The latter would have been true no matter whether these ascetic virgins had actual "front row seats" in the sanctuary or not.[3]

---

[1]    John Chrysostom, *Adversus eos qui apud se habent subintroductas virgines* 10 (PG 47:509). English translation by Elizabeth A. Clark in *Jerome, Chrysostom, and Friends: Essays and Translations*, 2d ed., Studies in Women and Religion 2 (New York: The Edwin Mellen Press, 1982), 194. For more on Chrysostom's treatise, see Livia Neureiter, "John Chrysostom's Treatises on Spiritual Marriage," *Studia Patristica* 41 (2006): 457–62.

[2]    Important for this: Blake Leyerle, *Theatrical Shows and Ascetic Lives: John Chrysostom's Attack on Spiritual Marriage* (Berkeley: University of California Press, 2001).

[3]    John Chrysostom, *Quod regulares feminae viris cohabitare non debeant* 1 (PG 47:513–16; English text in Clark, 209). I remain uncertain whether in this passage Chrysostom is referring to an actual ecclesial place arrangement, as Blake Leyerle (*Theatrical Shows and Ascetic Lives*, 90) thinks, or whether he invokes this place arrangement as a metaphor to indicate an ecclesial value judgment (or possibly, of course, both).

This glimpse of a gathering for worship, which Chrysostom offers in his treatise against ascetic cohabitation, has been available for over 1,600 years.[4] Yet without the development of gender history, we would in all likelihood continue to read this story as a marginal curiosity rather than as an intriguing witness to the complexity of gender differences as these are negotiated in lived liturgy. It is the latter reading that makes the story a fitting introduction to the task of the present chapter where I map the development in twentieth-century historiography from women's history to the broader workings of gender history. I then sketch gender history's key interpretive strategies, with a focus on their bearing on liturgical historiography, and conclude with some reflections on the commitments that ultimately motivate a gender-attentive inquiry into liturgy's past.

To put what will follow in a nutshell in relation to the above story: Early forms of women's history would have focused their interpretative energy on the women who become visible in Chrysostom's text. Who are these virgins who cohabit with ascetic men in sexual renunciation? Can we recover these women's own voices, or do we encounter them only through a "male gaze"? What can the broader cultural and ecclesial context tell us about their form of life? In contradistinction, gender historians, while continuing to be interested in these important women-specific questions, now attend to *all* the gender identities that become visible in this glimpse of worship life in Chrysostom's time. How the virgins in question enter the sanctuary, after all, cannot adequately be described without mentioning the ascetic men who accompany them. Furthermore, "women" is a rather complex category in this text. Where the ascetic virgins find their place in the sanctuary may separate them not only from male worshippers but also from the place of non-ascetic women, and, possibly, of widows. In addition, one cannot adequately represent Chrysostom's description of the role of the ascetic men who accompany the virgins without reference to a third gender present both in Chrysostom's text and in the worship life of the time, namely eunuchs. And no gender analysis of this story would be complete without reference to the gendered identity of the author himself, in this case a priestly ascetic preacher fiercely opposed to ascetic cohabitation. We encounter these past liturgical practices only through his eyes. Finally – to round off the gendered complexity of this text's life and reception history – the historian who inserts this story in her present book comes with her own gendered subjectivity and scholarly lenses.

How then did gender history, with its attention to a broad array of gender differences and their representations, develop? To this I now turn.

---

[4]    There has been much recent interest in what we can learn about congregational life from Chrysostom's sermons; see especially the work by Wendy Mayer and Pauline Allen, *John Chrysostom*, The Early Church Fathers (New York: Routledge, 2000), and Jaclyn Maxwell, "Lay Piety in the Sermons of John Chrysostom," in *Byzantine Christianity*, ed. Derek Krueger, A People's History of Christianity 3 (Minneapolis: Fortress Press, 2006), 19–38.

## Gender History: Beyond Women's Ways of Worship

The narrative of the emergence of gender theory—especially its relationship to women's history and feminist theory—is not only multifaceted but also contested.[5] With that caveat, and with my following remarks focused on the specific subject-matter of the present book, namely gender analysis for liturgy's past, I offer the following sketch.

Gender theory emerged out of both the deepening insights and the increasing difficulties produced by the vibrant growth of women's studies and feminist scholarship. The latter burst on the scene as scholarly fields in the early 1970s, on the heels of the second wave of the 1960s women's movement, which itself followed a first-wave women's movement in the nineteenth and early twentieth centuries. As regards the writing of history, second-wave feminist scholarship generated fundamental critical insights into the working of traditional historiography, a wealth of ground-breaking studies of women of the past, and a much greater visibility and recognition of particular women-identified contours and sites (e.g., female convents).

*Earlier Approaches and Their Weaknesses*

Two early forms of women's history and feminist historiography deserve recognition here even if they have been supplanted by more sophisticated approaches. I mention these two forms because the very difficulties they raised for the writing of history contributed to the emergence of gender history. Moreover, these approaches continue to inform historiographic work, not least of all in the writing of liturgy's past.[6]

The first of these approaches might be termed the "add-women-and-stir" approach. We owe to this approach the addition of a number of remarkable women to the mix of traditional characters of the past, women who had been invisible or marginal up to that time. For the history of Christianity, adding women like Faltonia Betitia Proba, Julian of Norwich, and Sor Juana Inés de la Cruz to the traditional narrative clearly expanded the conventional image of the tradition. Problematic in this approach was, and continues to be, its adherence to the traditional master narrative. Simply adding women to this narrative while leaving its interpretive strategies intact, renders visible only a handful of elite women. These women

---

[5]     One of the most succinct and (in my mind best) narratives available is the introduction by Roberta Gilchrist to her book, *Gender and Archaeology: Contesting the Past* (New York: Routledge, 1999), ch. 1.

[6]     Much of Susan J. White's book, *A History of Women in Christian Worship* (Cleveland: Pilgrim Press, 2003), is informed by this approach. I would also include here my own essay "Women in Worship," in *The Oxford History of Christian Worship*, ed. Geoffrey Wainwright and Karen B. Westerfield Tucker (New York: Oxford University Press, 2005), 755–68, even if its argument tries to move beyond this perspective.

are inserted into a traditional historiography whose fundamental givens are not reconfigured in any way by this addition.[7]

A second approach prevalent in early writings by historians of women focused on women as victims, that is, as objects of misogyny and patriarchal oppression, within the master narrative. Problems with this approach include the occlusion of female sites of agency and power, obliviousness to hierarchies between women of different social classes or ethnicities, and, not least, a fixation on an overarching explanatory category such as a historical meta-narrative of misogyny, for what ultimately are very complex and divergent gendering processes and workings of power. To put the matter differently: A "women-as-victims" approach trusted the facts generated by traditional historiography too much in that it took for granted the marginal, dependent, and subservient status of women in the past. Such an approach also misjudged how cultural materials actually circulate among historically marginalized groups. Marginalized peoples are not devoid of agency; they never simply receive, but also transform.[8]

*Gender as a Category of Historical Analysis*

In response to the growing complexities generated by feminist theory, and also by other intellectual shifts, gender history emerged in the mid-1980s. As a field of scholarly inquiry into the construction of gender, gender theory generated a vibrant expansion of perspectives and interpretive strategies, not least of all in the field of history.[9] Gender historians conveniently link the emergence of their field to the publication of Joan W. Scott's seminal essay "Gender: A Useful Category of Analysis" in the *American Historical Review* in 1986.[10] With the emergence of gender history, analyses of sexual difference—that is: gender, gender systems, and gender hierarchies as these have marked the past—come alive. The expansion and shift are usually linked to the beginnings of third-wave feminism. Influenced by postmodernist, and especially poststructuralist (largely Foucauldian), thought and

---

[7]    A case in point is the many courses in church history that have simply added a number of references to women or women's texts to an otherwise quite traditional narrative.

[8]    Max Harris, for example, has shown this in his studies of folk festivals, *Aztecs, Moors, and Christians: Festivals of Reconquest in Mexico and Spain* (Austin: University of Texas Press, 2000), and *Carnival and Other Christian Festivals: Folk Theology and Folk Performance* (Austin: University of Texas Press, 2003).

[9]    On gender history as a scholarly field of inquiry, see Laura Lee Downs, *Writing Gender History, Writing History* (New York: Oxford University Press, 2004); Claudia Opitz, *Um-Ordnungen der Geschlechter: Einführung in die Geschlechtergeschichte*, Historische Einführungen 10 (Tübingen: Edition Diskord, 2005). Johanna Alberti, *Gender and the Historian* (New York: Longman, 2002) maps the writings of historians of women from the late 1960s to the turn of the century.

[10]    See Joan Wallach Scott, "Gender: A Useful Category of Historical Analysis," *American Historical Review* 91 (1986): 1053–75.

the "linguistic turn,"[11] third-wave feminism moved away both from essentializing categories ("women's experience") and from meta-narratives ("women's oppression"), the weaknesses of which its own vibrant scholarship had rendered visible.[12]

Three new foci of analysis emerged and became critical to the workings of gender history. The first is an insistence on "difference"; this inscribes into the notion of gender the recognition that relational others are fundamental to the construction of a category in the first place. To put this concretely: one cannot invoke "women" without acknowledging that the word's meaning is constituted by what women are not, namely men. Similarly, the other of the category "gay" would be either a straight man or a lesbian woman, with bisexual, intersexed, and trans human beings queering the binaries. Difference, in other words, reigns in gendering processes. Not surprisingly, detailed analyses of gender differences—whether between women and men, or between men and women of differing sexualities, or of different genders beyond the traditional binary—became a dominant concern. These gender differences are seen as socially constructed. The older distinction between sex (as supposedly "natural," based in biological fact) and gender (as culturally constructed) had been rendered unworkable, not least because the biological differentiation of the sexes came to be seen as more complicated than what was believed to be a natural differentiation of two sexes. Cases in point are the six million human beings alive today with neither clearly identifiable female or male chromosomes.[13] Far from being marginal, the complexity of gender differences impacts contemporary life in a multitude of ways, from restroom access for the gender-ambiguous, to sex determination and Y-chromosome testing of female athletes, to Vatican deliberations on transgender surgery in a priest or anxieties over the "obscuring of the difference or duality of the sexes."[14]

---

[11]  For the discipline of history, this turn and its challenges for the field have been expertly delineated by Elizabeth A. Clark, *History, Theory, Text: Historians and the Linguistic Turn* (Cambridge, MA: Harvard University Press, 2004).

[12]  A telling acknowledgement of this shift appears in the introductory sentences of Daniel Boyarin's entry "Gender," in *Critical Terms for Religious Studies*, ed. Mark C. Taylor (Chicago: University of Chicago Press, 1998), 117–35, here 117.

[13]  For more on this see Anne Fausto-Sterling, *Sexing the Body: Gender Politics and the Construction of Sexuality* (New York: Basic Books, 2000), 51–4; Christine E. Gudorf, "The Erosion of Sexual Dimorphism: Challenges to Religion and Religious Ethics," *Journal of the American Academy of Religion* 69 (2001): 863–91, here 874f.

[14]  With regard to the former, *Catholic News Service* reported in January of 2003 that the Vatican had produced a document "*sub secretum*" in which sex change surgeries were declared irrelevant with regard to the true gender of a person; thus a priest who had undergone a sex-change operation was still a priest. For anxieties over "obscuring of the difference or duality of the sexes," see the 2004 document from the Vatican's Congregation for the Doctrine of the Faith, titled "Letter to the Bishops of the Catholic Church on the Collaboration of Men and Women in the Church and in the World," esp. # 2f. The text

As the seemingly natural category "women," which had anchored much of women's history, crumbled under the weight of evidence that the underlying binary division was neither universal nor stable, but was negotiated quite differently in different historical contexts, further fields of inquiry emerged, related to questions of gender now broadly conceived. Obviously, feminist historiography itself did not simply stop with the emergence of gender theory. Rather, it fine-tuned its tools, typically along the theoretical lines of gender theory, with the subject-matter continuing to be a particular female gendering process (e.g. adolescent girls, lesbian women, or subaltern female subjects).[15] Among the newly emerging fields, the most prominent were the study of masculinities, sexuality studies, and queer theory.

The study of masculinities is the most obvious complement to women's studies, especially in the field of history. Traditional historiography, after all, which came under criticism for its women-specific blindspots, had not attended to the "millions of men who were only men"[16] any more than it had attended to women. From its early search for the histories of "non-hegemonic males" the study of masculinities has evolved into an inquiry into the manifold historical formations of masculinity. The Christian tradition, with its own forms of masculine identities, has been a quite fertile field of inquiry.[17]

Sexuality studies emerged out of a different, although related, recognition, namely that one's gender and one's sexual practices are not necessarily co-terminous. This scholarly field of inquiry consequently focuses on sexual desires and *practices* rather than on gendered identities themselves. It has produced a wealth of studies, many of which are dedicated to non-dominant sexualities and cultures—e.g., gay, bisexual, or intersexed—without however leaving heteronormative sexualities unmarked.[18]

Queer theory, usually linked in one way or another with the 1990 publication of Judith Butler's *Gender Trouble*, emerged in the challenge to, and the undoing of, the distinction between sex as a stable biological reference point and gender as a cultural construction. For Butler, all gender identities were constructed in performance, and "doing gender" became the signpost for the scholarly inquiry into fundamentally unstable gender identities. Queer theory as it emerged from

---

can be accessed on the Congregation's website: http://www.vatican.va/-roman_curia/congregations/cfaith/documents/rc_con_cfaith_doc_20040731_collaboration_en.html.

[15]   The field has been mapped well in a reader; see *The Feminist History Reader*, ed. Sue Morgan (New York: Routledge, 2006).

[16]   The apt expression is Thelma Fenster's; see her "Why Men?," in *Medieval Masculinities: Regarding Men in the Middle Ages*, ed. Clare A. Lees et al., Medieval Cultures 7 (Minneapolis: University of Minnesota Press, 1994), IX–XIII, here X.

[17]   For an overview, see the reader *Men and Masculinities in Christianity and Judaism: A Critical Reader*, ed. Björn Krondorfer (London: SCM Press, 2009).

[18]   A good overview is provided by Robert A. Nye, "Sexuality," in *A Companion to Gender History*, ed. Teresa A. Meade and Merry E. Wiesner-Hanks, Blackwell Companions to History (Malden, MA: Blackwell Publishing, 2004), 11–25.

these roots has been committed particularly to alternative performances of gender identity, which challenge what has been constructed as (hetero-)normative.

So much for a first focus on gender differences as these came to the forefront in gender history. A second focus was a determined insistence on "intersectionality." Intersectionality focuses attention on the interrelatedness of various markers of difference such as gender, social class, ethnicity, and age. An example for the importance of intersectionality as an explanatory category is the case of Empress Maria Theresia, mentioned in the previous chapter. At a point in time when women did not have access to university education, Maria Theresia—solely because of her status as monarch—was able to authorize a curricular reform of theological faculties, in the process of which the (sub-)discipline of "liturgics" was established in catholic faculties.

A third focus that came to the forefront with the development of gender theory is an analysis of power, which was inscribed in the very definition of gender by Joan W. Scott's previously mentioned essay. In this essay, she famously described gender as a "primary way of signifying relationships of power."[19] Leaning on French deconstructive thought (Jacques Derrida as well as Michel Foucault), Scott sought to move away from a view of gender differences assumed to be self-evident and "in the nature of things" to a view of gender differences as historically constructed in ever-shifting ways. Along the way Scott also inscribed into gender analysis a basically oppositional understanding of power in gender hierarchies. This emphasis on oppositional power has recently been critiqued by Jeanne Boydston, a gender historian who argues—I think rightly—that the practice of gender is not inherently and always about power differentials, since gender is not practiced everywhere in oppositional binaries.[20] Boydston challenges gender historians to interrogate, ever anew, their own (universalizing) assumptions about gender, and to use gender as a "set of relatively open questions" applied to divergent processes of gendering in a multitude of specific times and places.[21] Gender history here comes to be recalibrated, away from a fixed inquiry into a single named process to a set of questions about variable, historically grounded processes of gendering.[22] Boydston's essay, a recent example of the vibrantly self-reflective nature of the field of gender history, seems to me to hold particular promise for the analysis of gender processes, not least of all in the history of Christianity.

---

[19]   Joan W. Scott, "Gender: A Useful Category of Historical Analysis," 1067.

[20]   See Jeanne Boydston, "Gender as a Question of Historical Analysis," *Gender and History* 20 (2008): 558–83.

[21]   Ibid., 559.

[22]   Ibid., 576.

**Why Gender History for Liturgy's Past?**

What relationship is there between gender history and the task of writing liturgical history? What work can a set of questions about gender processes do for liturgy's past? Did gender processes influence liturgical practices? And if yes, how can these processes be (re-)inscribed into the writing of liturgical history? Where and how did gendered identities mark liturgical life, when bodies gathered in sacred space, for example, in gender-specific forms of presence and participation, in gendered images or hagiographic texts, or in representations of the Holy One to be worshiped? These are some of the questions that *Gender Differences and the Making of Liturgical History* seeks to face, especially in the second part of the book. For now, it is important to take a closer look at the task that motivates this inquiry.

The *task* of bringing gender history to bear on liturgy's past centers on writing gender back into the "facts" of liturgical history. As I have insisted before, such work is *not* about discarding the writing of liturgical history to date, but about reconfiguring its gender-oblivious narrative and that narrative's explanatory and authorizing power. Methodologically, such reconfiguration happens by bringing the tools of gender history to the discipline of liturgical historiography. Two steps stand out, familiar from scholarly work in other fields that attended to these tasks earlier. First, the traditional interpretive strategies that have informed the writing of liturgical history become the subject of critical analysis (this was the burden of Chapter 1). Critical questions are raised about traditional liturgical historiography and its explanatory power: What is occluded in this history writing, given that what comes to be authorized as "facts of liturgical history" is always theory-specific? What assumptions about gender (or the unimportance of gender) are written into the liturgical record as we know it? How has gender-oblivion shaped our image of liturgy's past? These are some of the questions that help to destabilize the givenness of inherited ways of writing liturgical history, and to ask what has been occluded or rendered unintelligible in such history writing. The second step in restoring gender to liturgical history follows from this. If a critical engagement with the interpretive strategies that produced the traditional narrative is the first step, then the second is to reconceive the narrative of the past in more nuanced, gender-attentive ways. For such a reconceptualization, we have to establish a set of key methodological principles and interpretive strategies based on the insights of gender history, to be put to work for the writing of liturgy's past. I offer these below.

In the meantime, a comment on the timing of this task. Obviously, a scholarly inquiry that seeks to insert questions about gender into the writing of liturgical history is linked to broader intellectual trends, especially current developments in gender history. That said, it would be all too facile to dismiss *Gender Differences and the Making of Liturgical History* as being, at heart, in conversation merely with a currently fashionable scholarly theory that, in a decade or so, will have exhausted its appeal. I hope that my earlier sketch of the discipline of liturgical historiography, as one always in conversation with contemporary intellectual trends and theorizing (think of the influence of models of evolution on twentieth-century liturgical historiography), will suffice to put to rest such an easy dismissal of gender history. Liturgical history writing will always be shaped by the intellectual conversations of its own time. The best we can do is to enter into these conversations critically and self-critically; the alternative would be to let these conversations shape our thinking unbeknownst to us.

I am convinced that bringing together the vastly expanded and reconfigured field of gender history with the ongoing work of liturgical historiography holds great promise for the writing of liturgy's past. To date, nothing has been published on this subject in the field of liturgical studies. There are two reasons in particular why this should change, and why a gender-attentive historical narrative of the liturgy is of some urgency now. First, the field of gender history has produced sustained challenges to conventional forms of historiography, of which liturgical historiography is one. Liturgical historiography ignores to its own impoverishment these theoretical challenges, not least because the story it seeks to tell is at heart a story of human beings who gather in worship before God, and these human beings come, always and only, embodied—and that means living within some version of a gendering process.

A second reason for seeking to bridge the gap between gender history and the writing of liturgy's past lies in the fact that gender history, far from being merely a set of theoretical insights, has by now produced an astounding amount of historical material. This material is of profound relevance for liturgical historiography. One example is the recent vibrant scholarship on eunuchs.[23] Although this scholarship shows little interest in the liturgical lives of eunuchs, the findings nevertheless bear immediate relevance for liturgical historiography.[24] The baptism of an Ethiopian eunuch, recounted in Acts 8:27–39, already grants a glimpse of this "third-gender" presence in earliest Christianity. Why would liturgical historiography want to ignore the wealth of insights now available into the lives and worlds of those who worshiped?

It is high time to bring into conversation the two disparate versions of the past that originate from the writing of liturgical history, on the one hand, and the writing of gender history, on the other hand. Such conversation cannot but contribute to a deepened, richer understanding of the history of worship, and what on earth would *not* be desirable about that? In order to facilitate this conversation, I turn to the key methodological principles that inform *Gender Differences and the Making of Liturgical History*.

---

[23]   I will pursue this subject in greater depth in Chapter 6 of this book.

[24]   I am thinking here of the important essay by Robert F. Taft, "Women at Church in Byzantium: Where, When—and Why?," *Dumbarton Oaks Papers* 52 (1998): 27–87. The subject-matter, if defined as "women" alone, runs into gender trouble quickly because intersectionality (in this case: status) intervenes to complicate matters. Eunuchs, for example, would have had access to the women's space if the women were high-status Byzantine women.

## Methodological Principles: Gender History and the Writing of Liturgy's Past

The starting point for bringing into conversation gender history and the writing of liturgy's past has to be an account of what will guide this conversation. For the interests of the present book, such an account can be grounded in a set of methodological principles generated in gender history that aligns with the tasks of liturgical historiography. In many ways, principles earlier identified for the writing of women's liturgical history continue to be applicable here; I am thinking in particular of an expanded set of sources, a broadened understanding of what constitutes liturgical sites, and a fresh look at conventional periodizations.[25] The one methodological principle that demands a more sustained reconfiguration, not surprisingly, is the understanding of gender itself. As will be obvious from the sketch of the development from women's history to gender history, the category gender needs to be, first, freed from primarily meaning women, second, complexified, and third, unmoored from dominantly signifying binary oppositional power differentials.

First, gender is *not* a synonym for women. Gender difference is nothing if not a relational category, and it has to be displayed as such. In terms of the writing of liturgical history, for example, not only women but also "men who were only men" have been written out of this history. Traditional liturgical historiography with its attention to elite males—most of them monks and priests with a gendered particularity of their own—and their institutions and productions rendered invisible a number of other gendered particularities, millions of men who were only men among them. Fortunately for the latter, there has been a noticeable rise in scholarly interest in historical constructions of masculinity, enabling us to leave behind the illusion that masculinity was unmarked. A gender-attentive liturgical historiography, then, cannot leave men's cultures unmarked and invisible, as if women, more than anybody else, were gendered. In fact, gender history can never treat "women" as if that category can stand on its own and was not constituted by its relational other, men. An insistence on this fact is, I think, the most marked difference between earlier work and the present *Gender Differences and the Making of Liturgical History*.

Second, and following from this, gender applies not only to masculinity and femininity, but to all gendering processes and identities, including those that subdivide one of the sides of the traditional binary, for example virgins and widows,[26] or which defy the binary, as intersexed persons do. A gender-attentive rereading of the liturgical past thus will include attention to how the presence of

---

[25]  See Teresa Berger, *Women's Ways of Worship: Gender Analysis and Liturgical History* (Collegeville: Liturgical Press, 1999), 5–26.

[26]  Anke Bernau has argued that "holy virgin" functioned as a distinct gender identity in the Christian tradition; see her "Virginal Effects: Texts and Identity in *Ancrene Wisse*," in *Gender and Holiness: Men, Women and Saints in Late Medieval Europe*, ed. Samantha J.

eunuchs in Byzantium or castrati singers in the West shaped liturgical life, and how holy virgins and celibate priests signaled distinct gendering processes that complicate a simple binary notion of gender. Attention to all gendered identities as these intersect with liturgical life reveals a liturgical past much more intricate than one shaped exclusively by two sides of an oppositional binary, men and women.[27]

Third, "gender" is not a stable universal. Rather, gendering processes are invariably complex, configured with significant differences in diverse historical places and times. These differences can entail gendering processes that do not involve binary power differentials, and perhaps historical contexts exist where gender was not a primary signifier at all.[28] That said, gender theory's insistence on intersectionality is worth repeating here. Gender never stands by itself, but is always inflected by other markers of difference, such as ethnicity and race, age, and ecclesial affiliation, to name just a few. Last but not least, the lived experience of gender is forever shifting, as the gendered body is transformed by the life-cycle and its cultural codes. Thus, an 80 year-old man is a different kind of male from an eight-day-old infant with XY chromosomes.

Intersectionality, i.e. gender's relationship with other markers of difference, is quite obvious in liturgical history. For much of the history of the liturgy the dominant marker of difference might in fact be ascribed to a combination of gender and social status, rather than gender alone. In restoring gender to the writing of liturgy's past, we have to assume that there are multiple constructions of gender and gendering processes. An attempt to write gender back into the history of liturgy thus is an attempt to historicize, not to essentialize, gender differences as these mark liturgy.

Moreover, even if one common gender system in liturgy's past is binary masculinity and femininity, the Christian tradition has produced and been enriched by its own slippages and subversions of seemingly dominant scripts. There are rich variations on masculinity and femininity present when, for example, the Eucharist is seen as God's breast milk and communion as nursing, images that found liturgical expression in the ancient blessing over a milk-and-honey cup at the baptismal Eucharist.[29] Such gender variations are also present in texts and images that depict Mary as a priest, the first person to offer to humanity the body and blood of Christ. Other variations can easily be named, for example in relation to the sanctoral cycle, since sanctity not infrequently meant a break with reigning values, gendered identity among them. In fact, "constructing one's gender identity

E. Riches and Sarah Salih, Routledge Studies in Medieval Religion and Culture (New York: Routledge, 2002), 36–48.

[27] The Christian tradition might in fact just prove Jeanne Boydston's suggestion right, namely to see "variation as the rule and to understand categories with 'normative' claims as but instances of the epiphenomena of that variation." See Boydston, "Gender as a Question of Historical Analysis," 569.

[28] I follow Boydston here, ibid.

[29] I attend to this in greater detail in Chapter 4.

differently may be a marker of holiness."[30] The hagiographic tradition thus is quite familiar with gender-bending, gender-crossing, and gender slippage, from cross-dressers to male writers who imagine themselves as brides of Christ or as pregnant with the Word. The writing of liturgy's past will have to attend to these.

So much for a set of methodological principles that are able to guide gender analysis in liturgical historiography. I will leave further explication of gender-attentive interpretive strategies to the work on concrete materials in the chapters that follow.

## Lifting a Veil on Liturgy's Past: What for?

I wish to conclude this chapter with a first look at the larger vision that underlies the search for a gender-attentive writing of liturgy's past (I will return to this in more detail in the concluding chapter).

Mark Jordan, in a probing and insightful essay titled "Arguing Liturgical Genealogies," identifies a problem for this search by questioning the force of scholarly, historiographic work for contemporary gender issues in the church. He asks, "why fret about a more exact history when the real fight is over the institutions that will determine what counts as church history—and who gets to be counted in?"[31] Unquestioningly, this is a vexing issue. At the same time, the underlying division of labor implied here — namely the struggle for a more "exact" history, and the struggle over the meaning of the past—itself deserves to be questioned. Both tasks are important, each in its own way, and—since they are intertwined—do not have to be construed as mutually exclusive. The passion to seek a deeper truth about the liturgical past is not primarily about the historiographical "thrill of recovering the forgotten, the overlooked, or the repressed" (although I see no reason to deny such a thrill).[32] The margins, after all, always are constitutive of the definition of the center. But the historiographic passion behind *Gender Differences and the Making of Liturgical History* ultimately gestures toward theological commitments. In other words, making gender a critically important set of questions for liturgical historiography finally is not about "gender" alone. Rather, it is about the heart of critical liturgical inquiry as I understand it: namely about the truth claims that surround human beings who encounter the Holy One in liturgical symbols and practices. Within this grandest of theological claims about liturgical inquiry, three particular commitments stand out:

---

[30]    Samantha J. E. Riches and Sarah Salih in their introduction to *Gender and Holiness: Men, Women and Saints in Late Medieval Europe*, Routledge Studies in Medieval Religion and Culture (New York: Routledge, 2002), 5.

[31]    See his essay "Arguing Liturgical Genealogies, or the Ghost of Weddings Past," in *Canon, Tradition, and Critique in the Blessing of Same-Sex Unions*, ed. Mark D. Jordan et al. (Princeton: Princeton University Press, 2006), 102–20, here 112.

[32]    The apt wording is Mark Jordan's, "Arguing Liturgical Genealogies," 112.

First, there is a liturgical commitment to truthful ἀνάμνησις. Such *anamnesis*, the presence in retelling of God's redemptive power in history, plays a fundamental role in the liturgical assembly. One only has to think of the Blessing over Baptismal Waters, which recounts salvation history through the lens of this particular natural element,[33] or of the *anamnesis* of Jesus' passion in the heart of the Eucharistic Prayer, rendering present that self-giving of life. Narrating the past is fundamental for other liturgical speech acts beyond anamnetic prayers, such as in any confession of sins. At the same time, representations of the past are present in worship beyond the verbal level, e.g, in sacred images. Narrating the past, then, has always been a fundamental liturgical act. Surely, interrogating narratives of the past, identifying flaws, and striving for the most truthful narrative possible is an important part of liturgical reflection and practice.

Second, there is a theological commitment: Out of what is visible of the past, the church continues to lay claim to a particular construal of its past, namely tradition, understood as Spirit-inspired and Spirit-sustained. Such a tradition presumably cannot safely rest in accounts of the past that themselves are not safe, for example because they are based on conventionally androcentric readings of what matters. Even if one acknowledges that knowing "the truth" about the past is an impossibility, the unmasking of half-truths that pretend (if only through silence) to be all that needs to be said remains a fundamental task. Why not think of such unmasking as Spirit-inspired? Rendering visible the daring diversity of the liturgical tradition when it comes to gender processes may just be part of vibrant ecclesial discernment. Thankfully, the liturgical past (or at least what is visible of it to us) contains its own manifold subversions of established routines, thus enabling renewed confidence in the Spirit's presence within a past that might have to be acknowledged as, at points, irrevocably flawed.

Lastly, there is a contemporary ecclesial and pastoral commitment: Rendering visible the complex ways in which liturgy has always been shaped by changing gender constructions will I hope open a space for nuanced reflections in a world where gender differences continue to be alive and well in worship. Among the more publicly visible issues are continuing questions about women's ministries, questions surrounding the full ecclesial life of queer Christians, and popular discussions of the need for a more "muscular" Christianity in an otherwise "impotent" because "feminized" church. Clearly, gender is far from being a profound marker of *past* liturgical practice only. What the study of the past can offer to the present is a genealogy for contemporary struggles and questions, in the form of a history of liturgical life filled with gender as both a fundamental given and deeply contested. To unearthing the contours of such a history, I now turn.

---

[33] Reinhard Messner makes this Blessing central in his insightful thinking about the liturgical past and tradition; see his "Die vielen gottesdienstlichen Überlieferungen und die eine liturgische Tradition," in *Liturgische Theologie: Aufgaben systematischer Liturgiewissenschaft*, ed. Helmut Hoping and Birgit Jeggle-Merz (Paderborn: Schöningh, 2004), 33–56.

# PART II
# Tracing Gender in Liturgy's Past

Part II of *Gender Differences and the Making of Liturgical History* presents four in-depth case studies in order to demonstrate what a gender-attentive liturgical historiography entails. This part opens with two chapters on traditional fundamentals of liturgical historiography, one dedicated to liturgical space (Chapter 3) and one to eucharistic practice (Chapter 4). The following two case studies move beyond conventional fundamentals of liturgical history writing in order to imagine alternative ways of studying liturgy's past that are based on foregrounding questions of gender differences in worship. The first of these case studies inquires into gender differences as they shaped liturgical presence and participation by highlighting liturgical impediments based on bodily flows, including menstruation, nocturnal emissions, sexual relations, and childbirth (Chapter 5). The following chapter traces the emerging link between liturgical presiding and priestly masculinity, taking into account the concomitant questioning regarding liturgical leadership by other gender identities, among them women, eunuchs, and "in-continent" men (Chapter 6).

# Chapter 3
# Sacred Spaces and Gendered Bodies

It was the spring of A.D. 384. A pilgrim arrived at the shrine of Saint Thecla near the city of Seleucia in Asia Minor.[1] The pilgrim had journeyed from the distant Western parts of the Roman Empire to the Holy Land; now on her return journey, she wished to visit Hagia Thecla. Thecla, the itinerant, cross-dressing, self-baptizing, virginity-loving, legendary companion of the apostle Paul, had become a popular saint, venerated both as apostle and protomartyr.[2] Devotional objects bearing Thecla's image, such as pilgrimage flasks, were available, probably not least at the shrine near Seleucia, which had become the center of Thecla devotion in Asia Minor. Our pilgrim, upon reaching this shrine, entered into the liturgical routine she had followed at previous pilgrimage sites. She prayed at the shrine, then proceeded to read the text related to the pilgrimage site she was visiting, in this case the *Acts of Thecla*. On the following days, she enjoyed the hospitality of the guardians of the shrine. One of these, a deaconess named Marthana, our pilgrim already knew from their time together in Jerusalem. But why not let the pilgrim tell in her own words of meeting her friend again:

> At the holy church [Hagia Thecla] there is nothing but countless monastic cells for men and women. I met there a very dear friend of mine, and a person to whose way of life everyone in the East bears witness, the holy deaconess Marthana, whom I had met in Jerusalem, where she had come to pray. She governs these monastic cells of *aputactitae* [ascetics], or virgins. Would I ever be able to describe how great was her joy and mine when she saw me? ... There are many cells all over the hill, and in the middle there is a large wall which encloses the church where the shrine is. It is a very beautiful shrine. The wall is set to guard the church against the Isaurians [inhabitants of the region, with a reputation for banditry]. Having arrived there in the name of God, a prayer was said at the shrine and the complete Acts of Saint Thecla was read. I then gave unceasing thanks to Christ our God, who granted to me, an unworthy woman and in

---

[1]    As to the dating of Egeria's pilgrimage I follow the timeline now accepted by the majority of scholars.

[2]    My knowledge of early devotion to Saint Thecla is largely dependent on my colleague Stephen J. Davis's book, *The Cult of Saint Thecla: A Tradition of Women's Piety in Late Antiquity*, Oxford Early Christian Studies (New York: Oxford University Press, 2001). In what follows, I draw especially on part I of Stephen Davis's book.

no way deserving, the fulfillment of my desires in all things. And so, after spending two days there …, and after praying and receiving Communion [*facta oratione et communione*], I returned to Tarsus and to my journey.[3]

## Egeria: Gender and Sacred Sites

The story of this pilgrim's visit to the shrine of Hagia Thecla is of interest for an inquiry into gender and sacred space for a number of reasons. To begin with, the text is one of only a handful of extant texts written by women from the first thousand years of liturgical history. The author is now commonly identified as "Egeria" (the text itself does not give her name). Egeria's travelogue, hidden from historians until the late nineteenth century, has become one of the most important witnesses to the early history of the Jerusalem liturgy and to the development of a liturgical calendar. In terms of gender history, the text is remarkable not only because of its female author but also because of its intended audience. Egeria wrote for a group of women she had left at home, whom she addresses directly throughout her text as "venerable ladies," "sisters," or, repeatedly, "your affection" (*affectio vestra* [5.8 et al.], *dominae sorores* [46.1,4], *dominae sorores venerabiles* [20.5]). These women, most likely living together in some form of vowed community, seem to have been especially interested in liturgical details. That the women compared Egeria's descriptions with their own liturgical practices is one plausible explanation for this interest.[4]

Gender identities thus mark the document as a whole, as well as its intended readers, and, given that Egeria's travelogue is both women-identified *and* liturgy-focused, her pilgrimage to the shrine of Saint Thecla has to be seen within that larger context. Egeria's visit to Hagia Thecla then takes on particular meaning since here Egeria's dual motivations come into sharp focus. Devotion to Saint Thecla, with its links to the strongly women-identified narrative of the *Acts of Thecla*, seems to have flourished particularly among women.[5] By the time of Egeria's pilgrimage to the shrine, Hagia Thecla had become the site of a large ascetic-eremitic community. Egeria mentions one of its leaders, Marthana, by name (strikingly, this deaconess is the only contemporary explicitly named in the travelogue). Marthana governed [*regebat*] ascetics at Thecla's shrine; the text does

---

[3] Egeria, *Itinerarium* 23.2–6. A number of English translations of the Latin text in CCSL 175 are available. I quote from Gingras's here because he remains closest to the Latin original: *Diary of a Pilgrimage*, trans. and annotated by George E. Gingras, Ancient Christian Writers 38 (New York: Newman Press, 1970), 87f. For a discussion of this particular passage, see Davis, *Cult of Saint Thecla*, 64–71.

[4] See Hagith Sivan, "Holy Land Pilgrimage and Western Audiences: Some Reflections on Egeria and her Circle," *Classical Quarterly* 38 (1988): 528–35, and "Who was Egeria? Piety and Pilgrimage in the Age of Gratian," *Harvard Theological Review* 81 (1988): 59–72.

[5] Davis has argued this point convincingly in his *Cult of Saint Thecla*, 8–35.

not make clear whether she had oversight over both male and female ascetics, or over women only.[6] Egeria's text simply highlights the leadership of a woman at this particular shrine.

Historians of liturgy have shown little interest in Egeria's visit to Hagia Thecla with its gender-specific nuances. Instead, liturgical scholars have focused their attention on the detailed description of the Jerusalem liturgy in the second part of her *Itinerarium*. The overall gender-specific character of Egeria's writing then quickly disappears from view, despite the fact that she opens her description of the Jerusalem liturgy by emphasizing that she is writing down her astonishingly detailed liturgical observations precisely because that is what her sisters wish to understand. "Knowing how pleased Your Charity [*affectio vestra*] would be to learn what is the ritual observed day by day in the holy places, I consider it my duty to make known to you the details."[7] Moreover, throughout her description Egeria is careful to explain for her sisters aspects of the worship life of the Jerusalem church. She translates, for example, the Greek name for the evening office into the Latin her sisters know [*lucernare*], and the Greek *Kyrie eleison* into the familiar *Miserere Domine*.[8] Egeria's descriptions thus are clearly aimed toward the liturgical life of her female audience, including those descriptions of the Jerusalem liturgy which have rightly garnered Egeria a place among the key witnesses to liturgy's past.

Why Egeria's text stands at the beginning of this particular chapter on gender and sacred space has much to do with the kind of worship space that becomes visible in Egeria's pilgrimage to Hagia Thecla. This shrine serves as an example of a sacred site whose contours do not fit neatly into traditional histories of the development of sacred space. One of the reasons for this misfit is the prominently women-identified nature of the site: Hagia Thecla is the shrine of a female saint whose story seems to have circulated especially among groups of women; female ascetics live around this shrine, governed by a deaconess we know by name; the shrine is visited by a pilgrim who writes down her story for a community of women far away. This is a quite different story from the one usually told in narratives of the development of liturgical space. The conventional storyline, especially for the fourth century, typically focuses on the emergence of urban basilicas as the centers of Christian liturgical practice. With such a focus, what remains invisible are the many other sanctuary spaces, for example house chapels, relic shrines, cemetery churches, and estate churches, that continued to exist alongside the rising urban basilicas.[9] Finally, Egeria's visit to Hagia Thecla is a fitting starting point for this

---

[6]   Egeria, *Itinerarium* 23.3.

[7]   Egeria, *Itinerarium* 24.1: "*Ut autem sciret affectio vestra, quae operatio singulis diebus cotidie in locis sanctis habeatur, certas vos facere debui, sciens quia libenter haberetis haec cognoscere.*" The translation is from Gingras, *Diary of a Pilgrimage*, 89.

[8]   See Egeria, *Itinerarium* 24.4.

[9]   Kim Bowes has mapped this in detail in her *Private Worship, Public Values, and Religious Change in Late Antiquity* (New York: Cambridge University Press, 2008).

chapter because the narrative resonates with more recent scholarly analyses of space, which have shifted from a focus on space as such to questions of spatial movement and space as constructed by people moving within it. A pilgrim on the move like Egeria is a key witness to the spatial practice of holy places.

Taking Egeria's visit to Hagia Thecla as a point of departure, the task of the present chapter is to highlight a number of ways in which gender shaped sacred spaces, with particular attention to sites of liturgical practice typically underrepresented in more traditional accounts. The focus in what follows is on the early centuries of Christian worship.

## Interpreting Gender in Sacred Space

Before turning to a number of gender-specific elements that shaped the development of sacred space, we need to highlight some overarching interpretive principles for the inquiry that follows.

### Sacred Space: Pluriform and Porous

First, the nature of gendering processes in sacred space, narrowly conceived as a church building, cannot be mapped in isolation from other spaces, which themselves can become liturgical space. For much of liturgical historiography the dominant understanding of sacred space has been of public ecclesial spaces—early Christian basilicas, Romanesque monasteries, Gothic cathedrals, baroque chapels, and Neo-Gothic parish churches, to name a few examples. Such an understanding no doubt attends to fundamental sites of liturgical practice, but these are by no means all the sacred spaces there are. Neither are these sites isolated from other spaces that may be or can become sacred. Public, ecclesial space is interrelated with these other sites of liturgical practice, chief among them those in the domestic realm, and the public square. These are permeable or "porous" toward public ecclesial spaces in a variety of ways.

Processions are a prime example of this permeability and malleability of what comes to constitute sacred space. The oldest extant Roman ritual of dying, death, and burial, *Ordo Romanus* 49 (7th/8th century) and the mobile liturgical rite that becomes visible there, is a case in point.[10] That ritual begins in the house of the dying person. There, at the deathbed, the person dying is given *viaticum*, the

---

[10] This *Ordo* was edited and numbered *Ordo Romanus* 49 by Michel Andrieu in his *Les* Ordines Romani *du haut moyen âge* 4, Spicilegium Sacrum Lovaniense 28 (Louvain: Spicilegium Sacrum Lovaniense Administration, 1956), 529f. The text was later shown to be a torso, and was completed, on the basis of a recently discovered manuscript, by Hieronymus Frank, "Der älteste erhaltene *Ordo defunctorum* der römischen Liturgie und sein Fortleben in Totenagenden des frühen Mittelalters," *Archiv für Liturgiewissenschaft* 7 (1962): 360–415, here 362–5.

Passion narrative is read, and psalms and prayers are offered. When death has occurred, the corpse is washed and clothed, then taken in procession from the house to the church, where vigil is kept. After the funeral Mass the procession moves, with accompanying psalms and antiphons, to the place where the corpse is to be interred. Clearly, in this ritual journey sacred spaces are produced along the way by practices of a lived liturgy that begins in the home as death approaches, and extends all the way to the grave, and beyond, as the deceased continues to be remembered in prayer. Gradations of sacred space are inscribed into this liturgical practice: The hinge in this mobile liturgy is the sacred space of the church, set apart for liturgical use. The house of the deceased, where the procession to the church originates, returns to its function as a domestic space once the liturgical accompaniment of the death is over. The cemetery, the end point of the procession, is a space set apart for the dead, not only through the ritual of burial itself, but also through other rituals that come to be linked to this site, especially commemorations of the dead.

Gendered distinctions accompanied such spatial liturgical practices throughout, even if the ritual text of *Ordo Romanus* 49 itself does not make this obvious. More than an analysis of liturgical texts is required here to make such gendering evident, for example questions about clothes and clothing. Different dress and adornment codes for men and women—probably the most visible aspect of gendered difference in early medieval times—would have been evident in any liturgy. In the early medieval West, trousers and a short tunic had become "the universal basis for men's clothing" (except for clergy and religious), while women wore long robes.[11] Distinctions of dress and adornment marked not only the living but also followed the deceased into their graves. In terms of rituals of dying, death, and burial, other gender distinctions were inscribed into the process. The dressing of the corpse for burial, for example, and specific mourning practices such as wailing, seem to have been performed by women.[12]

Such gendered distinctions did not change significantly from one site to the next in a processional liturgy but simply accompanied it throughout. Processions are but the clearest example of what is true even for the most isolated or clearly bounded liturgical sites. Gender processes, as they are present in the larger culture, do not stop at church doors. Gender processes, moreover, also influence the intersections and relationships between spaces. Thus, in order to attend to the particular gendering of public ecclesial space, attention to both the domestic sphere and the public square is especially important, not least because these spaces are co-constitutive of each other: The "other" of the public square, after all, is not the sacred, but the domestic or private sphere. We cannot adequately map the

---

[11]   See Julia M. H. Smith, *Europe after Rome: A New Cultural History, 500–1000* (New York: Oxford University Press, 2005), 118–21.

[12]   Research in this area of liturgical history has only begun; see Michael S. Driscoll, "*Per Sora Nostra Morte Corporale:* The Role of Medieval Women in Death and Burial Practices," *Liturgical Ministry* 10 (2001): 14–22.

gendering of public ecclesial space without attention to the gendering of other spaces in which Christian life was ritualized. One of these spaces, namely natural sites, I will for the most part by-pass in this chapter, although the importance of natural sites is anything but negligible (e.g., the desert in early monasticism, mountains, wilderness, springs, rivers, and the sea).[13] The boundaries between all these spaces, moreover, are nothing if not porous.

*Beyond Public vs. Private*

A second point to be made here concerns the intersections between domestic, public, and ecclesial space. Clearly, these spaces, and spatial movement in and between them, are historically conditioned and ever-changing. Historians of gender have, for some time now, contested the usefulness of the binary categories of "public and private" as descriptors of the past. The domestic sphere for much of the time—including the formative periods of Christian liturgy—was not nearly as *private* as it is today. In order to move beyond a narrow focus on the categories of private vs. public, gender historians have begun to explore other ways of conceptualizing domestic space, traditionally a site of female presence and agency. I myself find the category "household" particularly productive for liturgical historiography. A household is broader than its familial inhabitants, since it can include not only extended family but also other dependents, slaves, and servants, as well as domestic animals. The household, in other words, is not equivalent to "the private side of an over-easy binary of public/domestic,"[14] and thus offers other ways of conceptualizing the domestic sphere. Moreover, "household" can also be applied to monastic houses, episcopal residences, and royal courts. It thus captures a breadth of domiciles that the "private" does not. Lastly, the household was also a formative image in early reflections on the nature of the gathered community of faith, with the church imaged as those belonging to the "household of the faith" [πρὸς τοὺς οἰκείους τῆς πίστεως, Gal 6:10].

*Acknowledging the Traditional Division of Spheres*

A third point to be made involves a particular understanding of space that is deeply inscribed in the Christian tradition, namely the conviction of a God-given gender-specific division of spheres as part of the created order. This gender-

---

[13]  See, for example, Trevor Johnson, "Gardening for God: Carmelite Deserts and the Sacralisation of Natural Space in Counter-Reformation Spain," in *Sacred Space in Early Modern Europe*, ed. Will Coster and Andrew Spicer (New York: Cambridge University Press, 2005), 193–210.

[14]  Anneke B. Mulder-Bakker and Jocelyn Wogan-Browne, "Introduction," in *Household, Women, and Christianities in Late Antiquity and the Middle Ages*, which they edited; Medieval Women: Texts and Contexts 14 (Turnhout, Belgium: Brepols, 2005), 1–10, here 4.

specific division of spheres, in the Christian tradition and beyond, was linked to a particular understanding of a sexual division of labor. The public square, and with it public ecclesial space, was coded as the superior male sphere, in which the presence of women was usually marked as inferior, for example by assigning women back seats. Women's space was the household, the domestic sphere with its particular labors (i.e, birthing, care of children, food production, clothing, etc.), which was understood to be inferior. The gender-specific division of spheres and the sexual division of labor were seen as a natural part of the created order and as God-given. To cite but one example, John Chrysostom articulates well this commonplace understanding of the sexual division of labor. It is worth quoting the passage at some length:

> Our life is customarily organized into two spheres: public affairs and private matters, both of which were determined by God. To woman is assigned the presidency of the household; to man, all the business of state, the marketplace, the administration of justice, government, the military, and all other such enterprises. ... if the more important, most beneficial concerns were turned over to the woman, she would go quite mad. Therefore God did not apportion both duties to one sex ... Nor did God assign both to be equal in every way, for *women in their contentiousness would deem themselves deserving of the front-row seats rather than the man*! But taking precautions at one and the same time for peace and decency, God maintained the order of each sex by dividing the business of human life into two parts and assigned the more necessary and beneficial aspects to the man and the less important, inferior matters to the woman.[15]

Here is a religiously authorized understanding of the sexual division of labor that marked the Christian tradition throughout much of its history. What happens when such a gendered understanding of space intersects with practices of sacred space? Before I turn to a look at some of the evidence, a note on liturgical historiography concludes this explication of interpretive principles.

## *Lacunae in Conventional Historiographies of Sacred Space*

Conventional liturgical historiography of developments after the third century, focused on *public ecclesial space*, thus mostly occludes, if only through silence, the domestic sphere—although the household arguably was the most basic, daily, and influential site for ritualizing faith.[16] The household, moreover, is also

---

[15]    John Chrysostom, *Laus Maximi et quales uxores ducendæ* 4 (PG 51:230f); English translation: *The Kind of Women Who Ought to be Taken as Wives*, in *Women in Early Christianity: Translations from Greek Texts*, ed. Patricia Cox Miller (Washington, DC: The Catholic University of America Press, 2005), here 271f. Emphasis added.

[16]    Balthasar Fischer pointed out this lacuna in his essay "Gemeinschaftsgebet in den christlichen Gemeinden und in der christlichen Familie in der alten Christenheit," first

permeable toward all other liturgical space, particularly in relation to life-cycle rituals. One example of this occlusion of the household is the standard account of the development of daily prayer. In this account, the focus is usually on two sites, namely the cathedral/parish, and the monastery. Largely occluded is the fact that Christians prayed daily and communally in households, well beyond the first three centuries in which the house-church was the dominant gathering site of the faithful. Equally invisible in traditional historiography is the fact that many domestic rituals were not only communal—involving the extended family of a household, as well as servants and slaves—but also tied to the larger liturgical life of the church. Communion consumed at home, home altars and shrines, personal relics, the veneration of images, and the celebration of ecclesial feasts and fasts are just a few examples of this. Other examples of the porous boundaries between public and domestic devotions can be added, especially for later periods, such as rituals around the deathbed and surrounding birth (with baptism not infrequently administered by midwives), and the existence of domestic chapels, private relics, oratories, altars, and domestic tabernacles. Moreover, public ecclesial space itself was not a unified space, as medieval understandings of gradations of sacred, holy, and religious space show. Nor was public ecclesial space tightly bounded; the existence of lodging spaces, vending activities, and legal proceedings in churches makes this abundantly clear.[17]

As I emphasized earlier, gender processes are present in all spaces, including public sanctuaries and the *ecclesia domestica*, but with marked differences. For now, suffice it to emphasize that when thinking about the impact of gender on sacred space, we do well to consider the domestic, the public ecclesial, and the public civic sphere together. In what follows, I provide some historical evidence to substantiate this claim.

### Fragments from the Biblical Foundations

In a study of the religious culture of women in ancient Israel, Carol Meyers has drawn attention to ritual practices in the household as central to Israelite faith. Meyers's focus on the household as a ritual site renders visible a space that for the most part was of little interest to the elite urban male authors of the Hebrew

---

published in 1974, now reprinted in *Frömmigkeit der Kirche: Gesammelte Studien zur christlichen Spiritualität*, ed. Albert Gerhards and Andreas Heinz, Hereditas 17 (Bonn: Borengässer, 2000), 1–17; see esp. 1, 11f. Most recently, Kim Bowes has made the domestic sphere the focus of her inquiry, see note 9.

[17]    Dawn Marie Hayes analyzes some of these records in "Earthly Uses of Heavenly Spaces: Non-Liturgical Activities in Sacred Space," in her *Body and Sacred Place in Medieval Europe, 1100–1389*, Studies in Medieval History and Culture 18 (New York: Routledge, 2003), 53–69. See also J. G. Davies, *The Secular Use of Church Buildings* (New York: The Seabury Press, 1968).

Scriptures, with their focus on tribal, national, and state interests. The dominant religious site for these biblical authors was cultic space outside of the home. As Meyers argues: "Biblical texts lead us to ask questions about whether women were allowed in the temple precincts or whether they could offer sacrifices at community festivals, not about religious acts women may have performed in their own households, every day."[18] Meyers focuses precisely on such household religious practices, especially those of women. She emphasizes that these practices were "arguably more prominent, in terms of the day-to-day experience of most people, than the extra household religious activities and cultic events."[19] Meyers concentrates on women-specific rituals surrounding pregnancy, birth, lactation, circumcision, and child-care, arguing that these ritual practices were dependent on specialized ritual knowledge (e.g., effective prayers against barrenness) as well as skilled practitioners (e.g., midwives), which were complementary to the priestly expertise of official cult personnel. By broadening the sources for reconstructing ritual practices for example by including archaeological finds such as household shrines and pillar-figurines—Meyers is able to render visible a "ritual culture surrounding reproduction" that was a part of Israelite household practices of faith.[20] Even if one does not want to follow Meyers's exclusionary concentration on women and reproduction—why would women not also have prayed for victory in a looming battle?—she redraws the picture of Israelite ritual practices. If we take household ritual practices into account, as well as the fact that Israelite women were not much more disadvantaged than non-priestly men in communal cultic activity,[21] then glimpses of richly textured ritual lives and sacred sites emerge that are a far cry from conventional images of Israelite faith.

I highlight Meyers's *Household and Holiness* here because her findings fit well with my own conviction that the conventional narrative of sacred space has occluded important sacred sites such as the household. In addition, Meyers draws attention to the fact that the image of sacred space in the Scriptures is already slanted toward the "elite urban male" configuration of sacred space, since this is the context of many of the authors of the Hebrew Bible.

The lines between household and public sacred space do not follow an unambiguous gender dichotomy. A case in point is the tradition of employing feminine images for Jerusalem, and especially for Zion. As Christl Mayer has recently shown, the female personification of Zion—as daughter, spouse, queen, whore, wailing mother, and widow—functions as a powerful metaphor for the

---

[18] Carol Meyers, *Households and Holiness: The Religious Culture of Israelite Women* (Minneapolis: Fortress Press, 2005), 7.

[19] Meyers, *Households and Holiness*, 11.

[20] Ibid., 57.

[21] For more on this, see Phyllis A. Bird, "The Place of Women in the Israelite Cultus," in her *Missing Persons and Mistaken Identities: Women and Gender in Ancient Israel*, Overtures to Biblical Theology (Minneapolis: Fortress Press, 1997), 81–102.

relationship between God, God's people, and a sacred space.[22] This female metaphor inscribes the image of a gendered body into the very notion of this space as sacred. A striking example in the Hebrew Bible of a female metaphor linked both to domestic space and to a ritual meal is found in the Wisdom literature. The text, Prov 9:1–5, represents an intriguing interplay between space, gender, and—at least in its reception history—liturgical practice (the Christian tradition has understood the text to point toward the church's eucharistic feast[23]). Proverbs 9:1–5 images God, in the metaphor of Lady Wisdom, building a house and hosting a meal:

> Wisdom has built her house,
>     she has hewn her seven pillars,
>     she has prepared her meat,
> she has spiced her wine,
> she has laid out her festive table.
>     She has sent out her servant girls
> to call from the town's highest places:
>     "You who are simple-minded, turn to me!"
>     To those lacking insight she says:
>     "Come, eat my festive meal and drink my spiced wine."[24]

This text is quite specific about Lady Wisdom's building project. She herself has put the stones in place, and wielded chisel and hammer; she herself has "hewn her seven pillars." Such construction work is not the typically feminine labor associated with houses and home-making. Lady Wisdom in fact does not seem to have any interest in the traditionally feminine domestic sphere associated with married responsibilities and child-raising. Instead, she is imaged as a host who wishes to provide food and drink for guests.

From such feminine images of sacred space and ritual meals I return to concrete quotidian spaces. Looking at Roman-era Palestine, it seems clear that Jewish households did not confine women in the narrow way that later rabbinic sources suggest. While rabbinic sources, in revisioning Judaism without the temple, surround women's public appearance with anxiety, the archaeology of earlier domestic space suggests that women participated extensively in the economic labors of the household, and that the household's boundaries were porous with the

---

[22]   Christl M. Maier, *Daughter Zion, Mother Zion: Gender, Space, and the Sacred in Ancient Israel* (Minneapolis: Fortress Press, 2008).

[23]   Documentation in Charles Kannengiesser, *Handbook of Patristic Exegesis: The Bible in Ancient Christianity* 1 (Boston: Brill, 2004), 309; *Ancient Christian Commentary on Scripture: Old Testament* 9, ed. J. Robert Wright (Downers Grove, IL: InterVarsity Press, 2005), 71–6.

[24]   The translation from the Hebrew is mine.

wider outside.[25] The lines between household and public sacred space thus did not necessarily follow a clear gender dichotomy.

What can be gleaned from these fragments in the Hebrew Bible as far as gender and scared space are concerned? Minimally, these fragments complicate the traditional image of Israelite ritual space as public space, outside of the home, with women and non-elite men appearing mostly at the margins of ritual practice. This increased complexity is particularly helpful as a backdrop to the New Testament images of the earliest Christian communities, which gathered to worship in their homes.

### Entering the Earliest Christian Sanctuaries: The Household as Sacred Space

The dominant gathering space of the ἐκκλησία in earliest Christianity, and thus the site of its liturgical practice, was the household, that is, the domestic sphere, broadly conceived. In claiming the household as ritual space, Christian communities were not substantially different from their Jewish neighbors and from the broader Graeco-Roman context in which they found themselves. Where early Christian communities differed from their Jewish neighbors and the broader culture was in the fact that the latter knew ritual space both in the domestic as well as in the public sphere. For Christian communities, public sanctuaries did not emerge prominently until the early fourth century. What does this mean for gendering processes in the earliest Christian sanctuary spaces?

In first-century Judaism, the domestic sphere, traditionally associated with female agency, continued to be an important ritual site especially for the observance of the Sabbath, of food and purity laws (such as ritual bathing for purification for both women and men), and of domestic celebrations of feasts and fasts.[26] Passover, the Feast of Tabernacles, and the Day of Atonement were celebrated in public as well as in the household. In the Jewish Diaspora, at least, no significant distinction existed between domestic and public rituals, but a "matching of the public and domestic spheres. ... Jewish festivals were simultaneously communal and domestic occasions."[27] Instruction in the Torah, above all, took place in both the synagogue and the home.

---

[25] See Eric M. Meyers, "The Problems of Gendered Space in Syro-Palestinian Domestic Architecture: The Case of Roman-Period Galilee," in *Early Christian Families in Context: An Interdisciplinary Dialogue*, ed. David L. Balch and Carolyn Osiek, Religion, Marriage, and Family (Grand Rapids, MI: Eerdmans, 2003), 44–69, esp. 59, 68f; and Tal Ilan, *Jewish Women in Greco-Roman Palestine* (Peabody, MA: Hendrickson Publishers, 1996), esp. 128–34, 178–90.

[26] In what follows I am indebted to John M. G. Barclay, "The Family as the Bearer of Religion," in *Constructing Early Christian Families: Family as Social Reality and Metaphor*, ed. Halvor Moxnes (New York: Routledge, 1997), 66–80, here especially 68–72.

[27] Barclay, "The Family as the Bearer of Religion," 72.

In Graeco-Roman households, domestic ritual space—especially the hearth and its goddess, *Hestia/Vesta*, together with the store-house and its deities—and practices such as prayers, libations, food offerings, and incense, were an important part of religious life. Both literary references and the archeology of domestic architecture give evidence of these domestic ritual sites and practices. At the same time the household shrines, the statuettes, the paintings of deities or deified ancestors, and domestic ritual practices were part of the larger religious life to which the Roman public civic cult also belonged.[28] Domestic worship and public cult, in other words, were interrelated in various ways.[29]

For Christian communities, which until the early fourth century had no legally recognized public worship spaces, the household was the main site of ecclesial gathering and liturgical practice.[30] Domestic space functioned—as needed, in the very act of the believers' gathering—as sanctuary space. To put this differently: The gathering of the ἐκκλησία *made* sanctuary space, within the domestic realm. After the gathering this sanctuary space returned to being the living quarters of a household.

How earliest Christianity was marked by its gathering in house-churches while also challenging basic familial solidarities has received much attention in recent years.[31] For gender-attentive liturgical historiography, a key question is how the domestic gendering processes of the time shaped ecclesial life in this space. What was the impact of domestic gender processes on domestic sanctuary space? A look at the broader Graeco-Roman context offers some insights here. To begin with, the late antique household—like the ancient Israelite household before it—was a sphere where women had particular agency.[32] This included economic agency, since the late antique household could be the space for buying, selling, and trading.[33] The household might also include not only the immediate family but slaves, freed servants, and clients. The domestic sphere thus was not closed off from the public sphere but porously interrelated with it.

This interrelationship is important to keep in mind when focusing on Graeco-Roman households as sites of earliest Christian worship. The homes in which

---

[28]   See Bowes, *Private Worship*, ch. 1, for more on this.

[29]   Ibid., esp. 33.

[30]   Bowes, ibid., 20, 48, makes this point well.

[31]   See, for example, the volumes edited by Moxnes, Balch and Osiek, and Mulder-Bakker and Wogan-Browne, notes 26, 25, and 14.

[32]   For more on women as leaders of households, see the chapter "Women Leaders of Households and Christian Assemblies," in Carolyn Osiek and Margaret Y. MacDonald, with Janet H. Tulloch, *A Woman's Place: House Churches in Earliest Christianity* (Minneapolis: Fortress, 2006), 144–63.

[33]   For more on women as economic actors, see Richard Saller, "Women, Slaves, and the Economy of the Roman Household," in *Early Christian Families in Context: An Interdisciplinary Dialogue*, ed. David L. Balch and Carolyn Osiek, Religion, Marriage, and Family (Grand Rapids, MI: Eerdmans, 2003), 185–204.

house-churches formed were not simply restricted private dwellings but might include workshops, some of them in women's hands (e.g., for wool dressing, embroidery, hairdressing, laundering, beautification, gold-leaf, ivory work, etc.). Households could also be headed by women. Such is the case with the household of the "ideal woman convert" Lydia,[34] who received baptism together with her household after hearing the Gospel (Acts 16:11–15). Lydia was a business woman, a dealer in purple goods. After being baptized, she opened her house to Paul and other Christians.[35] Similarly, Nympha hosted an ἐκκλησία in her house in Laodicea (Col 4:15). In the house of the mother of John Mark, believers gather for nocturnal prayer (Acts 12:12–17). It seems likely that in these house-churches women functioned as hosts, patrons, and leaders.[36]

Since in the earliest centuries "to step into a Christian house church was to step into women's world,"[37] it is not surprising that pagan opinion and criticism connected the new religion in a particular way with violations of gender boundaries. As Margaret MacDonald has emphasized: "Church groups are offensive because in them the public sphere is swallowed up by the private and women play a major role in defining the new ethos. The true purpose of the home is negated when it shelters church meetings and male responsibilities in public affairs are ignored or subverted."[38]

Even if pagan authors rely on quite traditional *topoi* when critiquing early Christian communities—that they attract and corrupt especially women and children (proof both of insidiousness and weakness)—there is enough evidence from within Christian sources themselves to support this picture.[39] Since households were important sites for the growth of the new faith, women and men, as well as children, servants, and slaves, will have played roles in the missionary expansion of Christianity. Looked at in this light, the household codes in the Pastoral Epistles

---

[34]   The term is Margaret Y. MacDonald's, "Was Celsus Right? The Role of Women in the Expansion of Early Christianity," in *Early Christian Families in Context: An Interdisciplinary Dialogue*, ed. David L. Balch and Carolyn Osiek, Religion, Marriage, and Family (Grand Rapids, MI: Eerdmans, 2003), 177.

[35]   See Valerie Abrahamsen, "Lydia," in *Women in Scripture: A Dictionary of Named and Unnamed Women in the Hebrew Bible, the Apocryphal/Deuterocanonical Books, and the New Testament*, ed. Carol Meyers, Toni Craven, and Ross S. Kraemer (Boston: Houghton Mifflin Company, 2000), 110–11.

[36]   See *A Woman's Place*, esp. 157–62.

[37]   Ibid., 163.

[38]   Margaret Y. MacDonald, *Early Christian Women and Pagan Opinion: The Power of the Hysterical Woman* (Cambridge: Cambridge University Press, 1996), 112f.

[39]   I agree here with Margaret Y. MacDonald; see "Was Celsus Right?," 157–84. She is responding to scholars like Kate Cooper and Judith Lieu who have cautioned that ancient texts about women's influence in early Christianization are rhetorical strategies rather than pointers to what actually happened. Without some real mooring in what happened, however, these claims would not have been credible.

can be read as evidence of gender contestations and a felt need to defend tenuous masculine authority and control in the house-church setting.[40]

Jorunn Økland has argued, in a study focused on Paul's exhortations to silencing and veiling of women in worship (1 Cor 11–14), that these exhortations render visible the pressure put on gender roles in a household when domestic space becomes sanctuary space in the gathering of the ἐκκλησία.[41] However Paul's exhortations are read (and this is contested scholarly terrain), it stands to reason that domestic gender roles were in play when living quarters became sanctuary space. Gender roles will not have been unaffected by the transformation, and indeed might have embodied it.

With the third century, material evidence emerges of Christians modifying household spaces not as temporary sacred spaces but as spaces permanently set apart, in the house, for worship, including the celebration of Baptism and Eucharist. The house-church excavated at Dura-Europos, a Roman outpost in Syria, is the much-studied example of this transition.[42] With it came a clearer separation between domestic and sanctuary space, which until then had been performed by time set apart, rather than as space set apart. Domestic and sanctuary spaces nevertheless continue to intertwine in myriads of ways. The domestic realm continued to be a site of personal and communal devotion, from individual prayers to mealtime rituals. Lay home-communion, for which we have evidence through the seventh century (at least in the East), is an example of a sacramental practice situated in the permeable space between domestic and sanctuary realms.[43] Archaeological excavation of Christian houses also has shown how Christian faith and devotion came to be deeply woven into the material culture of domestic space. Protective inscriptions, saintly images, personal relics, Christian symbols on lighting devices, on eating and drinking vessels, on clothing and jewelry make this abundantly clear.[44]

---

[40]  Cf. *A Woman's Place*, 132–6.

[41]  Jorunn Økland, *Women in Their Place: Paul and the Corinthian Discourse of Gender and Sanctuary Space*, JSNTSup 269 (New York: T&T Clark, 2004).

[42]  The literature on the *domus ecclesiae* of Dura-Europos is enormous. Good starting points are the description in L. Michael White, *The Social Origins of Christian Architecture* 2, Harvard Theological Studies 42 (Valley Forge, PA: Trinity Press International, 1997), 123–31, and Allan Doig, *Liturgy and Architecture: From the Early Church to the Middle Ages*, Ashgate Liturgy, Worship and Society Series (Burlington, VT: Ashgate, 2008), 10–18.

[43]  For more on this, see Robert F. Taft, "Home-Communion in the Late Antique East," in *Ars Liturgiae: Worship, Aesthetics and Praxis* (Festschrift Nathan D. Mitchell), ed. Clare V. Johnson (Chicago: Liturgy Training Publications, 2003), 1–25.

[44]  The material culture of early Christian domestic space is well illustrated in Eunice Dauterman Maguire et al., *Art and Holy Powers in the Early Christian House*, Illinois Byzantine Studies 2 (Urbana and Chicago: Krannert Art Museum and University of Illinois Press, 1989). My thanks to Jaime Lara for directing me to this book.

## Entering Public Sanctuaries

In the fourth century the public sphere emerges as a principal site for liturgical celebrations of the now officially recognized Christian religion. Yet older liturgical sites, such as household and burial sites, did not simply vanish with the rising Christian basilicas. Rather, these other spaces existed alongside the nascent public sanctuaries, and this co-existence was not tension-free.[45] Even if one does not want to go as far as to argue that the rising Christian churches were places where the elite worshipped while the majority—that is, "popular" Christianity— gathered in other settings, especially cemeteries beyond the city walls,[46] a diversity of sanctuary spaces clearly existed in the fourth century and beyond.

Such parallel ecclesial spaces become visible, for example, in the estate-based ascetic communities of the fourth century. Stephen Davis has raised the intriguing possibility that the ascetic community of women and men living at Hagia Thecla at the time of Egeria's visit might have been similar to the mixed ascetic community that Macrina (c. 327–79) had established at her family's rural estate at Annesi in Asia Minor a few decades earlier.[47] Macrina's vast estate housed two churches, one built by her mother at some distance from the house (for the relics of the Forty Martyrs), and another within the living quarters, probably built by Macrina herself.[48] In these two estate churches we find the liturgical spaces of a large domestic center, spaces that hosted liturgical practices that may not necessarily have been those of public sanctuaries. Macrina, for example, is described by her brother Gregory of Nyssa not only as assuming a number of liturgical postures— turning to the East and stretching her hands out in prayer; signing her eyes, mouth, and heart with the sign of the cross at the end of prayer – but also as reciting the evening thanksgiving for the light, and as performing a healing ritual on herself, involving a mixture made from her own tears and her chapel's dirt floor.[49]

---

[45] Kim Bowes has mapped this in her *Private Worship, Public Values, and Religious Change in Late Antiquity*, see note 9.

[46] This is the argument of Ramsay MacMullen in his recent book aptly titled *The Second Church: Popular Christianity A.D. 200–400*, SBL Writings from the Greco-Roman World Supplement Series 1 (Atlanta: Society of Biblical Literature, 2009). His argument, however, rests on a strict division between popular and elite Christianity, a dichotomy that many scholars now reject.

[47] See Davis, *Cult of Saint Thecla*, 56.

[48] Bowes, *Private Worship*, 208–12, offers a more detailed analysis of Macrina's community, churches, and liturgical practices.

[49] All texts relevant to Macrina's life, including Gregory of Nyssa's *Life of Macrina*, are now available in English translation in one volume edited by Anna M. Silvas, *Macrina the Younger, Philosopher of God*, Medieval Women: Texts and Contexts 22 (Turnhout, Belgium: Brepols, 2008). Gregory of Nyssa, *The Life of Macrina*, is pp. 109–48. See also Bowes, *Private Worship*, 208–12. Robert Taft's comment on Macrina's recitation of the thanksgiving over the light, namely that it shows that "the domestic lamp ritual was still in vogue in spite of its adoption into the church service," betrays a supercessionist sense of

We do not know whether the shrine of Hagia Thecla, visited by Egeria, had similarities to the ascetic community on Macrina's estate. Links between the two communities did exist: Macrina bore the secret name Thecla, and a close friend of Macrina's familiy, Gregory of Nazianzus, had sought shelter at the shrine of Hagia Thecla just ten years before Egeria's visit.[50] Whatever the precise relationship between the churches of Macrina's estate at Annesi and the shrine of Hagia Thecla near Seleukia, both sites remain largely invisible in conventional accounts of the development of sacred space in the fourth century, as these accounts focus squarely on the rising Christian basilicas. Yet at Annesi and at Hagia Thecla, given that they were women-identified, ascetic, and in the case of Macrina's community estate-based, gender differences may well have shaped worship in other ways than those of the public basilicas.

## Gender Separations in Liturgical Space

The rising Christian public buildings of the fourth century allow a clearer view of the increasing differentiations within sacred space itself, especially between apse and nave, clergy and laity. Gender is deeply inscribed into these differentiations, as ecclesial ministries and sanctuary space together come to be more visibly shaped along gender-specific lines. The altar space and placement within are an example. This space certainly is not gender-free. To highlight but two ways in which gender, ministerial leadership, and this sacred space intersect: there were clearly no men among the canonical widows, who in some communities had a privileged liturgical space. Evidence for women among the bishops also is scant, and the reading of the evidence continues to be contested. Gender, however, shapes not only the altar space and movement within it, but also the nave, the space where the congregation gathers. Of particular interest here are the forms of gender separation in this congregational space.

### *The* Didascalia Apostolorum

Evidence for gender separation in worship predates the fourth century, as the *Didascalia Apostolorum* demonstrates. This third-century Syrian church order has been a staple of liturgical historiography ever since its initial publication in the nineteenth century. Historians of early Christian worship have, however, paid little attention to the pronounced gender binary that frames this text. Especially when historians concentrate on select "liturgical portions of the Didascalia," the church order's overall gendering and its relevance for liturgical historiography are easily

---

the relationship between domestic and public ritual space. See Robert Taft, *The Liturgy of the Hours in East and West: The Origins of the Divine Office and Its Meaning for Today* (Collegeville: Liturgical Press, 1986; 2nd rev. ed. 1993), 37.

[50]   See Davis, *Cult of Saint Thecla*, 5, 62–4.

lost.[51] Thus, for example, when the gender-specific arrangement of the gathered assembly in Chapter 12 of the *Didascalia* is discussed, it is not located within the emphatic gender-specific frame with which the document began. This church order, after all, opens with a call to follow the law, which is immediately spelled out in remarkably gender-specific details, first for husbands and then for wives. The husband is instructed to be "pleasing solely to his wife"; he is not to "adorn himself and be a stumbling-block to women," or "bathe in the bath with women," or "give his life to the wickedness of prostitutes."[52] Wives are told to be "pleasing and respectful to their husbands alone," not to "wash together with the men," nor to "adorn themselves so that they become a stumbling-block to men, nor ensnare them." Finally, they are not to be "quarrelsome with their husbands."[53]

This opening is striking since the *Didascalia* here draws on the *Didache*, which also opened with a set of moral teachings. In the *Didache*, however, these moral teachings are not divided into gender-binary specifics; neither does gender, as an ecclesial ordering principle, play much of a role in this earlier church order. The *Didascalia* presents a marked development at this point, since the whole document is framed by gender-specific exhortations, ending with a critique of liturgical purity laws. I will return to these purity laws in a later chapter; suffice it here to note that the gender separation of the liturgical assembly in the *Didascalia* is part of a larger gender-specific ordering of ecclesial and domestic life.[54] When in Chapter 12 bishops are encouraged to order the assembly along lines both of ecclesial status and of gender, the church order has already performed the gendering of the assembly at the text's very opening. *Didascalia* 12 envisions the liturgical assembly ordered from east to west. In the east are the bishop's seat and the seats of the presbyters. Then come the lay men. Behind these men, toward the west and away from the altar and the bishop's seat, women have their place. The women are to be grouped according to marital status: young girls, married women with children, elderly women, and widows. There is no equivalent separation among the lay men (i.e. into groups of young, married, and elderly or widowed men). After these careful spatial arrangements, the *Didascalia* also provides elaborate instructions for deacons to find appropriate places for newcomers and latecomers

---

[51] Thus, the booklet *The Liturgical Portions of the Didascalia*, edited by Sebastian Brock and Michael Vasey, Grove Liturgical Study 29 (Bramcote: Grove Books, 1982), gives the introductory paragraph of this church order, as well as the following exhortation to married men; the subsequent exhortation to women, however, is omitted, thus rendering invisible the stark gender-binary which frames the *Didascalia*.

[52] *Didascalia Apostolorum* 2. English translation: *The Didascalia Apostolorum: An English Version*, ed. and translated by Alistair Stewart-Sykes, Studia Traditionis Theologiae 1 (Turnhout, Belgium: Brepols, 2009), 105.

[53] *Didascalia Apostolorum* 3. English translation: *The Didascalia Apostolorum*, 111f.

[54] Cf. also Charlotte Methuen, "'For Pagans Laugh to Hear Women Teach': Gender Stereotypes in the *Didascalia Apostolorum*," *Studies in Church History* 34 (1998): 23–35.

to the assembly. Clearly, separation of the sexes in worship is of basic importance for this church order.

## *The* Apostolic Tradition

The third-century *Didascalia Apostolorum* stands as an early witness to the liturgical practice of gender separation. The text is important not least because it offers specific directions as to how this gender separation is to be performed, namely by placing the women behind the men in the nave. In comparison, the *Apostolic Tradition* (in its oriental versions; the Latin has a lacuna at that point) and its Egyptian derivative, the *Canons of Hippolytus*, offers no such direction. These church orders simply indicate, respectively, that "the women are to stand in a place in the church and pray alone," and that "women are to be separated in a place."[55] Since these instructions appear in chapters describing the process of initiation, their particular focus is on the place of the female catechumens in church. Their place is said to be with the women believers. When the time for the actual baptism comes, the female catechumens are to be baptized last, after the children and the men.[56] Gender separation during the act of baptism is unsurprising, given that baptizands were nude.

The *Apostolic Tradition* does not specify how exactly the separation of women, both believers and catechumens, is to be performed in sacred space. Besides the arrangement known from the *Didascalia*, namely women behind the lay men, a second basic arrangement puts women and men on different sides of the nave. The *Testamentum Domini* witnesses to this arrangement.

## *The* Testamentum Domini

The *Testamentum Domini* is an enlarged derivative of the *Apostolic Tradition* (probably from Syria). This church order, dating in all likelihood from the fifth century, envisions a longitudinal gender separation. With this, the *Testamentum Domini* goes beyond its key source, the *Apostolic Tradition*, in specifying the form gender separation in worship is to take, namely "men on the right and the women on the left" side of the nave.[57] The *Testamentum Domini* also goes further in separating the women catechumens from the women faithful and the girls. The

---

[55]   *Apostolic Tradition* 18, Ethiopic version. *Canons of Hippolytus* 18. All versions of the *Apostolic Tradition*, together with their parallel passages in the *Apostolic Constitutions*, the *Canons of Hippolytus*, and the *Testamentum Domini*, are available in English translation in Paul F. Bradshaw et al., *The Apostolic Tradition: A Commentary*, Hermeneia (Minneapolis: Fortress Press, 2002), here 100–101.

[56]   Cf. *Apostolic Tradition* 21 (all oriental versions), in *The Apostolic Tradition: A Commentary*, 112f.

[57]   *Testamentum Domini* 2.4, in *The Apostolic Tradition: A Commentary*, 101.

latter are further divided, with faithful virgins coming first, and behind them those being instructed in virginity.[58]

The *Testamentum Domini* evidences some other peculiarities of detail when it comes to gender and sacred space. The text diverges from the *Apostolic Tradition* (and all other early church orders) in placing the canonical widows—who are explicitly said to receive an ordination—in closest proximity to the bishop in the liturgical assembly. These widows are repeatedly described as those "who sit in front."[59] The deaconesses, on the other hand, are placed at the very back, near the main door of the building (maybe as doorkeepers, with special responsibility for women who enter the church?). At the celebration of the Eucharist, the *Testamentum Domini* envisions a veil drawn, with widows *and* deaconesses standing within the veil along with the bishop, presbyters, and other ministers. Within the veil, however, the widows are placed behind the presbyters, and, if menstruating, are told to remain in the nave and not to approach the altar at all.[60]

*Patterns and Images of Gender Separation*

The increasingly detailed nature of all these instructions in early church orders indicates how the spatial arrangement of gendered bodies in the liturgical assembly grew in importance from the third century onwards. This spatial arrangement includes both a basic separation by binary gender—men separated from women in the nave—as well as intricate arrangements in which gender, ecclesial status, specific liturgical actions, and—last but not least—individual menstrual cycles intersect.

In the ensuing centuries, the separation of women and men in the nave became a dominant feature of the spatial practice of liturgy. We know of three main ways of performing this gender separation in worship. First, women's space could be behind that of the men, who directly faced the altar. This is the situation envisioned in the *Didascalia Apostolorum*. Second, men stood on the right, women on the left side in the nave. The *Testamentum Domini* witnesses to this form of gender separation. As noted, this particular division comes to dominate in the Western church.[61] *Ordo Romanus* I, which reflects the stational Eucharist at Rome ca.

---

[58]   Ibid.

[59]   Ibid.

[60]   *Testamentum Domini* 1.23; for the English text and for further discussion of the important liturgical ministries of women outlined in the *Testamentum Domini*, see *Ordained Women in the Early Church: A Documentary History*, ed. and trans. Kevin Madigan and Carolyn Osiek (Baltimore, MD: The Johns Hopkins University Press, 2005), 150–62, here 151.

[61]   More in Heinrich Selhorst, *Die Platzordnung im Gläubigenraum der altchristlichen Kirche* (Münster: Aschendorff, 1931), 24–35. I note in passing that Selhorst, who finished his dissertation on this subject in 1929, emphasizes in the Introduction (p. 3) that his particular interest is in the place of *women* in early Christian liturgy.

A.D. 700, presupposes not only this gender-specific division in the nave, but also a gender- (and status-)specific offertory and reception of communion, with women on the left and men on the right side of the nave.[62] This gender-specific division is by no means innocent, considering that for much of Christian history, the left [Latin: *sinister*] was coded as inferior and negative, while the right [*dexter*] was considered superior and positive.[63]

An early visual representation of this gendered division in the nave can be found in Sant' Apollinare Nuovo, the palatine chapel of Theoderic in Ravenna. The sixth-century mosaics to the right and left of the nave show two processions. On the right side (from the standpoint of a worshipper entering the church) is a procession of male saints and martyrs to the enthroned Christ in the front. To the left side is a procession of female saints and martyrs, who follow the Magi to the seated figure of the Virgin and Child in the front. A congregation gathering for worship in this church would have seen "permanent gender labels" for their particular side and aisle in the nave.[64] The women would have faced the Virgin and Child at the front, accompanied by the female saints above them; the men would have faced the enthroned Christ, accompanied by the male saints above them.

In a third arrangement of liturgical gender separation, attested to especially in Byzantine sources and sanctuaries, women found themselves in a gallery above, behind, or to the side of the main worship space where male worshippers gathered.[65] In the Western church, women's galleries appear especially in convents, as the place reserved for the nuns.[66] With gender separation through galleries, we have entered the realm of actual architectural forms that divide a sanctuary gender-specifically.

---

[62]   See the important essay by Thomas F. Mathews, "An Early Roman Chancel Arrangement and its Liturgical Functions," *Rivista di Archeologia Cristiana* 38 (1962): 73–95. My thanks to Byron Stuhlman for directing me to this essay.

[63]   See, for example, Corine Schleif, "Men on the Right—Women on the Left: (A) Symmetrical Spaces and Gendered Places," in *Women's Space: Patronage, Place, and Gender in the Medieval Church*, ed. Virginia Chieffo Raguin and Sarah Stanbury, SUNY Series in Medieval Studies (Albany: State University of New York Press, 2005), 207–49; and Margaret Aston, "Segregation in Church," in *Women in the Church*, ed. W. J. Sheils and Diana Wood, Studies in Church History 27 (Oxford: Basil Blackwell, 1990), 237–94.

[64]   Corine Schleif, "Men on the Right—Women on the Left," 220.

[65]   Cf. Robert F. Taft, "Women at Church in Byzantium: Where, When—and Why?," *Dumbarton Oaks Papers* 52 (1998): 27–87.

[66]   Important here is Hiltje F. H. Zomer, "The so-called Women's Gallery in the Medieval Church: An Import from Byzantium," in *The Empress Theophano: Byzantium and the West at the Turn of the First Millennium*, ed. Adelbert Davids (New York: Cambridge University Press, 1995), 290–306, and Gisela Muschiol, "Liturgie und Klausur. Zu den liturgischen Voraussetzungen von Nonnenemporen," in *Studien zum Kanonissenstift*, ed. Irene Crusius, Studien zur Germania Sacra 24 (Göttingen: Vandenhoeck and Ruprecht, 2001), 129–48.

## Gender Separation, Set in Stone

The basic liturgical gender separation, performed by separating gendered bodies spatially, could be reinforced structurally. In the late fourth century Chrysostom, preaching in Antioch, mentions "boards" [σανίδες] placed between the men and the women. He indicates that he heard from elders that such "barriers" [τειχία] were introduced into the sanctuary not long before, and he chastizes his male hearers for needing such boards because their own interior walls were not strong enough to keep them away from women.[67] Chrysostom's sermon is our earliest reference to a structural reinforcement of gender separation in sacred space. Since we do not know for certain how Chrysostom's church was ordered, it is unclear where the barriers dividing men and women were positioned. Wendy Mayer and Pauline Allen have argued that the Old Church in Antioch was a basilica and that the boards mentioned by Chrysostom bisected the nave cross-wise, with the men in front and the women behind them.[68] Nor can we say whether these boards were only high enough to mark an otherwise invisible boundary in the sanctuary, or actually prevented visibility. We have some later evidence of structural reinforcements of gender segregation, through boards, grilles, and curtains,[69] and Syrian churches are known to have had separate doors into the sanctuary, one for women, one for men. The late-fourth century *Apostolic Constitutions* (2.7), a composite church order probably compiled in Antioch, already indicates such gender-specific doorways into the church building. On the other side of the spectrum, we cannot be certain that gender separation in worship was practiced everywhere in the fourth century, or that such separation was not rather lax.[70]

---

[67]   John Chrysostom, *In Matthaeum homiliae* 73 (PG 58:677).

[68]   See their *John Chrysostom*, The Early Church Fathers (New York: Routledge, 2000), 24.

[69]   The evidence is collected in Selhorst, *Die Platzordnung im Gläubigenraum*, 38–51.

[70]   Robert Taft suggests that gender separation might not have been in force in Augustine's North Africa; see his "St. John Chrysostom, Preacher Committed to the Seriousness of Worship," in *The Serious Business of Worship: Essays in Honour of Bryan D. Spinks,* ed. Melanie Ross and Simon Jones (New York: Continuum, 2010), 13–21, here 17 n. 32. The evidence, however, is ambiguous. The passage in the *Confessions* (3.3.5) to which Taft points is anything but explicit. Augustine writes the following about his student days in Carthage: *ausus sum etiam in celebritate sollemnitatum tuarum, intra parietes ecclesiae tuae, concupiscere et agere negotium procurandi fructus mortis* (CCSL 27:29). "Even within the walls of your church, during the celebration of your sacred mysteries, I once made bold to indulge in carnal desire and conduct that could yield only a harvest of death" (I quote from Maria Boulding's translation of *The Confessions* [Hyde Park, NY: New City Press, 1997], 78). The assumption that Augustine's action —whatever its precise nature; the author veils it heavily—means that men and women were not separated in the sanctuary is a stretch. Augustine could be describing a homoerotic experience (not least of all in light of his description in Book 4.6–8), but, more importantly, such a reading of the passage in question is contradicted directly by a remark in *De civitate Dei* (2.28)

Even where there is doubt about strict gender separation in the gathered assembly, spatial separations between the genders are visible in other ritual contexts. A remark by Augustine might indicate that women and men had their separate exit ways out of the baptismal pool [*City of God*, 22.8]. Gender separations certainly shaped the actual choreography of baptism as witnessed to in the *Apostolic Tradition* (21), which requires that women be baptized after the men. Some early baptisteries, such as that of Aosta in Italy, had a second font in an annex, leading scholars to suggest that this baptistery used entirely separate fonts for men and for women.[71] Going even further, Milan had two baptisteries that, at least in later centuries, were used gender-specifically, one for the baptism of women, the other for the baptism of men.[72] All these baptismal gender separations are stark witnesses to the intersections between liturgical practice, gender identity, and the architecture of sacred space.

## Why Gender Separation in Sacred Space?

The reasons given in the sources for the importance of gender separation in sacred space focus almost exclusively on the need for "decency and order." This need is based on an apostolic injunction, namely Paul's in 1 Cor 14:40 that "all things should be done decently and in order" [πάντα δὲ εὐσχημόνως καὶ κατὰ τάξιν γινέσθω]. The *Didascalia Apostolorum*, for example, begins its instructions for spatial arrangements in the gathered assembly with an appeal to "good order."[73] A much more elaborate reasoning for liturgical gender separation, and its biblical precedents, can be found in an intriguing passage in Cyril of Jerusalem's *Procatechesis*. Cyril, bishop of Jerusalem from ca. 350–87, delivered this series of pre-Lenten catechetical instructions for those to be baptized at Easter. The *Procatechesis* is a document crucial for the history of worship in fourth-century Jerusalem, and also noticeable for the way gender is inscribed into it. The passage regarding gender separation at a prebaptismal exorcism is worth quoting at some length:

> And when the Exorcism is made, until the rest who are exorcised be come, let the men stay with the men, and the women with the women. Here I would allude to Noah's ark; in which were Noah and his sons, and his wife and their wives; and though the ark was one, and the door was shut, yet had things been arranged suitably. And though the Church be shut, and all of you within it, yet let there

---

indicating that the genders were segregated in church: "*quia populi confluunt ad ecclesiam casta celebritate, honesta utriusque sexus discretione*" (CCSL 47:14.1–2).

[71]    See Everett Ferguson, *Baptism in the Early Church: History, Theology, and Liturgy in the First Five Centuries* (Grand Rapids: Eerdmans, 2009), 836 and 852.

[72]    See Terence Bailey, "Ambrosian Processions to the Baptisteries," in *Plainsong and Medieval Music* 15 (2006): 29–42, here 30.

[73]    *Didascalia Apostolorum* 12, pp. 174f (see note 52).

be a distinction, of men with men and women with women. Let not the ground of your salvation become a means of destruction. Even though there be good ground for your sitting near each other, yet let passions be away.[74]

Cyril's reason for liturgical gender separation is the assumed gendered ordering of Noah's ark. This is not a far-fetched connection when we take into account early Christian readings of the story of the flood: Noah's rescue from the flood waters was taken to prefigure God's saving acts in baptism (1 Peter 3:20f already makes that connection). Noah's ark, moreover, also becomes a key symbol of early Christian ecclesiological thinking.[75] Even where Noah's ark is not invoked, ship imagery can dominate instructions on how to gather the liturgical assembly. The *Apostolic Constitutions*, a composite church order thought to be written in Syria around A.D. 380 and drawing, *inter alia*, on the *Didache*, the *Didascalia Apostolorum*, and the *Apostolic Tradition*, is a case in point. In the document's instruction to the bishop on how to order the liturgical assembly, the ship metaphor dominates throughout. Since the *Apostolic Constitutions* draws on Old Testament materials more frequently than its (known) sources do, the image of Noah's Ark may well underlie the following text, even without the Ark being mentioned:

> When thou callest an assembly of the Church as one that is the commander of a great ship, appoint the assemblies to be made with all possible skill, charging the deacons as mariners to prepare places for the brethren as for passengers, with all due care and decency. And first, let the building be long, with its head to the east, with its vestries on both sides at the east end, and so it will be like a ship. In the middle let the bishop's throne be placed, and on each side of him let the presbytery sit down; and let the deacons stand near at hand, in close and small girt garments, for they are like the mariners and managers of the ship: with regard to these, let the laity sit on the other side, with all quietness and good order. And let the women sit by themselves, they also keeping silence. ... Let the porters stand at the entries of the men, and observe them. Let the deaconesses also stand at those of the women, like shipmen. ... Let the younger women also sit by themselves, if there be a place for them; but if there be not, let them stand behind the women. Let those women which are married, and have children, be placed by themselves; but let the virgins, and the widows, and the elder women, stand or sit before all the rest.[76]

---

[74] Cyril of Jerusalem, *Procatechesis* 14 (PG 33:354–6). English translation, together with the Greek text, in *St. Cyril of Jerusalem's Lectures on the Christian Sacraments*, ed. F. L. Cross (reprint: Crestwood, NY: St Vladimir's Seminary Press, 1986), 48f.

[75] Hugo Rahner has analyzed this in detail in his *Symbole der Kirche: Die Ekklesiologie der Väter* (Salzburg: Otto Müller Verlag, 1964), 504–47.

[76] *Constitutiones Apostolorum* 2.7. English translation by James Donaldson, *Constitutions of the Holy Apostles*, ANF 7 (Grand Rapids, MI: Eerdmans, 1978), 421.

Cyril and the *Apostolic Constitutions* are not alone in connecting the ordering of a ship/ark with the ordering in church.[77] A century later, the Syriac *Cave of Treasures* will know of a quite specific gender arrangement in the Ark: Noah and his sons occupied the east side while their wives were placed on the western side.[78] In all these instances, gender separation functions as a basic form of ordering, in space. Gender differences, then, are one way of expressing and performing spatial ordering, including that in sacred space. I note in passing that the Ark as an image for the church also fed into specifically feminine ecclesial metaphors, for example when the ark, and with it the church and its baptismal font, are understood as a maternal womb, birthing the new community of the saved.[79]

Beyond Noah's ark, however, questions of origin for the various gender separations in worship will have to take into account several factors. To begin with, we have to acknowledge the silence of the New Testament and of the post-biblical witnesses until the early third century. This silence precludes a clear picture of how gendered bodies assembled for worship in the earliest Christian communities, when sanctuary space was within the domestic sphere. References to a ritual separation of men and women in Judaism come from a later period and can thus not explain the origins of the (earlier) Christian practice.[80] The late-antique context is more helpful here, since it knows various forms of gender separation. Men and women were kept separate in a number of settings, for example by excluding one gender altogether from a particular ritual (e.g., men from the Greek festival of *Thesmoforia*) and by spatial separation of the genders in civic festivals with both female and male participation.[81] Men and women also had their separate spaces in the theater and in the circus. Christian communities thus in all likelihood simply participated in broader cultural gendering processes when separating women and men in worship, and when privileging men with closer proximity to the center. When exactly this gender separation in Christian communities begins is unclear. Such separation becomes visible in the sources by the early third century, but whether there ever was a time when it was not practiced remains an open question.

---

[77]    For other examples, see Selhorst, *Die Platzordnung im Gläubigenraum*, 14–17.

[78]    *The Book of the Cave of Treasures*, English translation of the Syriac *Spelunca Thesaurorum*, by E. A. Wallis Budge (London: The Religious Tract Society, 1927), 110f.

[79]    More on this in Rahner, *Symbole der Kirche*, 531–4.

[80]    See Sharon Lea Mattila, "Where Women Sat in Ancient Synagogues: The Archaeological Evidence in Context," in *Voluntary Associations in the Graeco-Roman World*, ed. John S. Kloppenborg and Stephen G. Wilson (New York: Routledge, 1996), 266–86.

[81]    More on this in Økland, *Women in their Place*, ch. 4.

## Beyond Sanctuary Binaries

I have so far inquired into liturgical gender separation as if binary gender is the dominant concern. But as the sources highlighted above already signal, gender separations involve more than women from men. That gender is not simply a binary category is obvious from how gender is intertwined, for example, with status and age (e.g., a young girl is a different kind of female from a widow, a female catechumen different from a vowed virgin), not to mention the existence of cross-dressing ascetic women, of whom the Christian tradition knows more than a few. Other gender complexities deserve to be looked at, for example gender-slippages in sacred space when it comes to the presence of eunuchs. Eunuchs had access to spaces where "bearded men" could not enter. Little research has been done on these gendered identities and how they intersect with liturgical space and practices, even though ancient sources offer hints of how some of these lives intersected with Christian worship practices.[82] An early biblical example is the baptism of the Ethiopian eunuch on the Gaza road, recounted in Acts 8:26–40. For an inquiry into the intersections between gendered bodies and liturgical sites, this story is intriguing. It shows, to begin with, that baptism was open to eunuchs. This was not a given, in light of Deut 23:1 and Lev 21:17–21, which exclude eunuchs from the covenant community; both Is 56:3–5, and the fact that the Ethiopian eunuch seems to have been a Jewish believer, contradict the deuteronomic law. The story of the baptism by Philip stresses the Ethiopian's gender identity, mentioning no less than five times that he is a eunuch. Furthermore, the story locates the baptism of this "third gender" person not in a house church but in a transitional space, in the middle of nowhere, so to speak, and on the move. Despite this unstable site, the Ethiopian eunuch stands at the beginning of a long story of Christian congregations that included eunuchs; funerary inscriptions in early Christian burial sites, and the fact that castrati sang in the Vatican's Sistine Chapel Choir until the beginning of the twentieth century, mark two points of that long story.[83]

That being a eunuch shaped one's movements in worship is evident in the famous chancel mosaics in San Vitale, Ravenna. These mid-sixth-century mosaics show, on one side, Emperor Justinian, holding a golden paten. On the other side Empress Theodora stands, with a golden chalice. The two mosaics invoke imperial presence, if not participation in the offertory procession. On his side, Emperor Justinian is accompanied by a male entourage of both ecclesial and court dignitaries, seemingly about to process toward the sanctuary. The Empress, who stands in a more courtly context (with a richly ornamented fountain), is accompanied by a group of elegantly-dressed women to her left, and two beardless men, in all likelihood court eunuchs, to her right. One of the eunuchs holds open the curtain of the doorway through which the Empress seems about to pass with

---

[82]　I treat this in more detail in Chapter 6.

[83]　See Robert Muth, "Kastration," *Reallexikon für Antike und Christentum* 20 (2004): 285–342.

the chalice. If nothing else, the mosaic makes clear that simply mapping binary gender in worship occludes the more complex realities of Byzantine life, in this case eunuchs and their presence in women's spaces. Alas, we continue to know all too little about how the presence of eunuchs in sacred space shaped liturgical movements and practices.

### Outside the Bounds of the Nascent Public Church[84]

Given the various gender separations in public sanctuaries, we may ask how gender might have marked liturgical practices in other sites, not only Macrina's estate churches mentioned above, but also the shrines of the martyrs, cemetery churches, and processions to and from them. In *The Cult of the Saints*, Peter Brown argued that during processions and pilgrimages, traditional gender-based separations might temporarily be eased. In his own inimitable description:

> It was on such occasions ... that the greatest cleavage of all in late-antique urban society was bridged: for a delightful and perilous moment, the compartment segregating the sexes in public broke down. If not actually mixed with the men in the crowds, women were certainly available to the public gaze in a manner rare in a late-antique urban context.[85]

It may thus not be a coincidence that the most important liturgical document written by an early Christian *woman* is precisely the diary of the pilgrimage described at the beginning of this chapter—one that shows its author moving about rather freely.

In the context of pilgrimages and processions, one site and gathering space of Christians deserves particular mention, namely cemeteries and their shrines. Throughout the ancient world burial sites were outside the city walls, and thus beyond the urban public square. The cemeteries' gender scripts appear to have been more flexible than those of the public square, since cemeteries as well as funerary chambers underground were spaces beyond both the domestic and public spheres. Peter Brown, continuing his argument cited above, suggested that for late-antique women "the cemetery areas had always been a zone of 'low gravity,' where their movements and choice of company were less subject to male scrutiny."[86] More recent research suggests that funerary ceremonies and commemorative rites after burial provided a ritual space where women could exercise agency and

---

[84]    Bowes, *Private Worship*, 2, uses this helpful descriptor to name the ritual spheres to which her inquiry is devoted.

[85]    Peter Brown, *The Cult of the Saints: Its Rise and Function in Latin Christianity* (Chicago: The University of Chicago Press, 1981), 43.

[86]    Brown, *Cult of the Saints*, 44.

leadership.[87] One scholar studying the role of women in Rome as patron "bone gatherers" of martyr saints argues that burial places, tombs, epitaphs, and funerary images are an "untapped gold mine of information," especially about non-elite women, since "death provided the only opportunity for hundreds of thousands of otherwise unknown Roman women or their loved ones to leave some sort of physical record of their existence."[88]

These arguments are of interest for an inquiry into sacred space and gendering processes, since Christians are known to have gathered from earliest times at the burial places of the departed, especially those martyred for their faith. By the fourth century, and in tandem with the entry of the church into the public square and the concomitant rise of urban basilicas, cemeteries had become a focus of a grandiose redefinition of sacred space. The primary reason for this redefinition was popular devotion to the martyrs and saints, and by extension to their graves, relics, and shrines. Ramsey MacMullen, in fact, claims that well into the fourth century, martyr-memorials and cemetery churches far outnumbered urban churches. He estimates that for Rome "the space available for worship in-city, compared with the space available in cemeteries, was as one to ten or one to fifteen."[89] During the fourth and fifth centuries these cemetery shrines and their relics—initially outside the bounds of the city and thus at a distance from the newly public urban churches—became part of the ecclesial topography of a city. Bishop Ambrose's initiatives in Milan, linking devotion to the martyrs to the urban churches through the translation of relics, are a particularly well documented example of a much larger trend.[90] Depending on one's scholarly lenses, this process can be described in various degrees of conflict and tension, gender-specific ones included.[91]

---

[87]    See especially Janet H. Tulloch, "Women Leaders in Family Funerary Banquets," in Carolyn Osiek and Margaret Y. MacDonald, with Janet H. Tulloch, *A Woman's Place: House Churches in Earliest Christianity* (Minneapolis: Fortress, 2006), 164–93. Kathleen E. Corley argues in her recent book *Maranatha: Women's Funerary Rituals and Christian Origins* (Minneapolis: Fortress Press, 2010) that women's roles in funerary practices, especially in meals and ritual lament, are at the heart of Christian communities, including the oral traditions behind the New Testament passion accounts in the gospels.

[88]    Nicola Denzey, *The Bone Gatherers: The Lost Worlds of Early Christian Women* (Boston: Beacon Press, 2007), XIX. My thanks to Byron Stuhlman for directing me to this book.

[89]    MacMullen, *The Second Church*, 111.

[90]    See Jean-Michel Spieser, "Ambrose's Foundations at Milan and the Question of Martyria," in his *Urban and Religious Spaces in Late Antiquity and Early Byzantium*, Variorum Collected Studies Series (Burlington, VT: Ashgate, 2001), ch. 7.

[91]    If Peter Brown's *Cult of the Saints* is on the nuanced side, Felice Lifshitz in her "The Martyr, the Tomb and the Matron: Constructing the (Masculine) Past as a Female Power Base" in *Medieval Concepts of the Past: Ritual, Memory, Historiography*, ed. P. Geary, G. Althoff, and J. Fried (Cambridge: Cambridge University Press, 2002), 311–41, sees above all gender-specific conflicts and power struggles.

Augustine provides us with a glimpse of this process in the description of his mother Monica's practice of visiting cemeteries. While still in North Africa, Monica was in the habit of bringing a basket full of meal-cakes, and bread and wine, to the shrines of the saints on their memorial days. She would consume some of the food herself at the shrine of the saint, and give the rest away. When Monica moved to Milan, she found that this devotional practice of her North African Church was discouraged by Ambrose. In fact, a shrine doorkeeper [ostiarius] prevented Monica from following her devotional practice in this regard (Confessions 6.2.2).

This incident as reported by Augustine gives us a glimpse into mounting constraints on women's visits to the cemeteries and their shrines. Peter Brown describes this development more starkly as a "universal suspicion with which women's visits to the cemeteries were regarded."[92] This is especially true in relation to all-night vigils. A canon of the Synod of Elvira held in Spain in A.D. 306 for example stipulates: "Women are forbidden to spend the night in a cemetery since often under the pretext of prayer they secretly commit evil deeds."[93]

In this context it is worth remembering that the Christian witness to the Resurrection began with such a visit of women to a tomb. The baptistery at Dura-Europos holds a visual reminder of this: a surviving fresco, at an angle to the baptismal font, shows three women with lights held high approaching a sarcophagus-like structure, in all likelihood an image of the women visiting the tomb on Easter morning.[94]

## Leaving the Sanctuary

What has come to light in this inquiry into the relationship between sacred space and gendered bodies? At the most basic level, the answer simply is this: no gender-free space exists in liturgical history, not least because Christian communities emerged out of, and developed in, cultural contexts in which space was clearly gendered. Relationships are there to be explored, then, between sacred space and gendered bodies, or rather many such relationships. These relationships are discernable across a wide range of early Christian sanctuary spaces: the household, burial sites, pilgrimage centers, private chapels, estate churches, and urban basilicas. Gendering processes marked the spatial practice of liturgy in all of these sites. These liturgical gendering processes themselves are many: from the basic gender separation between men and women to the gender-specific peculiarities of widows' places and eunuchs' movements, gender intersects with sacred space

---

[92]   See also Brown, *Cult of the Saints*, 147f.

[93]   Canon 35. I am quoting from the English translation by Samuel Laeuchli in his *Power and Sexuality: The Emergence of Canon Law at the Synod of Elvira* (Philadelphia: Temple University Press, 1972), 130. Laeuchli devotes a section of his study to "The Clerics and Women" (pp. 97–101).

[94]   For more on this, see the literature on Dura-Europos mentioned in note 42.

in myriads of ways. And gendering processes, as they mark spatial practice, can be identified across a number of liturgical rites, from eucharistic assemblies, to prebaptismal exorcisms, to the choreography and architecture of baptism itself. Even if the evidence for the early centuries remains fragmentary and disparate, we have enough to indicate that gender and sacred space did intersect in manifold ways from earliest times.

In conclusion, I offer some insights to carry us beyond late antique Christianity. First, as we move beyond the early centuries, gender and sacred space will continue to have to be mapped across a broad array of sites, from the sacred space of public ecclesial sanctuaries to everyday spaces.[95] Gender scripts in all likelihood will function in somewhat different ways in these different sites.

Second, it seems safe to assume that gender will remain a fundamental marker of the spaces used for liturgical practice, and of movement therein. If there is one underlying theme in the manifold and complex ways in which gender intersects with sacred space, it might be this: Anxieties and constraints surround the presence of gendered bodies across a whole range of sacred spaces (Chapter 5 will highlight some of these).

Third, especially for lay women, gender separation in the sanctuary usually meant keeping a greater distance from the altar than men, including lay men. This distancing could go so far as forbidding women even to *enter* a particular sanctuary, as in the village church of Menat with which this book began.[96] Barring access to sacred space to women was common in the case of relic shrines located in monastic houses of men, but there were also many ways of subverting these regulations.[97] There did not seem to be similar gender-specific exclusions of men from women's communities that housed shrines and relics, at least in Merovingian and Carolingian times.[98] This agrees with recent scholarly work on convent histories as a whole, work that has shown how porous convent walls were and

---

[95] See, for example, Diana Webb, "Domestic Space and Devotion," in *Defining the Holy: Sacred Space in Medieval and Early Modern Europe*, ed. Andrew Spicer and Sarah Hamilton (Burlington, VT: Ashgate, 2005), 27–47, and Gabriela Signori, *Räume, Gesten, Andachtsformen: Geschlecht, Konflikt und religiöse Kultur im Mittelalter* (Ostfildern: Jan Thorbecke Verlag, 2005), 134–45.

[96] For more on this, see Jane Tibbetts Schulenburg, "Gender, Celibacy, and Proscriptions of Sacred Space: Symbol and Practice," in *Women's Space: Patronage, Place, and Gender in the Medieval Church*, 185–205.

[97] For more, see Julia M. H. Smith, "Women at the Tomb: Access to Relic Shrines in the Early Middle Ages," in *The World of Gregory of Tours*, ed. Kathleen Mitchell and Ian Wood, Cultures, Beliefs and Traditions: Medieval and Early Modern Peoples 8 (Boston: Brill, 2002), 161–80.

[98] See Jane Tibbetts Schulenburg, "Women's Monasteries and Sacred Space: The Promotion of Saints' Cults and Miracles," in *Gender and Christianity in Medieval Europe: New Perspectives*, ed. Lisa M. Bitel and Felice Lifshitz, The Middle Ages Series (Philadelphia: University of Pennsylvania Press, 2008), 68–86, esp. 84.

remained, even after the strict enclosure for all women religious demanded by the Council of Trent (convent plays are a case in point).

Finally, the position of women and men in the sanctuary is only one of the numerous indicators of the interplay between gender and sacred space. Many more deserve to be studied, such as the gendered organization of pilgrimage sites and anchoritic enclosures, of walls and tombs, of commemorative and devotional objects, of pew arrangements, and of the positioning of donors in donor images, to name just a few. And as mentioned above, mapping the positions of women and men in Christian worship by no means provides a complete map of gendered identity and sacred space. What if the "man" in question was a priest? For much of the past, a layman was much more restricted in his movements in church than a man who was a priest. And, in more recent times, what if the "woman" in question was an African American slave? She would not have sat with her white mistress in a nineteenth-century church in the American South, but rather found herself in a slave gallery. Clearly, "woman" and "man" are not stable or uniform categories, and we will have to do more than describe where women and men were positioned in church in order to map the many intersections between gender and sacred space. With the present chapter, I have offered a first sketch for the topography of this terrain.

# Chapter 4

# Eucharistic Fragments: Gender on and under the Table of Tradition

It was around A.D. 1455. In Siena, Tuscany, the painter Giovanni di Paolo (+ 1482) created a small panel, using tempera and gold, titled "Saint Clare of Assisi Blessing the Bread before Pope Innocent IV."[1] Clare, who had forsaken the world for a life of radical poverty, was canonized in 1255, less then two years after her death. Maybe Giovanni di Paolo wished to mark the bicentenary of the canonization with his painting. In it he represented a well-known story, which has Clare ask the pope, on the occasion of his visit to her community at San Damiano, to bless bread that had been set out on a table.[2] According to the story Innocent IV insisted that Clare herself bless the bread, and make the sign of the cross over it. Clare reluctantly obeyed. Miraculously, the sign of the cross appeared, stamped on the bread she blessed. The pope, having witnessed this miracle, is said to have taken with him and kept some of the bread blessed by Clare.

In Giovanni di Paolo's painting the tensions in this story of Saint Clare and Pope Innocent IV—especially those surrounding gender and status—take center stage in ways that remain hidden if we take the story primarily as a pious legend about Clare's obedience. The painter depicts a woman with her right hand authoritatively stretched out in priestly blessing over the three small, round loaves on the table. The miraculously transformed bread, with the cross now imprinted, resembles the large eucharistic hosts reserved for priests.[3] The painting frames these three host-like breads: on the right stands the pope, bowing both to the blessed bread and to Clare, with the remainder of that side filled with the papal entourage: three clerics, two of them cardinals. The men wear color-intense vestments and exude power. The left side of the painting is filled by Clare, alone, with the bread she has transformed. As she kneels, clad in her colorless monastic habit, her body

---

[1]    The painting is on view in the Yale University Art Gallery in New Haven, CT [1871.59]. I thank Linsey LaFrenier, Senior Museum Assistant at the Yale University Art Gallery, for information regarding the dating of this painting.

[2]    We know, however, from eyewitnesses whose testimonies are captured in the *Acts of the Process of Canonization* that Clare herself, for much of her life, practiced severe food asceticism; see *Clare of Assisi: Early Documents*, ed. and trans. Regis J. Armstrong (Mahwah, NJ: Paulist Press, 1988), 131 et al.

[3]    See Edward Foley, *From Age to Age: How Christians Have Celebrated the Eucharist*, rev. and expanded ed. (Collegeville; Liturgical Press, 2008), 114, 167–9, 221.

is upright, while her hand is outstretched in blessing over the bread. Clare's head is surrounded by a large golden halo. The pope, on the other side, wears his tiara, and the cardinals their red hats.

Giovanni di Paolo has painted a bread-miracle in the midst of a profound contrast: on one side a woman, kneeling, in simple dress, alone. On the other side a man, accompanied by his male entourage, standing, in lavish vestments. Yet inscribed in this visible imbalance of power are three elements that turn it on its head. Clare, and she alone, bears the sign of sanctity, a halo in the form of a full golden disk. On her side is the miraculously transformed bread that now resembles the priest's eucharistic host. Lastly, Clare's outstretched hand of blessing indicates her powerful connection to the bread on the table, a power authenticated miraculously through the sign of the cross that appears on the bread.

Rather than painting a narrative of female obedience, Giovanni di Paolo has chosen to display the power of female sanctity in the face of male clerical power, and God's surprising authentication of this female power over bread, to which a pope can only bow.

## Introduction

Giovanni di Paolo's painting is a tiny element of the complex history of eucharistic themes in images, stories, texts, music, and devotion. This history is much richer than most people realize. Gender complexities are a part of this richness, as di Paolo's painting so masterfully reveals. In what follows, I will explore some early eucharistic fragments that belong to these gender complexities that are hidden in our tradition. At the outset of this chapter, I want to clarify what will *not* be under discussion in what follows. My focus here is not on the history of the Eucharist as such, nor am I interested in looking in detail at one particular eucharistic rite, a single region, or a specific time period. Rather, I will concentrate on a limited number of early eucharistic fragments that have gender deeply inscribed into them, and have remained largely under the table of tradition, that is, invisible to most scholars, never mind believers. These fragments, in the order of exploration below, are a possible feminine image embedded in the Johannine eucharistic chapter; a maternal image in early eucharistic thinking and practice; and a fourth- or fifth-century prayer for an ascetic virgin's "eucharistizing." I place these fragments (others could be added[4]) next to each other in this chapter, in order to ask what

---

[4]    For example, the invocation of the Spirit as "mother" in what seems to be the earliest eucharistic epicleses extant to date, in the apocryphal *Acts of Thomas* (probably third-century, East Syrian), on which see Reinhard Messner, "Zur Eucharistie in den Thomasakten: Zugleich ein Beitrag zur Frühgeschichte der eucharistischen Epiklese," in *Crossroad of Cultures: Studies in Liturgy and Patristics in Honor of Gabriele Winkler*, ed. Hans-Jürgen Feulner et al., Orientalia Christiana Analecta 260 (Rome: Pontificio Istituto Orientale, 2000), 493–513; and, most recently, Susan E. Myers, *Spirit Epicleses in the Acts*

vision of the eucharistic tradition emerges with these gendered elements when placed on the table and in plain view. (I hasten to point out that a crucial gender-specific fragment of the tradition, namely the potent link between masculinity and eucharistic presiding, will come into sharp focus in the next chapter.)

In what follows I presuppose the recent scholarly work on eucharistic origins that has significantly redrawn our understanding of the early centuries.[5] Briefly, contemporary scholarship has moved away from a narrowly linear model, which had imagined an original *Urtyp*, that is, one basic form of eucharistic praying, rooted directly in Jesus' Last Supper. The idea of such an *Urtyp* (never mind an *Urtext*), traceable from apostolic origins through the fourth-century eucharistic prayers and beyond, has lost favor among many contemporary scholars who have instead begun to acknowledge, first, the fragmentariness of the available sources; second, the diversity of the evidence, which defies harmonization; and third, the local nature of the ancient texts and the communities to which they point. From this has emerged an image of eucharistic origins marked by historiographic caution: "we know much, much less ... than we once thought that we did."[6] Contemporary scholarship now mostly suggests that eucharistic origins lie in a number of relatively independent strands of early Christian meals, with variable elements of prayer, theological meaning, and indeed eucharistic elements. These meals, celebrated quite differently in various early Christian communities, are seen as growing out of the many communal meals Jesus shared with those around him—including, but not limited to, the meal on the night before he died, as well as post-resurrection meals—and the different interpretations given them in earliest Christianity.

The new appreciation of the diversity of early Christian meal practices has included a reevaluation of "the obscure category of the *agape*," which earlier scholarship had interpreted as a ritual meal separate from the *eucharistia*. Contemporary scholars are much less certain of this, and are ready instead to acknowledge how the category served—bluntly put—as "a convenient dumping ground for the unwanted meal evidence of the first few centuries."[7] That said,

---

*of Thomas*, Wissenschaftliche Untersuchungen zum Neuen Testament II, 281 (Tübingen: Mohr Siebeck, 2010), esp. 94–6, 132–8, 189–94, 216–18.

[5]     Three of the most important contributors are Reinhard Messner, "Über einige Aufgaben der Erforschung der Liturgiegeschichte der frühen Kirche," *Archiv für Liturgiewissenschaft* 50 (2008): 207–30, especially 214–16, 220–22, and his "Grundlinien der Entwicklung des eucharistischen Gebets in der frühen Kirche," in *Prex Eucharistica* 3/1, ed. Albert Gerhards et al., Spicilegium Friburgense 42 (Freiburg, Schweiz: Academic Press Fribourg, 2005), 3–40; Paul F. Bradshaw, *Eucharistic Origins*, Alcuin Club Publication (New York: Oxford University Press, 2004); and Andrew McGowan, *Ascetic Eucharists: Food and Drink in Early Christian Ritual Meals*, Oxford Early Christian Studies (Oxford: Clarendon Press, 1999).

[6]     Paul F. Bradshaw, *The Search for the Origins of Christian Worship: Sources and Methods for the Study of Early Liturgy*, 2d ed. (New York: Oxford University Press, 2002), X.

[7]     McGowan, *Ascetic Eucharists*, 21f.

there is consensus that diverse strands of eucharistic praying begin to intersect and converge during the second and third centuries, with "classical" eucharistic liturgies emerging in the fourth century.

What can gender history achieve here? Most importantly, gender-historical tools can be brought to bear on some fragments within the history of eucharistic practice and reflection, fragments that deserve to be teased out in greater gender-attentive depth than has been accorded them to date. In analyzing them, the historian confronts indicators of the power of gender in the history of eucharistic praying, which raises the question of how these gendered fragments, taken together, might reshape the image of eucharistic tradition as we know it. To answer this question, the gendered fragments on and under the table of tradition first need to be gathered and brought into plain view. To this task I now turn.

## Jesus as Both Host and Food

As mentioned above, contemporary research into eucharistic origins has emphasized the importance of Jesus' many shared meals for the practice of communal meals among the earliest Christians. Rare in this renewed attention to Jesus' meals is the recognition that in a first-century Jewish context food production was largely in women's hands. The making of bread especially was a distinctly female, often communal, and overall time-intensive labor.[8] Thus, when Jesus multiplied loaves – a meal moment remembered in all four Gospels, with Mark and Matthew telling versions of this feeding story twice—Jesus took a distinctly female labor upon himself. In the Gospel according to John, the story of the multiplication of loaves and the feeding of the multitude is of particular importance, since this Gospel does not have an "institution narrative" at the Last Supper. John 6 thus constitutes the "eucharistic" chapter of the fourth Gospel.[9] For my purpose here, the possible echo in John 6 of a distinctly feminine image of divine feeding and food is of particular interest. This image is rooted in Israel's Scriptures, which deeply influence John's Gospel at this point. Not only does the chapter gesture toward the memory of the gift of manna in the wilderness (Exod 16; Ps 78), the five loaves of the "bread of the Presence" that sustained David (1 Sam 21:3–6), and the prophetic promise of a banquet of bread, wine, and milk (Isa 55),[10] but it also seems to echo the invitation

---

[8]     See Carol Meyers, "Having Their Space and Eating There Too: Bread Production and Female Power in Ancient Israelite Households," *Nashim: A Journal of Jewish Women's Studies and Gender Issues* 5 (2002): 14–44.

[9]     For some of the rich exegetical debates around this key chapter in the Gospel according to John, see *Critical Readings of John 6*, ed. R. Alan Culpepper, Biblical Interpretation Series 22 (New York: Brill, 1997).

[10]     Diana Swancutt has argued forcefully for the last of these: see her "Hungers Assuaged by the Bread from Heaven. 'Eating Jesus' as Isaian Call to Belief: The Confluence of Isaiah 55 and Psalm 78(77) in John 6.22–71," in *Early Christian Interpretation of the Scriptures*

of Lady Wisdom—a feminine metaphor of Divine Presence in the Hebrew Bible— to the feast of life, for which she has prepared bread and wine (Prov 9:5).

In John 6, the feeding of the multitude leads to Jesus' claim that he himself becomes food, the true Bread of Life, which "gives life to the world" (John 6:33). The Biblical scholar Angelika Strotmann has recently argued in great detail that John here draws on images of Wisdom as both host and food, since Jesus not only feeds the multitude but also self-identifies as the bread of life.[11] The startling confluence between Lady Wisdom and Jesus as both host and ultimately food, taken together with the fact that bread production was women's work, substantiate Strotman's claim. One of the roots of the Johannine eucharistic vision would thus be Lady Wisdom as both the banquet's host and the one who gives herself as nourishment. As Strotmann points out, the image of Wisdom as host of a feast in Proverbs 9 reappears in Sirach 14:20–15:8, and is subsequently developed with a decisive twist: Sirach imagines Wisdom not only as the one who provides nourishment but as the one who seeks to give *herself* as food:

> Come to me, you who desire me,
>   and eat your fill of my fruits.
> For the memory of me is sweeter than honey,
>   and the possession of me sweeter than the honeycomb.
> Those who eat of me will hunger for more,
>   and those who drink of me will thirst for more (Sir 24:19–21).

The Johannine Jesus as one who not only provides food but himself claims to be food certainly embodies Lady Wisdom's invitation. With Jesus' invitation to his followers comes a heightening of the claim: "I am the bread of life," he says. "Whoever comes to me will never be hungry, and whoever believes in me will never be thirsty" (John 6:35).[12] Given the broader realities of first-century Judaism, a link between the eucharistic Jesus of John 6 and Lady Wisdom, or Wisdom theology, is not far-fetched. As Daniel Boyarin has shown, variations on Wisdom theology were widely held by both Jews and Christians in the first century, and beyond. Boyarin argues forcefully that such Wisdom or Logos theology shaped in particular the Gospel according to John.[13]

---

*of Israel: Investigations and Proposals*, ed. Craig A. Evans and James A. Sanders, JSNT Supplement Series 148 (Sheffield : Sheffield Academic Press, 1997), 218–51.

[11] Angelika Strotmann, "Die göttliche Weisheit als Nahrungsspenderin, Gastgeberin und sich selbst anbietende Speise," in *"Eine gewöhnliche und harmlose Speise?" Von den Entwicklungen frühchristlicher Abendmahlstraditionen*, ed. Judith Hartenstein et al. (Gütersloh: Gütersloher Verlagshaus, 2008), 131–56.

[12] For more on this, see Jane S. Webster, *Ingesting Jesus: Eating and Drinking in the Gospel of John*, Academia Biblica 6 (Atlanta: Society of Biblical Literature, 2003), 65.

[13] Cf. Daniel Boyarin, *Border Lines: The Partition of Judaeo-Christianity*, Divinations: Rereading Late Ancient Religion (Philadelphia: University of Pennsylvania

If John's eucharistic chapter richly reflects themes from the Hebrew Bible, the text also echoes the language of early eucharistic theology and practice. Thus, Jesus is described as taking the loaves, giving thanks [εὐχαριστήσας], and distributing them (John 6:11); and the term for the fragments of bread to be gathered, τὰ κλάσματα (John 6:12f), is the term used for the broken bread in *Didache* 9:3, 4.

Among the different New Testament meanings associated with Jesus' meals, this echo of a feminine image for God—Wisdom as both host and food—is only one, but at a point when scholarship emphasizes the diversity of eucharistic origins, this particular strand deserves heightened attention, not least in a gender-attentive re-reading of the evidence. Such attention is especially important given the fact that there is a strand in early Christian eucharistic thought and practice that continues to understand the eucharistic food through a feminine metaphor, namely as God's milk.

## The Eucharist as Mother's Milk

As foreign as this maternal eucharistic metaphor may be to most people today, it was an obvious and, indeed, compelling one in the context of early Christianity. To begin with, giving one's own body as food is precisely what mothers do when nursing, and a child nursing at the breast would have been "an everyday scene" for early Christians.[14] Breast milk was the first nourishment of every newborn, whether from the mother or from a wet nurse. Not coincidentally, the Greek verb τρέφω means not only "to nourish" and "to feed" but also "to nurse at the breast." Furthermore, pre-modern medical knowledge assumed that breast milk was the mother's blood (on which the unborn had already fed in the womb) now "heated" and thus turned white. Clement of Alexandria described this transformation of maternal blood into milk as follows:

> It is blood which is changed by the heat of the body once the mother has conceived, and in a maternal response develops and matures, for the well-being of the child. ... Of all the organs of the body, the breasts are the most sensitive to the condition of the womb. After childbirth, when the vein through which the blood was carried to the embryo has been cut off, then, with the passage obstructed, the blood is forced up into the breasts ... and the blood begins to turn into milk.[15]

---

Press, 2004), esp. 30–31, 93–111.

[14]   Margaret R. Miles, *A Complex Delight: The Secularization of the Breast 1350–1750* (Berkeley: University of California Press, 2008), 8.

[15]   Clement of Alexandria, *Paedagogos* 1.39.3–5. English translation in *Christ the Educator*, trans. Simon P. Wood, The Fathers of the Church (New York: Fathers of the Church, Inc., 1954), 38. For milk as maternal blood, see also Caroline Walker Bynum, *Wonderful Blood: Theology and Practice in Late Medieval Northern Germany and Beyond*

Thus, early Christians could easily link Jesus shedding his own blood, eucharistic food, and nourishment through breast milk. As Clement put it: "There can be no doubt that we can find nothing more nourishing, more palatable, or whiter than milk. But heavenly food is similar to milk in every way. ... Therefore, it is more than evident that the Blood of Christ is milk."[16] In addition, believers were able to appreciate a spiritual and liturgical progression here: if one key metaphor for baptism was that of new birth, then the first nourishment of the newborn would be breast milk, or—as the *Epistle of Barnabas* (17) as well as the *Canons of Hippolytus* (20) suggest—both breast milk and honey. Last but not least, Christians lived in a context where both the use of a ritual milk and honey cup (*melicraton*) and the metaphor of maternal breastfeeding as an image for a life-giving deity were already present. The most prominent and popular image of the goddess Isis, found throughout the Mediterranean world, was that of *Isis lactans*, the deity nursing her son at her breast.[17]

*Breast Milk as Eucharistic Metaphor*

Taking all these factors together, the use of milk and breastfeeding imagery in some early Christian eucharistic reflections should cause no surprise. Johannes Betz, in a 1984 essay titled "Die Eucharistie als Gottes Milch in frühchristlicher Sicht" (dedicated to the memory of Josef Andreas Jungmann), analyzed in detail this image and its possible liturgical implications.[18] He suggested that the image of the Eucharist as God's milk was not only echoed, but underlay, the blessing of a cup with milk and honey in the baptismal Eucharist. Betz's essay has received little attention in English-speaking scholarship to date.[19] Given this fact, together

---

(Philadelphia: University of Pennsylvania Press, 2007), 158f; and her essay "The Female Body and Religious Practice," in her *Fragmentation and Redemption: Essays on Gender and the Human Body in Medieval Religion* (New York: Zone Books, 1992), 181–238, esp. 214.

[16]     Clement of Alexandria, *Paedagogos* 1.40.2; *Christ the Educator*, 39.

[17]     Gail Paterson Corrington has studied this subject in "The Milk of Salvation: Redemption by the Mother in Late Antiquity and Early Christianity," *Harvard Theological Review* 82 (1989): 393–420.

[18]     Johannes Betz, "Die Eucharistie als Gottes Milch in frühchristlicher Sicht," *Zeitschrift für Katholische Theologie* 106 (1984): 1–26, 167–85.

[19]     Bradshaw (*Eucharistic Origins*), McGowan (*Ascetic Eucharists*), and Engelbrecht (see below) seem unfamiliar with this text. Paul F. Bradshaw et al., *The Apostolic Tradition: A Commentary*, Hermeneia (Minneapolis: Fortress Press, 2002), 134 n. 68, refers to Betz's essay, but does not engage its thesis. The author who did engage Betz's essay in some detail (although with different conclusions than I), is Edward J. Kilmartin, see his "The Baptismal Cups: Revisited," in *Eulogema: Studies in Honor of Robert Taft, S.J.*, ed. Ephrem Carr et al., Studia Anselmiana 110; Analecta liturgica 17 (Rome: Pontificio Ateneo S. Anselmo, 1993), 249–67.

with the author's stature as a scholar of early eucharistic theology,[20] I will pursue his argument in some detail here.

Betz began his inquiry into the early Christian evidence with a close reading of a New Testament text, 1 Peter 2:2–3: "Like newborn infants, long for the pure, spiritual milk, so that by it you may grow into salvation—if indeed you have tasted that the Lord is good." Betz argued that the text should, minimally, be considered open to the image of the Eucharist as God's milk, not only because of its emphasis on new birth through baptism, but also because of the use of Psalm 34:8 in 1 Peter 2:3; this Psalm verse early Christianity read eucharistically. About a century later (if one accepts 1 Peter to be a pseudonymous document, written sometime between A.D. 80 and 100[21]), a link between Eucharist and breast milk is not only explicit but also highly developed. Clement of Alexandria (c. 150–c. 215), in the first book of his *Paedagogos*, focuses on the image of breastfeeding to describe God's nurturing care toward the believer growing in faith. It is worth following Clement's thinking at some length here. Pondering the fact that a mother's blood turns into breast milk to nourish her child—a natural transformation Clement credits to divine nurturing care—he writes:

> There is a spiritual nourishment corresponding to this [physical] food, a food satisfying the needs of the re-created, reborn child; it also is prepared by God, the Nourisher and Father not only of those who are born, but also of those who are born again. This food is of the same kind as the manna which He made to rain down from heaven upon the ancient Hebrews, the celestial food of angels. In fact, even to this day, nurses still call the first flow of milk by the name manna, ... now that the loving and kind Father has rained down the Word, it is He Himself who has become the spiritual nourishment of the saints. O mystic wonder![22]

Clement goes on to describe the church as providing "milk that is holy" to her children, but rather than developing an ecclesial maternal image, he insists that the church imparts the milk that is Christ:

> she [the church] has no milk, because this Son of hers, beautiful and all hers, the Body of Christ, is milk. ... The Word is everything to His little ones, both father and mother, educator and nurse. "Eat My flesh," He says, "and drink My blood." He is Himself the nourishment that He gives. He delivers up His own flesh and

---

[20] For more on this see Lothar Lies, "Zur Eucharistielehre des Johannes Betz (1914–1984)," *Zeitschrift für katholische Theologie* 128 (2006): 53–80.

[21] See Paul J. Achtemeier, *A Commentary on First Peter*, Hermeneia (Minneapolis: Fortress Press, 1996), especially 49f.

[22] Clement of Alexandria, *Paedagogos* 1.41–42.1; *Christ the Educator*, 39f. See also Verna E. F. Harrison, "The Care-Banishing Breast of the Father: Feminine Images of the Divine in Clement of Alexandria's *Paedagogus* I," *Studia Patristica* 31 (1997): 401–5.

pours out His own blood. There is nothing lacking His children, that they may grow. What a mysterious paradox![23]

Clement, acknowledging that his readers may find this thinking startling, then moves on to another line of argument. He suggests that Christ is the maternal breast of the Father, nursing the believers with his shed blood, turned into breast milk:

> This is our nourishment, the milk flowing from the Father by which alone we little ones are fed. I mean that He, the "well-beloved," the Word, our provider, has saved mankind by shedding His blood for us. Therefore, we fly trustfully to the "care-banishing breast" of God the Father; the breast that is the Word, who is the only one who can bestow on us the milk of love. Only those who nurse at the breast are blessed.[24]

Clement's images, if somewhat jumbled, are clear enough, and his guiding insight remains stable: Christ's blood shed for us is received as mother's milk, on which believers feed/nurse. As biblical warrant, Clement quotes 1 Peter 2:2 and interprets the biblical text as follows:

> We are nourished with milk, the Lord's own nourishment, as soon as we leave our mother's womb; and as soon as we are born anew we are favored with the good tidings of hope of rest, that heavenly Jerusalem in which, as it is written, "milk and honey rain down."[25]

Clement here witnesses to an early connection between the biblical promise of milk and honey and God's nursing us, after natural birth, and after our new birth. He concludes his ruminations by insisting that imaging Christ's (eucharistic) self-giving as nursing is not strange:

> In all these various ways and figures of speech is the Word spoken of: solid food, flesh, nourishment, bread, blood and milk. The Lord is all these things for the refreshment of us who believe in Him. Let no one think it strange, then, that we speak of the blood of the Lord also under the figure of milk.[26]

Clement's reflections on breast milk as a metaphor for Christ's redemptive self-giving may be the most elaborate, but the Alexandrian theologian is by no means alone. The *Odes of Solomon*—an (early second century?) collection of poems, possibly Syrian, with Jewish influence and a Gnostic tinge, yet a "Christian

---

[23]  Clement of Alexandria, *Paedagogos* 1.42.1–2; *Christ the Educator*, 40.

[24]  Clement of Alexandria, *Paedagogos* 1.43.2–4; *Christ the Educator*, 41.

[25]  Clement of Alexandria, *Paedagogos* 1.44.2; *Christ the Educator*, 42.

[26]  Clement of Alexandria, *Paedagogos* I.47.2; *Christ the Educator*, 44.

whole"[27]—repeatedly invokes milk imagery, and also draws on Wisdom imagery throughout (Wisdom and Sirach are the most often quoted apocryphal books in the *Odes*). Metaphors of milk and of honey appear several times.[28] *Ode* 40, for example, in language reminiscent of the psalms, invokes hope in God thus:

> As honey drips from the honeycomb of bees,
> and milk flows from the woman who loves her children,
> so also my hope is on thee, my God.[29]

Earlier in the *Odes* the Redeemer identified himself as a nursing mother, offering believers her breast milk:

> And before they yet were,
> I perceived them.
> And on their faces I set a seal.
> I fashioned their members,
> And my own breasts I prepared for them,
> that they might drink my holy milk to live by it.[30]

The language (especially that of a "seal") is at least suggestive of new birth in baptism. A liturgical scholar familiar with later evidence for a milk and honey cup in the baptismal Eucharist may rightfully wonder about the sequence of birthing and sealing to nursing images ("holy milk") in this text.

The most pronounced use of milk imagery comes in *Ode* 19. The image of maternal milk, offered in a cup no less, is here invoked within a proto-Trinitarian vision built on "dissonant gender imagery."[31]

> A cup of milk was offered to me,
> and I drank it in the sweetness of the Lord's kindness.
> The Son is the cup,
> and he who was milked, the Father,
> and [the one] who milked him, the Spirit of holiness.
> Because his breasts were full

---

[27]   The description of the *Odes* is Michael Lattke's, *Odes of Solomon: A Commentary*, transl. Marianne Erhardt, Hermeneia (Minneapolis: Fortress Press, 2009), 13.

[28]   Cf. also Edward Engelbrecht, "God's Milk: An Orthodox Confession of the Eucharist," *Journal of Early Christian Studies* 7 (1999): 509–26. Engelbrecht's point that the image of God's milk is not primarily a Gnostic or heterodox one is well made. Unfortunately the author does not seem to know the essay by Johannes Betz.

[29]   *Ode* 40. English translation in *Odes of Solomon: A Commentary*, 557.

[30]   *Ode* 8; *Odes of Solomon: A Commentary*, 111.

[31]   The expression is Jennifer A. Glancy's, see her *Corporal Knowledge: Early Christian Bodies* (New York: Oxford University Press, 2010), 96.

and it was not desirable that
his milk should be poured out/discharged
for no reason/uselessly,
the Spirit of holiness opened his [viz., the Father's] bosom
and mixed the milk of the two breasts of the Father.
And she/it gave the mixture to the world.[32]

This text, with its mention of a "cup of milk" that is "given," has invited scholarly speculation about a specific ritual underlying this *Ode*.[33] My own interest in the text is less speculative. I cite the *Odes* primarily as evidence that milk imagery was present in early Christianity beyond Clement's use, and that this imagery appeared in a variety of contexts, across the assumed divides between Syrian, Greek, and Latin christianities. To substantiate the geographic spread of the image, another example deserves to be added. This text comes from Irenaeus of Lyons, who was born in Asia Minor, studied in Rome, and eventually became bishop of Lyons in southern France (+ ca. 200). In his major treatise against Gnostic thinking, *Adversus Haereses*, Irenaeus refers to Christ's incarnation as the "perfect bread of the Father" becoming milk for us. In this way, according to Irenaeus, Christ is able to nourish believers "from the breast of His flesh" with the "Bread of immortality," which otherwise they would not have been able to receive. Irenaeus writes:

> For as it certainly is in the power of a mother to give strong food to her infant, [but she does not do so], as the child is not yet able to receive more substantial nourishment; so also it was possible for God Himself to have made man perfect from the first, but man could not receive this [perfection], being as yet an infant. And for this cause our Lord ... came to us, not as He might have come, but as we were capable of beholding Him. He might easily have come to us in His immortal glory, but in that case we could never have endured the greatness of the glory; and therefore it was that He, who was the perfect bread of the Father, offered Himself to us as milk, [because we were] as infants. He did this when He appeared as a man, that we, being nourished, as it were, from the breast of His flesh, and having, by such a course of milk nourishment, become accustomed

---

[32] *Ode* 19; *Odes of Solomon: A Commentary*, 557. Interestingly, the Ethiopian "Anaphora of the Virgin Mary, Daughter of God" also knows a Trinitarian milk image, at the end of a long list of possible Trinitarian images: "The Father is the milk, the Son its taste, the Holy Spirit its fragrance: one is the milk that is unmixed." Translation mine, from the Latin text of this Anaphora in *Prex eucharistica: Textus e variis liturgiis antiquioribus selecti*, ed. Anton Hänggi and Irmgard Pahl, Spicilegium Friburgense 12 (Freiburg, Schweiz: Éditions Universitaires Fribourg Suisse, 1968), 164.

[33] Lattke, *Odes of Solomon: A Commentary*, 270.

to eat and drink the Word of God, may be able also to contain in ourselves the Bread of immortality, which is the Spirit of the Father.[34]

Even if Irenaeus does not explicitly invoke the Eucharist here, the nexus of images (and their eucharistic overtones) is very similar to the ones in Clement. And the link between incarnation and Eucharist is an ancient one, already evident in Justin's eucharistic thinking (e.g., *Dialogue with Trypho, a Jew* 70.4). The recurring language of Christ's "flesh" also suggests the influence of John 6 on this link.[35] Christ, the heavenly bread, offers his incarnated flesh to us as breast milk—in the same way in which a mother feeds her child with food adequate to the newborn's needs—because we could not otherwise ingest this Bread of immortality.

The image of Christ becoming mother's milk in order to feed us with the bread of life does not die with Irenaeus. Some two hundred years later, in North Africa, it reappears in Augustine. The bishop of Hippo, in his exposition of Psalm 130/131, which describes the relationship between God and the believer as one of a child being at the mother's breast, claims that "Our Lord Jesus Christ made the bread that was himself into milk for us [*Dominus ergo noster Iesus Christus panis, se fecit nobis lac*] by becoming incarnate."[36] Like Irenaeus, Augustine here imagines the incarnation through a maternal image as Christ's gift of his body as nourishment, namely breast milk: Christ who is bread, flesh, and meat (John 6!) becomes milk to feed us. Augustine writes:

> When a mother sees that her child is not yet capable of eating solid food, she gives him solids, but only through the medium of her own flesh. What nourishes the baby is the same bread that nourishes the mother, but because the baby cannot cope with an adult meal, the bread from the table is transformed and reaches the child through the mother's breast.[37]

This quite specific description (one imagines Augustine watching such maternal food production) appears repeatedly in the *Expositions*. Reflecting on Christ granting us salvation in his body and blood, Augustine claims that no human is fit

---

[34]  Irenaeus of Lyons, *Adv. Haer.* 4.38.1. English translation: *Irenaeus Against Heresies*, in *The Writings of the Fathers down to A.D. 325*, ed. Alexander Roberts and James Donaldson, ANF 1 (Grand Rapids, MI: Eerdmans, 1979, American reprint of Edinburgh ed.), 521.

[35]  Cf. Bradshaw, *Eucharistic Origins*, 87–91.

[36]  Augustine, *Enarr. in Ps.*, 130.11 (CCSL 40, 1907). English translation: *Expositions of the Psalms*, 121–150, trans. Maria Boulding, The Works of Saint Augustine III:20 (Hyde Park, NY: New City Press, 2004), 149. See also Margaret R. Miles, "Infancy, Parenting, and Nourishment in Augustine's *Confessions*," *The Journal of the American Academy of Religion* 50 (1982): 349–64.

[37]  Augustine, *Enarr. in Ps.*, 130.9 (CCSL 40, 1905); *Expositions of the Psalms*, 148.

for such food, which is the eternal food of angels and celestial powers. Therefore, it was "necessary for that banquet to be converted to milk":

> This is what a mother does. What a mother eats the baby eats too, but since the baby is unable to digest bread, the mother turns the bread into her own flesh, and through the humility of the breast and its supply of milk she feeds her baby with the same bread.[38]

This, Augustine argues, is how the Wisdom of God feeds us with heavenly bread. The passages are intriguing not least because Augustine here has found a way to interpret mother's milk as a transformation of *bread*, rather than of maternal blood, as we saw in Clement of Alexandria. The locus of transformation, however, remains the same in both theologians, namely the maternal body, as do the end product and its source: milk from the maternal breasts. In his *Confessions*, Augustine makes a similar link between milk and the body of Christ: "what am I but a child suckled on your milk and fed on you, the food that perishes not?"[39] The link between breast milk and the eucharistic Wisdom-inspired language of John 6 is quite evident here.

Taking all these various textual references together (and more could be added),[40] one might say that although the image of God nursing the faithful with mother's milk is sporadic in early Christian writings, the image does appear repeatedly, in diverse contexts, and in key writers—Clement of Alexandria, Irenaeus of Lyons, and Augustine of Hippo are not marginal figures in the Christian tradition. In several instances, eucharistic overtones are unmistakable in the use of this image.

In addition to these textual witnesses, milk metaphors in early Christianity may also be embedded in visual culture. Johannes Betz pointed to catacomb images of Christ as the Good Shepherd, who, according to Psalm 23:5, not only leads to the waters but also prepares a table with food. This Good Shepherd is repeatedly represented in early Christian art as carrying a milk pail, or as milking. Given that in the world of early Christianity a shepherd was a key provider of (animal) milk, these visual representations may also gesture toward the metaphor of eucharistic milk. With this in mind, we may find in other Christian writings traces of this

---

[38] Augustine, *Enarr. in Ps.*, 33.6. English translation: *Expositions of the Psalms*, 33–50, trans. Maria Boulding, The Works of Saint Augustine III:16 (Hyde Park, NY: New City Press, 2000), 17. Similarly, in *Enarr. 2 in Ps.*, 30.9, Augustine writes: "He who has promised us the food of heaven has nourished us here below with milk, in his motherly mercy ... the Lord put on flesh and came to us, to make his wisdom palatable to us as milk," *Expositions of the Psalms*, 1–32, trans. Maria Boulding, The Works of Saint Augustine III:15 (Hyde Park, NY: New City Press, 2000), 329. My thanks to John Leinenweber for pointing me to these passages.

[39] Augustine, *Confessions*, 4.1.1 (CCSL 27:40). I quote from Maria Boulding's translation of *The Confessions* (Hyde Park, NY: New City Press, 1997), 92.

[40] E.g., the *Epistle of Barnabas*, 6.

metaphor. I am thinking here especially of the vision of the martyr Perpetua, who was put to death in the amphitheater of Carthage in A.D. 203. The account of her martyrdom preserves an autobiographic text in which Perpetua recounts a vision she had in prison where she was still breastfeeding her infant son. In this vision Perpetua sees a white-haired shepherd milking sheep. From the shepherd's hands, Perpetua receives, in her folded hands, a piece of cheese, that is, coagulated milk.[41] Those around her, all in white robes, respond "Amen." Perpetua eats, and when she awakens from her vision still tastes the sweetness of the food the Shepherd had given her. Even if I cannot here delve in detail into this particular account of a martyrdom—in which women, birthing, and breastfeeding play a crucial role – there clearly is a connection in this vision between a Good Shepherd, a milk product, and a ritualized form of eating.

*Milk and Honey: Liturgical Practice*

With these textual and visual witnesses as background, we now turn to the actual liturgical use of milk in early Christianity. In what follows, I focus on the blessing of a milk and honey cup at the baptismal Eucharist, and leave aside the broader use of milk in some early Christian communities.[42] Johannes Betz argued that evidence for a milk and honey cup could be mapped, in terms of geographic range, to the textual evidence for the metaphor of God's milk as eucharistic food.[43] He noted that the relationship between the two—the metaphor on the one hand, and the liturgical practice on the other—cannot be determined with any precision, but suggested that the metaphor might have preceded liturgical practice.[44] The evidence for this is not strong, but evidence for the liturgical practice of a milk and honey cup given to the newly baptized, at least in Christian communities in North Africa and Rome, certainly is. The first clear evidence for such a cup comes in the writings of Tertullian.[45] In a lengthy argument for liturgical practices authorized by ecclesial tradition rather than by Scripture itself, Tertullian lists the milk and honey

---

[41]    For more on cheese as an element of a eucharistic meal, see McGowan, *Ascetic Eucharists*, 95–107.

[42]    For the broader use of milk as an element in the eucharistic meal, see McGowan, *Ascetic Eucharists*, 107–15.

[43]    See Betz, "Eucharistie als Gottes Milch," 1–26, 167–85.

[44]    This suggestion is not surprising, given that Betz's scholarly field was the history of eucharistic thought, rather than of liturgical practice. Betz defines the *Apostolic Tradition* as the hinge, reading the text (which he still believed to reflect early third-century Roman practice) as a witness to his thesis of "metaphor become liturgy"; see esp. 179 and 184.

[45]    Whether one can read the reflections of Tertullian's contemporary Clement of Alexandria as witnessing to such a liturgical practice remains contested, with Betz arguing for and McGowan against. The editors of *The Apostolic Tradition: A Commentary*, 134, declare it to be "possible, but by no means certain." My own position is that Clement, although he does not mention a milk and honey cup, is likely to have known it, especially

mixture given to the newly baptized as one example of such a practice.[46] Since Tertullian claims that this practice is authorized by tradition rather than found in Scripture we can presume that the milk and honey cup is not a recent invention in his early third-century ecclesial context. This would move the origins of the practice back to at least the second century. Tertullian gives this example in a long list of traditional practices, and details about this milk and honey mixture remain unclear, especially the theological understanding of this ritual and its precise place between Baptism and Eucharist.

The earliest example of a liturgical source that mentions a milk and honey cup is the *Apostolic Tradition*, in a chapter dedicated to baptismal initiation (Chapter 21). Here, the milk and honey cup is an integral part of the baptismal Eucharist, and, indeed, of the eucharistic prayer itself. The cup is blessed and distributed together with the bread and the wine.[47] The textual evidence, however, presents several challenges. To begin with, it is no longer clear that we have a reflection of early third-century Roman practice here (as Betz still believed). Furthermore, Chapter 21 might in fact be made up of different strata; the section in question may belong to a remnant of a mystagogical instruction interpolated into an older text.[48] The different versions of the *Apostolic Tradition* (Latin, Sahidic, Arabic, and Ethiopic) also offer quite different details with regard to the milk and honey cup. Finally, the derivatives of the *Apostolic Tradition* diverge considerably at this point. The Latin version of the *Apostolic Tradition* is the most elaborate, even if, like the other versions, it does not offer an actual text of a blessing over the cup. The bishop simply is instructed to pray, not only over bread and wine but also over a cup of water and a cup of milk and honey, which are then given to the newly baptized. The milk and honey cup follows the water cup and precedes the wine cup. The oriental versions and the derivative *Canons of Hippolytus* diverge in various ways from the Latin version, including in the number of cups and the sequencing of their distribution. Given the divergences, however, the stability of the theological themes connected with the milk and honey cup is especially noticeable, and deserves particular attention. In the Latin version, the theological explanation of a cup of "milk and honey mixed together" fuses three themes:

> for the fulfillment of the promise that was to the fathers, which he said,
> "a land flowing [with] milk and honey"

---

given his tying together of water, milk, honey, and wine in *Paedagogos* I.50–51; *Christ the Educator*, 46–8.

[46]   Tertullian, *De Corona* 3.3. Tertullian's description seems to suggest that a mixture of milk and honey is offered the newly baptized immediately following their water baptism, thus well before the eucharistic celebration proper.

[47]   *Apostolic Tradition* 21. English text in *The Apostolic Tradition: A Commentary*, 120–22.

[48]   Such is the suggestion of the editors of *The Apostolic Tradition: A Commentary*, 128f.

and which Christ gave, his flesh,
        through which, like little children, those who believe are nourished [*nutriuntur*].[49]

The density and fusion of theological themes in this one sentence is rather remarkable: the biblical promise of a land flowing with milk and honey is said to point to Christ's own body, which is seen as feeding believers with sweet milk. Christ's body here is imaged as a maternal body which breastfeeds, in fulfillment of the promise of milk and honey. The oriental versions of the *Apostolic Tradition* all witness to these same themes. The derivative Egyptian *Canons of Hippolytus* even heightens the centrality of the maternal image by dropping the biblical reference behind the milk and honey cup/s, which are said to be offered "so that those who partake may know that they are born again like little children, because little children partake of milk and honey."[50]

Given the explicitly maternal interpretation of the milk and honey cup in all versions of the *Apostolic Tradition*, it seems curious that recent interpreters show no particular interest in this image, and focus instead on possible messianic and eschatological themes.[51] Just as curious is the suggestion that milk as a liturgical symbol in the *Apostolic Tradition* is not least a "sign of wealth and plenty, ... abundance and luxury."[52] This argument assumes that the milk at the baptismal Eucharist points primarily to animal milk. Maternal milk, on the other hand, rather than being a sign of luxury, simply was the most basic foodstuff of every newborn, analogous to bread as the basic foodstuff of adults.

Witnesses to a milk and honey cup at the baptismal Eucharist do not end with the *Apostolic Tradition*, although the theological interpretation of this cup begins to move away from the maternal meaning. Whether *Apostolic Tradition* 21 witnesses to Roman practice or not, Jerome (c. 345–420) clearly attests the existence of a milk and honey cup at the baptismal Eucharist there.[53] He also assumes that this practice is common among the churches. In the text in question, Jerome argues,

---

[49]     *Apostolic Tradition* 21.28, in *The Apostolic Tradition: A Commentary*, 120 (the arrangement of the lines is mine). Latin text in Jean Michel Hanssens, *La Liturgie d'Hippolyte: Documents et Études* (Rome: Libreria Editrice dell'Università Gregoriana, 1970), 116.

[50]     In *The Apostolic Tradition: A Commentary*, 121. The *Testamentum Domini* does not have a milk and honey cup at that point.

[51]     *The Apostolic Tradition: A Commentary*, 139, for example, describes the "theological sophistication" of the Latin version's description of the milk and honey cup, yet makes no mention whatsoever of the maternal image embedded in the text.

[52]     McGowan, *Ascetic Eucharists*, 112, 114.

[53]     Justin Martyr, describing a baptismal Eucharist in Rome about A.D. 150, does not mention a milk and honey cup (*First Apology* 65.1). However, as Bradshaw has pointed out (*Eucharistic Origins,* 64), given that Justin himself was from Samaria and probably belonged to a Christian community in Rome with Eastern membership, his description does not necessarily reflect what all the other Christian assemblies in Rome practiced.

like Tertullian before him, for the power of tradition to authorize practices that have no Scriptural warrant, citing the milk and honey cup as one such practice: "after leaving the water, of tasting mingled milk and honey in representation of infancy."[54] Note that Jerome does not speak of "*baptismal* infancy or new birth,"[55] but rather of milk as a "representation of infancy" —which is a nursing rather than a birthing image. Jerome's theological thinking thus is quite close to the Latin version of the *Apostolic Tradition*.

A reference to a milk and honey cup may also be provided by Zeno, bishop of Verona from about A.D. 362 to about 380. In a sermon delivered at the Paschal Vigil, Zeno invites his hearers "to be babes at the breast together."[56] Though not a clear reference to a milk and honey cup, this certainly is not far from the image of breast milk linked to the baptismal Eucharist. Zeno, who uses birthing imagery intensely throughout his baptismal reflections, focuses on mother church as the one who gives birth in baptism, which will indeed become the dominant theme, at least in the West. It is worth asking, however, whether underneath this ecclesial-maternal image there is not an older, theologically more precise image, which acknowledges God as the One birthing believers to new life in the church's baptismal font.

A further witness to the practice of a milk and honey cup in Rome given to the newly baptized is provided by a letter of John the Deacon, in which he answers questions a certain Senarius posed regarding baptismal initiation. In this letter, written ca. A.D. 500, John offers a lengthy explanation for the milk and honey cup at the baptismal Eucharist. He thinks of this cup in strongly sacramental terms, with his theological explanation of the cup focused on the eschatological land of promise. The image of this land of promise as Christ's own body—as maternal and breastfeeding—has all but disappeared here. Instead, it is the eschatological body of the believer that has now become the promised land:

> You ask why milk and honey are placed in a most sacred cup and offered with the sacrifice at the Paschal Sabbath. The reason is that it is written in the Old Testament and in a figure promised to the New People: *I shall lead you into a land of promise, a land flowing with milk and honey* [Lev. 20.24]. The land of promise, then, is the land of resurrection to everlasting bliss, it is nothing else

---

[54]   Jerome, *Dialogue against the Luciferians*, 8 (PL 23:153–82B). English translation, by W. M. Fremantle, in NPNF series 2, 6:324.

[55]   As in the paraphrase of this passage given by the editors of *The Apostolic Tradition: A Commentary*, 135.

[56]   Zeno of Verona, *Baptismal Homilies* 2.28. English translation in Gordon P. Jeanes, *The Day Has Come! Easter and Baptism in Zeno of Verona*, Alcuin Club Collection 73 (Collegeville: Liturgical Press, 1995), 54–99, here 97. In another homily (1.12), Zeno connects the "sweet murmur of the stream of nectar" with the "milky water of the life giving font," encouraging his hearers "to drink deeply" (ibid., 59). The baptismal waters, in other words, are seen as streams of milk and honey.

than the land of our body, which in the resurrection of the dead shall attain to the glory of incorruption and peace. This kind of sacrament, then, is offered to the newly-baptized so that they may realize that no others but they, who partake of the Body and Blood of the Lord, shall receive the land of promise: and as they start upon the journey thither, they are nourished like children with milk and honey, so that they may sing: *How sweet are your words unto my mouth, O Lord, sweeter than honey and the honeycomb* [Ps. 119.103; 19.11]. As new [human beings], therefore, abandoning the bitterness of sin, they drink milk and honey: so that they who in their first birth were nourished with the milk of corruption and first shed tears of bitterness, in their second birth may taste the sweetness of milk and honey in the bowels of the church, so that being nourished upon such sacraments [*ut nutriti talibus sacramentis*] they may be dedicated to the mysteries of perpetual incorruption.[57]

Similarly to this explanation by John the Deacon, the slightly later *Verona (Leonine) Sacramentary*, whose materials witness to sixth-century Roman practice, betrays no trace of the maternal christological imagery that marks earlier texts. The *Verona Sacramentary* does however provide the text of an actual blessing to be said over a water, milk, and honey cup, at the baptismal Eucharist on Pentecost:

Bless also we ask you, O Lord, these your creatures of water, honey, and milk, and give your servants drink of this fount of water of everlasting life, which is the spirit of truth, and nourish them with this milk and honey according as you promised to our fathers, Abraham, Isaac, and Jacob, to lead them into the land of promise, a land flowing with milk and honey. Therefore, O Lord, unite your servants to the Holy Spirit, as this honey and milk is united, wherein is signified the union of heavenly and earthly substance [*substantia*] in Christ Jesus our Lord.[58]

Such a blessing of a milk and honey cup lives on in medieval liturgical manuscripts in the West, even if this cup becomes increasingly distanced from the baptismal Eucharist and the elements of bread and wine. The late fourth-century North African councils already had insisted that milk and honey, although offered at the altar, should have their own separate blessing so as to distinguish them clearly from the eucharistic elements.[59] In medieval liturgical manuscripts from England, as Pierre-Marie Gy has noted, the blessing of a milk and honey cup often

---

[57]    John the Deacon, *Letter to Senarius* 12. English translation in E. C. Whitaker's *Documents of the Baptismal Liturgy*, rev. and expanded ed., ed. Maxwell E. Johnson (London: SPCK, 2003), 211.

[58]    *Documents of the Baptismal Liturgy*, 207.

[59]    Third Council of Carthage, canon 24. English text in *Documents of the Baptismal Liturgy*, 141.

is placed within the Maundy Thursday Mass;[60] thus it had a very explicit link to the Eucharist, although no longer to Baptism. By the thirteenth century, however, the blessing of milk and honey had become simply one part of the blessing of Easter foods, with no direct link to a baptismal Eucharist or its eucharistic prayer.

*Milk Metaphors—Early Meanings and Later Migrations*

To conclude, what has this inquiry into eucharistic milk-images and practices shown? Beginning on the most basic level, simply this: that a strand exists within the rich diversity of early eucharistic thinking that images God's gift of food/drink as the maternal gift of breast milk. To put this differently: Christ's body given and his blood shed are understood as a mother's gift of her own body, in nurture of a child's life (a quite different image from, say, that of sacrificial offering[61]). Manifold theological themes are interwoven into this image, among them the biblical promise of a land of milk and honey; Lady Wisdom as the one who offers herself as food; Jesus giving his body and blood to nurture life; and images of baptism as new birth. These themes, taken together, lend themselves to the baptismal Eucharist—the first feeding after the new birth—being understood as the offer of maternal breast milk. The liturgical practice, attested to in at least some churches (North Africa, Egypt, Ethiopia, and Rome), of a milk and honey cup given to the newly baptized is linked to that image, even if the question of which came first—theological reflection or liturgical practice —is futile, and possibly misguided (why posit a dividing line between these two practices of faith?).

What does gender analysis offer in a rereading of this early Christian image of eucharistic food/drink as God's milk? Three aspects stand out. First, this image becomes a focus of scholarly analysis, with its gendered particularity (the maternal body, post partum) receiving specific attention. Such attention challenges a (quite common) reading of the ancient texts that largely occludes their gendered images—and thus misses key theological points. Gender analytical tools also correct readings of these texts that do highlight but misinterpret the embedded gendered image, for example by seeing references to God's breasts as "starkly feminine" (when it is really the maternal lactating body that is the focus) or as "downright sexual."[62] The latter assessment ignores the fact that an intense sexualization of the breast took place only with the Renaissance and early modernity. Gender history here safeguards against reading contemporary, intensely sexualized, views of the human body back into ancient sources.

---

[60]  See Pierre-Marie Gy, "Die Segnung von Milch und Honig in der Osternacht," in *Paschatis Sollemnia: Studien zur Osterfeier und zur Osterfrömmmigkeit*, Festschrift Josef Andreas Jungmann, ed. Balthasar Fischer and Johannes Wagner (Freiburg i.B.: Herder, 1959), 206–12, here 207.

[61]  Although, as most mothers know, the two are not entirely unrelated.

[62]  Engelbrecht, "God's Milk" (note 28), 525.

Finally, gender history leads us to inquire into what happened to the image of God nursing believers with mother's milk—an inquiry made not for antiquarian purposes, but as a question about processes of ecclesial traditioning. The image, after all, does not simply disappear, but rather migrates. It can be traced, even if not in official liturgical texts, until at least the sixteenth century, a time in Western culture when the image of the female breast becomes both eroticized and medicalized, and is thus more difficult to sustain as an image of spiritual realities.[63] A few examples of the continuing use of the image of God's breasts and milk beyond late antique Christianity must suffice at this point. Such images of God breastfeeding the believer appear especially in mystical writings, and prominently in those by women. This reception history is not surprising: Milk and honey, after all, are already on the lovers' table in the Song of Songs. "I eat my honeycomb with my honey, I drink my wine with my milk. Eat, friends, drink, and be drunk with love" (Song of Songs 5:1). That the image of God's milk is appealing not *only* to women mystics is evident in a letter written by the early Cistercian monk Aelred of Rievaulx (1109–67) to his *confrères*. Insisting on the importance of having a crucifix on the altar, Aelred writes:

> On your altar let it be enough for you to have a representation of our Savior hanging on the cross; that will bring before your mind his Passion for you to imitate, his outspread arms will invite you to embrace him, his naked breasts will feed you with the milk of sweetness to console you.[64]

Even if Aelred does not explicitly connect the Eucharist and God's milk here, the fact that he stresses the placing of the crucifix on the altar is suggestive. A very explicit connection between the Eucharist and God's breast milk is evident two hundred years later in another English spiritual writer, Julian of Norwich (c. 1342– after 1416). Julian meditates:

> But our true Mother Jesus ... must needs nourish us, for the precious love of motherhood has made him our debtor. The mother can give her child to suck of her milk, but our precious Mother Jesus can feed us with himself, and does, most

---

[63]   Margaret R. Miles has mapped this development in *A Complex Delight* (note 14). Cf. also the detailed study by Carlene Villaseñor Black, "The Moralized Breast in Early Modern Spain," in *The Material Culture of Sex, Procreation, and Marriage in Premodern Europe*, ed. Anne L. McClanan and Karen Rosoff Encarnación (New York: Palgrave, 2002), 191–219.

[64]   Aelred of Rievaulx, quoted by Caroline Walker Bynum, "'... And Woman His Humanity': Female Imagery in the Religious Writing of the Later Middle Ages," in *Fragmentation and Redemption* (note 15), 151–79, here 158f, with further examples from male medieval authors.

courteously and most tenderly, with the blessed sacrament, which is the precious food of true life.[65]

Metaphors of nursing continue to appear in spiritual writings well into the sixteenth century on both sides of the growing confessional divide. The image of Christ's gift of self in the Eucharist as breast-feeding finds an echo, for example, in the sixteenth-century Protestant lay reformer Katharina Schütz Zell of Strasbourg. In her interpretation of the Lord's Prayer, Zell writes about Christ's passion:

> [Christ] gives the analogy of bitter labor and says: "A woman when she bears a child has anguish and sorrow" [Jn. 16:21] and He applies all of this to His suffering, in which He so hard and bitterly bore us, nourished us and made us alive, gave us to drink from His breast and side with water and blood, as a mother nurses her child.[66]

Katharina Schütz Zell's Catholic contemporary, the Spanish reformer Teresa of Avila (1515–82), repeatedly uses this image of breast-feeding to describe how God sustains her soul or grants her the heights of mystical experiences. In her *Meditations on the Song of Songs*, for example, she writes:

> it seems to the soul it is left suspended in those divine arms, leaning on that sacred side and those divine breasts. It doesn't know how to do anything more than rejoice, sustained by the divine milk with which its Spouse is nourishing it … An infant doesn't understand how it grows nor does it know how it gets its milk, for without its sucking or doing anything, often the milk is put into its mouth. Likewise, here, the soul is completely ignorant. … It doesn't know what to compare His grace to, unless to the great love a mother has for her child in nourishing and caressing it.[67]

So much, briefly, for the continuing presence of images of God's maternal milk in the Christian tradition. The image has recently re-appeared, especially among women. An example is the Milk and Honey Ritual celebrated at the Re-Imagining Conference, which was held in Minneapolis in 1993 to mark the half-point of the Ecumenical Decade of Churches in Solidarity with Women. The woman who

---

[65]   Julian of Norwich, *Showings*, trans. Edmund Colledge and James Walsh (New York: Paulist Press, 1978), 298.

[66]   Quoted by Elsie Anne McKee, "Katharina Schütz Zell and the 'Our Father'," in *Oratio. Das Gebet in patristischer und reformatorischer Sicht*, ed. Emidio Campi et al., Forschungen zur Kirchen- und Dogmengeschichte 76 (Göttingen: Vandenhoeck & Ruprecht, 1999), 239–47, here 242–43.

[67]   Teresa of Avila, "Meditations on the Song of Songs," 4:4, in *The Collected Works of St. Teresa of Avila* 2, trans. Kieran Kavanaugh and Otilio Rodriguez (Washington, DC: Institute of Carmelite Studies, 1980), 244f. Cf. also *The Interior Castle* 7.2.6, in ibid., 435.

crafted the ritual had sought to celebrate women's bodies and sensuality, not least by invoking the feminine symbol of milk for the Creator God's abundant goodness and care. After the Re-Imagining Conference, this ritual became a focal point of indignant reaction since it was seen as transgressing the boundaries of the Christian tradition. Both the critics and the creators of the ritual seemed unaware that in the early centuries, there were Christian communities that blessed a chalice filled with milk and honey at the baptismal Eucharist and offered the consecrated cup to the newly baptized together with bread and wine.

### Breaking Bread and Blessing It, in Women's Hands?

Given contemporary scholarly appreciation for the diversity of early Christian meal practices, it is worth revisiting a text here that suggests such diverse ways of eucharistic praying extended beyond the first three centuries. The text is a eucharistic blessing from the late fourth or fifth century, to be performed by a female ascetic. The blessing appears in a Greek treatise on ascetic virginity titled *Discourse on Salvation to a Virgin*, better known by its Latin name, *De virginitate*.[68] Traditionally ascribed to Athanasius, the text now is thought to be pseudo-Athanasian, even if its content is "consistent with a fourth-century date."[69] Its geographic provenance is as doubtful (Asia Minor? Egypt?) as its central focus is clear, namely the daily round of prayers that the virgin addressed in the treatise is to follow. It remains uncertain whether this virgin lives in her family's household or in a community of ascetic women—or in the fluid space where these two are not yet separate sites. *De virginitate* focuses on the virgin's individual prayer life, but there is also mention of the possibility of other ascetic women being with her, and indeed of visitors to the house, including male visitors. The virgin is cautioned not to go out in public and to avoid the baths unless absolutely necessary, yet she does go to church, as a brief instruction to "keep silent in church, and ... pay attention only to the readings" makes clear.[70] The major part of the ascetic virgin's spiritual life, however, is focused on a daily house-based round of prayers and devotions. As a part of the detailed instructions for the latter, the virgin is told to eat her daily meal of bread and vegetables following the prayers of None. She is to "eucharistize" (εὐχαριστήσασα) the bread on her table, beginning with the following blessing:

---

[68] An English translation of the text, together with a brief introduction, can be found in Teresa M. Shaw, "Pseudo-Athanasius: *Discourse on Salvation to a Virgin*," in *Religions of Late Antiquity in Practice*, ed. Richard Valantasis, Princeton Readings in Religion (Princeton: Princeton University Press, 2000), 82–99. The English translation appears on pp. 85–97. Shaw's translation does not conform exactly to the Greek text in PG 28:265A since she draws on later editions of the Greek original.

[69] Ibid., 85.

[70] *De virginitate* 23; *Discourse on Salvation to a Virgin*, 96.

Blessed be God who nourishes me from my youth, "who gives nourishment to all flesh" [Ps. 136:25]. My heart is full with joy and glad thoughts, that "having enough of everything at all times we might abound in every good work" [2 Cor. 9:8] in Jesus Christ our Lord, with whom to you be glory, honor, and power together with the Holy Spirit unto the ages of ages. Amen.[71]

The virgin is then instructed to sit down at table and to break the bread. After making the sign of the cross over the bread three times,[72] she is to "eucharistize" (εὐχαριστοῦσα) the bread with this prayer:

We give thanks to you [εὐχαριστοῦμέν σοι] our Father for your Holy resurrection, for through Jesus your Son [παιδός] you have made it known to us; and just as this bread, which is at first scattered, becomes one when it is gathered together on this table, in this way may your church be gathered together from the ends of the earth into your kingdom, for yours is the power and the glory unto ages of ages. Amen.[73]

There is no wine to be blessed, which is unsurprising given that this meal is an "ascetic eucharist."[74] The virgin's food and drink (water?), however, are explicitly said to be "sanctified" (ἡγιασμένον) by her prayer. After the meal, the virgin is to speak a concluding prayer and thanksgiving which include a petition for "heavenly nourishment." The opening of this thanksgiving is quite close in wording to the postcommunion prayer in the eucharistic liturgy of chapter 8 of the *Apostolic Constitutions*.[75] In this late fourth-century composite church order (which contains the *Didache*, to which *De virginitate* also points), the bishop is instructed to pray: "We give thanks to you, because you consider us worthy to partake of your holy mystery."[76] *De virginitate* similarly directs the virgin to pray after the meal:

---

[71]     *De virginitate* 12; *Discourse on Salvation to a Virgin*, 91. I see no need to rearrange the original prayer texts, as Bradshaw does in his *Eucharistic Origins*, 118f. One and the same prayer could be said both before and after the meal, and the rubrics in question could be read as moving from the general instruction—following None prayers, eat!—to the specific: when you sit down at table and come to break the bread, eucharistize the bread with the prayer that follows.

[72]     This is clearly the correct translation of the text as edited by Eduard von der Goltz in the series *Texte und Untersuchungen zur Geschichte der altchristlichen Literatur Neue Folge* 14:2a (Leipzig: J. C. Hinrich'sche Buchhandlung, 1905), here 47. Shaw in her recent English translation understands the virgin to make the sign of the cross on herself.

[73]     *De virginitate* 13; *Discourse on Salvation to a Virgin*, 91.

[74]     Andrew McGowan has ably mapped this phenomenon in his *Ascetic Eucharists*.

[75]     Reinhard Messner pointed this out in his "Grundlinien der Entwicklung des eucharistischen Gebets in der frühen Kirche," 17, n. 59.

[76]     *Constitutiones Apostolorum* 8.15.2. Translation mine, to show the precise wording that is identical with that of *De virginitate*, as translated by Shaw, *Discourse on Salvation to*

"O God ... we give thanks to you and praise you, because you consider us worthy to partake of your goods."[77]

Gregory Dix, who offered an English translation of *De virginitate*'s eucharistic blessing in his *The Shape of the Liturgy*, expressed surprise that the "whole technical terminology of the liturgical eucharist" was applied to this "obviously purely domestic meal of women alone"—and that in the fourth century, as he dated the document.[78] Dix's interest in and underestimation of the text (a "purely domestic meal of women alone") was mainly focused on the site and shape of this prayer—namely a meal in a domestic setting—not on the gender of the presider, a female ascetic. Given his primary interest, Dix insisted – despite his surprise at the technical eucharistic terminology present in this blessing—that by the fourth century there was absolutely no "confusion of ideas between agape and eucharist" anymore.[79] The picture of the relationship between eucharist and agape is less clear to contemporary scholars, not least because the early texts themselves (*De virginitate* included) do not distinguish between an "*agape*" and the church's Eucharist. Instead, *De virginitate* applies "the whole technical terminology of the liturgical eucharist" (as Dix himself noted) to the ascetic virgin's meal prayer.[80] A fresh look at the eucharistic blessing in *De virginitate* seems called for.

To begin with, it should come as no surprise, given my previous chapter, that two specifics of this eucharistic prayer—namely, the domestic setting of the blessing and the gender of the presider—are linked. As Chrysostom made so very clear: to woman is assigned, by God, the "presidency of the household" [τήν τῆς οἰκίας προστασίαν].[81] Besides the context and the gender of the presider, a number of other elements are worth highlighting about the eucharistic blessing envisioned in *De virginitate*. There is the closeness, both in wording and in ritual action, to eucharistic praying in other liturgical sources. In terms of wording, the thanksgiving prayer over the bread contains an echo of the petitionary prayer in *Didache* 9:4 (a version of which also appears in the anaphoras of the *Apostolic Constitutions* 7, of the *Sacramentary of Sarapion*, a mid-fourth-century compilation of prayers, and

---

*a Virgin*, 92. Greek original in *Les Constitutions Apostoliques. Introduction, texte critique, traduction et notes* 3, ed. Marcel Metzger, Sources chrétiennes 336 (Paris: Les Éditions du Cerf, 1987), 212.

[77]   *De viriginitate* 14; *Discourse on Salvation to a Virgin*, 92.

[78]   Gregory Dix, *The Shape of the Liturgy* (London: Dacre Press, reprint of 2d ed., 1970), 95.

[79]   Ibid.

[80]   Ibid.

[81]   John Chrysostom, *Laus Maximi et quales uxores ducendæ* 4 (PG 51:230f). English translation: *The Kind of Women Who Ought to be Taken as Wives,* in *Women in Early Christianity: Translations from Greek Texts*, ed. Patricia Cox Miller (Washington, D.C.: The Catholic University of America Press, 2005), 271f.

of the Deir Balyzeh fragments, the latter of which witness to Egyptian usage[82]). *De virginitate*'s prayer also includes language usually associated with very early texts, especially the reference to Jesus as God's "child" [παιδός].[83] The thanksgiving prayer after the meal resembles the postcommunion prayer in the eighth book of the *Apostolic Constitutions*. There are thus a number of links between *De virginitate*'s eucharistic praying and other early liturgical sources.

Furthermore, the ascetic virgin not only recites a eucharistic blessing, but also makes the sign of the cross and then breaks the bread—an act with early eucharistic overtones in Christian communities (e.g., Acts 2:42, 46).[84] Moreover, *De virginitate*'s blessing may also hold an echo of the link between God's provision of food for the believer and mother's milk. The opening blessing is directed toward a God who "nourishes" (τρέφω: to nourish, feed, or nurse at the breast) the believer since childhood. Finally, *De virginitate* envisions a female concelebration in eucharistizing the bread should more than one virgin be present at the meal. The virgins, however, are forbidden to bless the bread if a catechumen is with them. The *Didache* already contains a similar prohibition, namely an injunction not to let an unbaptized person partake. By the fourth century, such a prohibition had become part of the public Eucharist where catechumens would be dismissed before the eucharistic prayer. Kim Bowes, noting this link, suggests that the virgin's household here parallels the table fellowship of the public church, "but it is *she* who sits at its head."[85] This is certainly correct, yet warnings that the faithful are not to eat with non-believers or catechumens mark many texts earlier than those of the fourth-century public eucharistic liturgies.[86] In other words, such warnings apply to a range of ritual meal practices in early Christianity, not only to those that come to be celebrated in the rising basilicas.

What are we to make of this text of a eucharistic prayer, from the fourth or fifth century, for women? We are obviously not faced with a text easily dismissed as belonging to some "heretical" group; the longstanding attribution

---

[82]   Texts of these eucharistic prayers, in English translation, can be found in *Prayers of the Eucharist: Early and Reformed,* ed. R.C.D. Jasper and G. J. Cuming (New York: Pueblo Publishing Company, 1987, 3d ed., rev. and enlarged), 74–81. Jonathan Schwiebert has mapped the ongoing influence of the *Didache*'s meal ritual in his *Knowledge and the Coming Kingdom: The* Didache's *Meal Ritual and its Place in Early Christianity*, Library of New Testament Studies 373 (London: T & T Clark, 2008), see esp. 212–38.

[83]   The term παιδός does, however, appear in the eucharistic prayer of the *Apostolic Tradition* (4) and—derived from the *Apostolic Tradition*? —in the *Apostolic Constitutions*.

[84]   For some of the scholarly debates about this phrase, see Bradshaw, *Eucharistic Origins*, 55–9.

[85]   Kim Bowes, *Private Worship, Public Values, and Religious Change in Late Antiquity* (New York: Cambridge University Press, 2008), 205.

[86]   See also the instructions for a communal meal in the *Apostolic Tradition* 27.

to Athanasius already indicates that.[87] Equally clearly, this text is not simply a eucharistic prayer "of women." Rather, the gender identity of the presider is that of an ascetic virgin, and *De virginitate* states explicitly—with reference to Gal 3:28, no less—that "all well-pleasing women take on the rank of men." The text in fact encourages the virgin to "[p]ut away the womanish mentality and take up courage and manliness."[88] Whatever the "gender of origin" of the pray-er of this blessing, her ascetic renunciation entailed a step up the gender ladder, toward masculinity. A final note on this eucharistic prayer: given that it is the only actual prayer text included in *De virginitate* and that it echoes other liturgical texts, it is unlikely that the author of the treatise composed this prayer *ex nihilo*. Presumably set oral traditions of praying, or previously established texts, were woven into *De virginitate* in the chapters dealing with the meal.

Given these characteristics of the text in question, what kind of "Eucharist" is envisioned here? The meal probably is best understood as a home communion of ascetic women, that is, women who both eucharistize the bread on their table every day, and also attend public worship, presumably a Sunday eucharistic liturgy. How these women thought of the relationship between the two Eucharists we will in all likelihood never know. However, these women certainly add another facet to home communion practices in the Late Antique East as mapped by Robert Taft. In his essay Taft noted the case of women solitaries who, in his mind, forwent the Eucharist for years because for ascetic reasons they did not go to church. (Bowes has termed this phenomenon "basilica abstinence."[89]) But looking at the witness of *De virginitate*, the choice—basilica Eucharist or no Eucharist at all— may not have been so stark, given that some ascetic virgins eucharistized, broke, and consumed sanctified bread in their homes every day. Given this practice, can one really argue that such women forwent "the Eucharist" as such for years? The nuanced language of eucharistizing, sanctifying, and consuming the bread in *De virginitate* suggests otherwise.

As to the new appreciation in contemporary scholarship of the diversity of eucharistic meal practices in early Christianity: a text such as *De virginitate* would advance the continuing diversity of eucharistic meals well into the fourth century and, if one follows scholars who date the text to the fifth century, even later. This matches nicely with one of the findings of the previous chapter, namely that

---

[87]    An early claim by Pierre Batiffol that the text was related to ascetic communities condemned by the Council of Gangra, held sometime between 341 and 355, has been rejected by most scholars, most recently by Shaw, "Pseudo-Athanasius," 84f.

[88]    *De virginitate* 10; *Discourse on Salvation to a Virgin*, 90.

[89]    See Robert F. Taft, "Home-Communion in the Late Antique East," in *Ars Liturgiae: Worship, Aesthetics and Praxis*, Festschrift Nathan D. Mitchell, ed. Clare V. Johnson (Chicago, IL: Liturgy Training Publications, 2003), 1–25, here 8f. For Bowe's term, see her *Private Worship*, 207.

domestic liturgical practices did not simply stop with the rising Christian basilicas. Ascetic women eucharistizing the bread on their table are a case in point.[90]

## Gathering the Fragments, "that nothing may be lost" (John 6:12)

The three eucharistic fragments lifted up here—a possible link between Jesus and Lady Wisdom as both banquet's host and its food, the Eucharist as mother's milk, and a fourth- or fifth-century prayer for an ascetic virgin's eucharistizing—are obviously quite distinct *tesserae* in the mosaic of eucharistic origins. Yet they do share at least two commonalities. First, these fragments have largely remained under the table of tradition, that is, hidden not only from most believers but also from the perceived image of eucharistic history and tradition. These fragments also have gender inscribed into their very being, in this case various constructions of femininity, including the maternal and the ascetic. As we take these fragments into account as parts of the (necessarily incomplete) mosaic of eucharistic origins, our view of this ancient mosaic can only be enhanced. First, the fragments point to the importance not only of the body of Christ in the Eucharist, but of the bodies of those who gather for the eucharistic meal. Those bodies always come to the table within, and never outside of, particular gendering processes. Second, the fragments lifted up here can be adequately understood only within heightened attention to their specific materiality, a materiality that is always related to broader aspects of lived human lives, including food production and nursing practices at a given point in time. Finally, there is the question of eucharistic tradition: what in this richly diverse history of eucharistic origins can lay claim to being "normative tradition"? How does that tradition relate to new knowledges about the past? And if normative tradition—such as bread and wine as eucharistic elements—is "one profound possibility among others,"[91] what authority do the other profound possibilities (e.g., milk? honey? women who eucharistize?) have?

---

[90]    Such practices might have continued longer than we think. Jean Leclercq, in his "Eucharistic Celebrations without Priests in the Middle Ages," *Worship* 55 (1981): 160–68, points to an *ordo* from the tenth or eleventh century whose communion prayers are in the feminine. For an argument that these are a (eucharistic) prayer of a women's community, see Gary Macy, *Treasures from the Storeroom: Medieval Religion and the Eucharist* (Collegeville: Liturgical Press, 1999), 174f.

[91]    McGowan, *Ascetic Eucharists*, 31.

# Chapter 5

# Presence at Worship: Bodily Flows as Liturgical Impediments

It was A.D. 1535. In the Tower of London, one of the prisoners prays with an inexpensive Book of Hours that he was able to take with him when arrested. At the back of this Book of Hours is a Latin Psalter in which the prisoner has highlighted and annotated passages that hold particular meaning for him.[1] Psalm 22 [Vulgate 21], for example, has a line next to the verses in which the psalmist reminds God of the care and midwifery God extended since before birth.[2] At the beginning of Psalm 84 [Vulgate 83], words are scribbled alongside the psalm verses, expressing longing to be able to attend worship again.[3] At some point the prisoner jots down a prayer of his own in the margin of his Book of Hours, beginning with these words:

Gyve me thy grace good lord
To sett the world at nought
To sett my mynd faste upon the.[4]

The prisoner at prayer is Sir Thomas More, Catholic layman, former Lord Chancellor of England, husband and father, soon-to-be a martyr for his Roman Catholic faith. To this day his written prayers appear in official prayer books and devotional guides.

When in the summer of 1535 Thomas More is brought to the scaffold for execution on charges of treason, a 20-year-old daughter of the minor nobility in Spain prepares to join a Carmelite monastery in her hometown Avila. She knows many of the traditional prayers and devotions with which Thomas More is familiar. Unlike the learned humanist, however, she is probably no more than

---

[1]   Eamon Duffy first drew my attention to this prayer book in his wonderful *Marking the Hours: English People and their Prayers 1240–1570* (New Haven: Yale University Press, 2006), 107–18.

[2]   Beinecke Library, Yale University, RSTC 15963, Ms Vault, More, Psalter, folio xvj. The marginalia are much more readable in the 1969 facsimile edition than they are in the original; see *Thomas More's Prayer Book: A Facsimile Reproduction of the Annotated Pages*, ed. Louis L. Martz and Richard S. Sylvester, The Elizabethan Club Series 4 (New Haven, CT: Yale University Press, for the Elizabethan Club, 1969), 40.

[3]   More, Psalter, folio lxvj; *Thomas More's Prayer Book*, 139; see the transcription on p. 200.

[4]   More, Psalter, folio xvij; *Thomas More's Prayer Book*, 3; transcription on p. 185.

phonetically literate in Latin. And her deepest experiences of prayer take place in a realm beyond words, in mystical ecstasies. At some point, she, like Thomas More, jots down a prayer of her own. It begins:

Nada te turbe,
Nada te espante,
Todo se pasa,
Dios no se muda.[5]

The writer of these lines is the monastic reformer Teresa de Jésus, better known as Teresa of Avila. To this day her prayer appears in official Catholic prayer books and is now also sung by millions around the world as a Taizé chant. Teresa was named a *doctor ecclesiae* in 1970 and is known in particular as the "Doctor [i.e., Teacher] of Prayer."

What can Thomas More and Teresa of Avila contribute to the writing of liturgical history? The answer will be "nothing much" if we take traditional histories as our point of reference. Neither Thomas' nor Teresa's practices of prayer, documented as they are, appear as sources in conventional liturgical historiography. As Herman Wegman noted more than a quarter century ago, the history of liturgy has been written "too exclusively from the part the clergy plays in it."[6] If we ask broader questions about liturgical presence and participation, Thomas More and Teresa of Avila may thus have insights to offer. The two—a prominent layman and a female monastic reformer—allow glimpses into liturgical lives that historically are under-documented, the lives of those who are present and do not preside. They, of course, make up the vast majority of worshippers. It is no accident of liturgical history that detailed descriptions of those present without presiding are rare until early modernity. Even then, such descriptions continued to be linked quite closely to status, education, and influence. In Thomas and Teresa we encounter two such worshippers who by virtue of their status (a powerful politician and a vigorous monastic reformer), education (both were literate), and reception history as saints (ensuring the preservation of their writings) can voice how they participate in worship, and also hand down to us some of their own personal prayers.

Thomas' and Teresa's stories may suggest hope for a historian of liturgy interested in the liturgical lives of "the people."[7] One problem for that hope is the fact that even first person narratives of those in the pews do not render visible all

---

[5]    Teresa of Avila, "Nada te turbe." Quoted from *The Collected Works of St. Teresa of Avila* 3, trans. Kieran Kavanaugh and Otilio Rodriguez (Washington, DC: Institute of Carmelite Studies, 1985), 386.

[6]    Quoted at the opening of the *Festschrift* dedicated to Herman Wegman, *Omnes Circumadstantes: Contributions toward a History of the Role of the People in the Liturgy*, ed. Charles Caspers and Marc Schneider (Kampen: J. H. Kok, 1990), VII.

[7]    See the subtitle of the *Festschrift* for Herman Wegman, mentioned above.

there is to know about liturgical presence and participation. Thus, there are areas of liturgical life neither Thomas nor Teresa unveil in their writings, an indication that autobiographical voices reveal as well as conceal some of the past. Among these hidden elements in the lives of Thomas and Teresa are liturgical constraints caused by longstanding prohibitions related to bodily discharges, especially those of menstruation, nocturnal emissions, and sexual relations. Rather than being obscure marginalia of liturgical history, these prohibitions deeply shaped presence and absence at worship for centuries. Since these prohibitions are related to distinctly personal embodiment, they are, however, not well documented in first person narratives of attendance or absence from worship. Rather, our first glimpses of the liturgical impediment of bodily discharges come in early church orders, ecclesial legislation, and episcopal letters. Gender differences figure prominently here, given that liturgical prohibitions related to bodily flows are rooted in the particulars of sexed embodiment. In order to inquire into these prohibitions, we thus—counter-intuitively—need to set aside the autobiographical narratives and return to many of the traditional sources of liturgical historiography. As we will see, these sources still have much to offer when asked gender-specific questions.

The present chapter focuses on this interplay between gender differences, bodily flows, and liturgical constraints. Its task is to highlight, through an analysis of liturgical anxieties surrounding bodily discharges, one of the many ways in which gendered embodiment conditioned and constrained liturgical presence. The chapter seeks to show that anxieties surrounding bodily discharges surface early in liturgical history, persist and deepen over time, and shape the liturgical lives of the faithful in manifold ways. In what follows, I will concentrate on liturgical regulations in the early centuries up to, and including, their particular construal by Pope Gregory the Great (+ 604).

## Liturgical Anxieties about Bodily Flows

Attendance at worship, in Christian faith communities as in others, was often surrounded by anxieties, constraints, and prohibitions. Not a few of these were related to the kind of bodies worshippers brought into sacred space, in particular to apprehensions about bodily flows.[8] Gender differences obviously play a fundamental role here. For women, bodily flows with profound consequences for liturgical participation were those of menstruation and of birthing. For men, nocturnal emissions were of particular concern. For both women and men, sexual relations were disciplined in a number of ways in relation to attendance at worship.

In many Christian writings, proscriptions concerning different bodily flows were treated together as part of an overarching anxiety about bodily discharges and liturgical propriety, regardless of whether they were related to female, male, or sexually entwined bodies. (The exception is ascetic literature, which often is

---

[8]    The key concern is with genital discharges as distinct from other bodily discharges such as tears, saliva, or a runny nose.

gender-specific to begin with.) Bodily discharges, in other words, were by no means a "woman's issue" only.[9] At the same time, anxieties over bodily discharges and liturgical proprieties obviously affected men and women in gender-specific ways. Before looking at this evidence in more detail, four overarching points need to be made.[10] First, the liturgical evidence in this case is quite genre-specific. It comes in a particular kind of early Christian texts, namely liturgical how-to literature, primarily church orders and episcopal pronouncements and correspondence. Other voices are mute for the historian of liturgy, such as the voices of women themselves who embodied (or circumvented?) menstrual and postpartum proscriptions about attendance at worship. Second, the early extant evidence is concentrated in certain regions, especially Egypt, Syria, and the reach of the *Apostolic Tradition*. We must not generalize too quickly from this. Third, liturgical anxieties around bodily discharges take different forms, are contested, and may not be applied uniformly even in a single text. Thus, a source may argue either for or against the observation of liturgical prohibitions regarding bodily discharges, and at the same time describe sexual relations as pure and therefore no hindrance to liturgical presence while also surrounding childbirth with significant liturgical constraints.[11] Finally, in addition to the sources that contain liturgical prohibitions regarding bodily discharges, we must acknowledge others that remain loudly silent on the matter. The pseudo-Athanasian *De virginitate* (discussed in Chapter 4), for example, makes no mention of menstrual proscriptions for the prayer life of an ascetic virgin. What then are we to make of other sources that do?[12]

## Liturgical Constraints Related to Menstruation

Menstruation affected women's liturgical presence and participation for much of the church's history; in some Christian communities menstrual taboos continue

---

[9]    Pun intended.

[10]    Three earlier studies continue to be important for the subject-matter at hand: Mary Douglas's groundbreaking anthropological work, *Purity and Danger: An Analysis of Concepts of Pollution and Taboo* (New York: Praeger, 1966); Peter Browe, *Beiträge zur Sexualethik des Mittelalters*, Breslauer Studien zur historischen Theologie 23 (Breslau: Verlag Müller & Seiffert, 1932), which is at heart an inquiry into purity regulations in medieval liturgy; and the influential study by Peter Brown, *The Body and Society: Men, Women and Sexual Renunciation in Early Christianity*, Columbia Classics in Religion (New York: Columbia University Press, 1988; 20th anniversary ed. 2008).

[11]    Cf. *Canons of Hippolytus*, 27 vs. 18. More on this below.

[12]    I leave aside the questions of why and how Christians came to adopt levitical purity regulations in the first place, especially given Jesus' own stance *vis-à-vis* causes of impurity (see Mk 7:15–23). Dorothea Wendebourg has addressed this question in "Die alttestamentlichen Reinheitsgesetze in der frühen Kirche," *Zeitschrift für Kirchengeschichte* 95 (1984): 149–69.

in effect to this day.[13] For what follows, it is important to distinguish constraints related to menstruation from those related to birthing. The two are connected, yet distinct, not least in their liturgical consequences. Every pregnancy and every birth develop out of a particular woman's menstrual cycle, but not every woman after menarche becomes pregnant and gives birth. The distinction is important especially with regard to the liturgical lives of women in ascetic communities. In ascetic communities, every healthy woman between menarche and menopause would be affected by liturgical prohibitions related to menstruation, while liturgical constraints around birth-giving would have little relevance.

When we inquire into the origins of proscriptions regarding bodily flows in Christian liturgy—proscriptions that are visible by the third century— one influence clearly is that of the Hebrew Bible read as Scripture. Menstrual separation is legislated in the Book of Leviticus in a chapter dedicated to the ritual impurity caused by bodily flows of both men and women.[14] For women, Leviticus distinguishes between the "regular" discharge of menstruation and other, irregular discharges owing to illness or injury. Both of these result in ritual impurity, an impurity that does not carry overtones of moral wrongdoing. Regarding menstrual impurity, Leviticus specifies: "When a woman has a discharge of blood that is her regular discharge from her body, she shall be in her impurity for seven days, and whoever touches her shall be unclean until the evening" (Lev 15:19). The menstruant's ritual impurity is understood to be contagious in that it renders everything she comes in contact with impure. This includes her sexual partner: "If any man lies with her, and her impurity falls on him, he shall be unclean seven days; and every bed on which he lies shall be unclean" (Lev 15:24). This prohibition of sexual intercourse is repeated in a subsequent chapter in Leviticus: "You shall not approach a woman to uncover her nakedness while she is in her menstrual uncleanness" (Lev 18:19). More starkly still: "If a man lies with a woman having her sickness and uncovers her nakedness, he has laid bare her flow and she has laid bare her flow of blood; both of them shall be cut off from their people" (Lev 20:18). The ritual impurity associated with menstruation here seems to have moved toward moral impurity based on a sense of transgression—and thus

---

[13]  See for example Vassa Larin's description of menstrual taboos observed in her Russian Orthodox convent, in "What is 'Ritual Im/purity' and Why?," *St Vladimir's Theological Quarterly* 52 (2008): 275–92, esp. 275.

[14]  As Lawrence A. Hoffman has emphasized, the main distinction in Leviticus 15 is not between men and women but between regular and irregular genital discharges; see his *Covenant of Blood: Circumcision and Gender in Rabbinic Judaism*, Chicago Studies in the History of Judaism (Chicago: University of Chicago Press, 1996), 147–50, especially 148: "what this carefully constructed Levitical essay does *not* provide is a delineation of impurity along male/female lines. Normal/abnormal is the structural key. ... neither men nor women stand out as a more serious case of pollution concern."

repugnance—independent of any association with the sanctuary.[15] The scriptural notion of impurity and repugnance at menstruation is not confined, in the Hebrew Bible, to the book of Leviticus. The prophet Ezekiel, who relies heavily not only on the priestly tradition but also on the metaphor "woman" to describe profanation, indicts the house of Israel in a word from the Holy One: "their conduct in my sight was like the uncleanness of a woman in her menstrual period" (Ezek 36:17b).

When it comes to the New Testament, codes of ritual impurity and purification were in place in the world Jesus was born into, and accepted as a given in the life of his mother Mary. The Gospel according to Luke describes Mary's purification after the birth of Jesus (Lk 2:22–4), and a widely read second-century apocryphal text, the *Protoevangelium of James*, inscribed the acceptance of ritual purity laws into Mary's childhood. Not only did Mary's mother Anna cleanse herself of the flow of blood after birth, but when Mary—depicted as living in the Temple since the age of three—turns twelve, the priests wonder what to do with her "so she won't pollute the sanctuary of the Lord."[16] (Mary's betrothal to Joseph and subsequent move into his house provide the solution). As far as ritual purity laws are concerned, the *Protoevangelium of James*—with its "obsession with purity, blood, and pollution"[17] —suggests that earliest Christian communities did not simply break with Jewish notions of ritual purity, any more than did Jewish communities themselves after the destruction of the Temple, even if the key reference point for ritual notions of purity, i.e. the Temple, was no more.[18] Broader cultural imaginings about menstruation's negative powers will have contributed to this.[19]

Finding evidence for liturgical anxieties around menstruation in Christian communities by the third century is not surprising, then. These anxieties affect a number of liturgical rites. I begin with the effect of menstruation on a woman's baptism. This issue largely disappears with the growing trend toward infant baptism, but until then a female catechumen, starting her period as her baptism approached, will have been a rather regular occurrence. Given that baptism took place with the baptizand undressed, the prohibition against a menstruant entering the baptismal font might have been simply a question of propriety, that is, of

[15]   Christine Hayes stresses this distinction in her review of Fonrobert's *Menstrual Purity* in *Journal of the History of Sexuality* 10:3–4 (2001): 547–53, here 548.

[16]   *Protoevangelium of James* 8.2. English translation in *The Infancy Gospels of James and Thomas*, ed. Ronald F. Hock, The Scholars Bible 2 (Santa Rosa, CA: Polebridge Press, 1995), 47.

[17]   Jennifer A. Glancy, *Corporal Knowledge: Early Christian Bodies* (New York: Oxford University Press, 2010), 108.

[18]   See also the essay by Shaye Cohen, "Menstruants and the Sacred in Judaism and Christianity," in *Women's History and Ancient History*, ed. Sarah B. Pomeroy (Chapel Hill, NC: University of North Carolina Press, 1991), 273–99.

[19]   More on this in *Menstruation: A Cultural History*, ed. Andrew Shail and Gillian Howie (New York: Palgrave Macmillan, 2005), esp. 13–37. Cf. also Glancy, *Corporal Knowledge*, 110–12.

keeping baptismal waters free of menstrual flow.[20] Baptism in this regard was a particular site for anxieties about menstrual blood.

When early liturgical sources addressed the problem of a menstruating catechumen stepping into baptismal waters, the issue was resolved by a postponement of the baptism. The texts suggest that such a postponement was a matter of days, with the baptism taking place once menstruation had ended. The first clear evidence for this comes in the *Apostolic Tradition* (in its oriental versions; the Latin has a lacuna at this point), in a chapter dedicated to "those who are to receive baptism." The text stipulates that "if a woman is in her time of menstruation, let her be set aside and receive baptism on another day."[21] The Egyptian *Canons of Hippolytus*, derivative of the *Apostolic Tradition*, directs: "If there is a woman and she has her menstrual period, she is not to be baptized on that occasion but she is to wait until she is purified."[22] I note the language of "purification" here for the end of menses; this language is also used in the text with regard to postpartum separation from worship. The *Canons of Hippolytus* spells out the period of baptismal postponement: baptism is to take place when the woman's period is over. The fifth-century Syrian *Testamentum Domini*, a significantly enlarged version of the *Apostolic Tradition*, specifies that a menstruating catechumen should take "another day, washing and bathing" before her baptism.[23] The language once again is reminiscent of traditional postmenstrual ritual purification. The three church orders highlighted here—the last two being derivatives of the first—are the earliest liturgical sources prohibiting the baptism of a menstruating woman, but they do not stand alone. Bishop Timothy of Alexandria (+ 385), in answers—considered canonical—to questions about liturgical constraints for menstruants, prohibits the baptism of a woman who has her period. Baptism is to be postponed until the woman is purified.[24] Thus

---

[20]   This explanation seems to me as likely as the "simplest" explanation that the editors of *The Apostolic Tradition: A Commentary*, Hermeneia (Minneapolis: Fortress Press, 2002), 110, offer, namely that postponement of baptism for a menstruant is a "baptismal extension of the inherited notion of the ritual impurity encountered elsewhere in relationship to the Eucharist." If it were a baptismal extension of inherited notions of ritual impurity one would also expect nocturnal emissions and sexual relations to be mentioned as reasons for postponement of baptism.

[21]   *Apostolic Tradition* 20.6. I am quoting from the Sahidic version here. English text in *The Apostolic Tradition: A Commentary*, 104. One wonders how the need for this postponement was determined. Was there a pre-baptismal interrogation of women concerning their menses? Were women expected to know that they should not come forward if the day of baptism happened to coincide with their menses?

[22]   *Canons of Hippolytus* 19; *The Apostolic Tradition: A Commentary*, 105.

[23]   *Testamentum Domini* 2.6; *The Apostolic Tradition: A Commentary*, 105.

[24]   Timothy of Alexandria, *Canonical Answers* 6–8. Greek text (with French translation) in *Discipline Générale Antique 2*, ed. Périclès-Pierre Joannou, Fonti 9 (Grottaferrata: Tipografia Italo-Orientale S. Nilo, 1963), 240–58, here 244–5. English text in *The Seven Ecumenical Councils of the Undivided Church, Their Canons and Dogmatic Decrees,*

in fourth-century Egypt, two sources testify to prohibitions related to baptism at the time of menstruation. Since Egyptian influence in matters liturgical was pronounced at the time, especially in Jerusalem, and since Timothy's stipulations were adopted by the bishops present at the Council of Constantinople in 381, these menstrual prohibitions may in fact have been observed much more broadly than their Egyptian ties signal.[25]

In his canonical response to questions raised by fellow priests and bishops, Timothy also speaks to menstruation and eucharistic attendance, forbidding a woman to approach the sacred mysteries until she be purified. Both earlier and later sources find much to say about menstruation as it constrains liturgical presence at the Eucharist. Menstruation had already surfaced as an obstacle to attendance at worship a good century before Timothy pronounced on the issue. His predecessor Dionysius of Alexandria (+ ca. 264) assumed that women themselves knew better than to come to church during their menses. (Given this position, one can wonder whether during Dionysius's episcopate women were not also excluded from entering the baptismal pool when menstruating, which would push the evidence for this prohibition back into the third century). Concerning attendance at worship, Dionysius writes to his fellow bishop Basilides around A.D. 262:

> The question touching women in the time of their [menstrual] separation, whether it is proper for them when in such a condition to enter the house of God, I consider a superfluous inquiry. For I do not think that, if they are believing and pious women, they will themselves be rash enough in such a condition either to approach the holy table or to touch the body and blood of the Lord. Certainly the woman who had the issue of blood of twelve years' standing did not touch *the Lord* Himself, but only the hem of His garment, with a view to her cure. For to pray, however a person may be situated, and to remember the Lord, in whatever condition a person may be, and to offer up petitions for the obtaining of help, are exercises altogether blameless. But the individual who is not perfectly pure both in soul and in body, shall be interdicted from approaching the holy of holies.[26]

---

*Together with the Canons of All the Local Synods Which Have Received Ecumenical Acceptance*, ed. Henry R. Percival, NPNF 2.14, 613.

[25]  For Egyptian liturgical influence, see, most recently, John Paul Abdelsayed, "Liturgical Exodus in Reverse: A Reevaluation of the Egyptian Elements in the Jerusalem Liturgy," in *Issues in Eucharistic Praying in East and West: Essays in Liturgical and Theological Analysis*, ed. Maxwell E. Johnson (Collegeville: Liturgical Press, 2010), 139–59, esp. 157.

[26]  Dionysius of Alexandria, *Ep. ad Basilidem* 2. English translation: *The Epistle to Bishop Basilides*, in *Fathers of the Third Century*, ed. Alexander Roberts and James Donaldson, ANF 6, 96.

Given that Dionysius had studied with Origen, who delivered a series of *Homilies on Leviticus* sometime between 238 and 244,[27] the position of the Alexandrian bishop is not surprising. Origen (like Philo before him) had interpreted most of the levitical purity regulations (i.e., those regarding foods, leprosy, and contact with death) allegorically, yet largely failed to do so with purity regulations pertaining to sexuality.[28] Dionysius justifies his own position with language reminiscent of purity in the Temple: "the individual who is not perfectly pure both in soul and in body, shall be interdicted from approaching the holy of holies."[29] Basilides seems to have been less certain in this matter. As the beginning of Dionysius' letter indicates, Basilides had written to ask for advice on a number of liturgical matters. Questions about bodily discharges and liturgical propriety—which take up most of Dionysius' letter—must have been virulent in Basilides' North African diocese.

In a vein similar to his predecessor Dionysius, Timothy of Alexandria also explicitly forbade a menstruating woman from coming to communion.[30] In fifth-century Syria the *Testamentum Domini* prohibits canonical widows from taking their rightful place around the altar where they would normally gather at the celebration of the Eucharist together with the bishop, presbyters, and other ministers. The widows are instructed to remain in the nave and not to approach the altar at all during their menses.[31]

The scattered evidence so far has pointed to liturgical constraints and prohibitions surrounding menstruation. One text, however, shows that the issue was vibrantly contested, at least in the author's own community. The *Didascalia Apostolorum* argues at length against women who practice menstrual separation. In this argument a group of baptized women becomes visible that insists on observing regulations concerning ritual purity. The length to which the author goes in arguing against such observance indicates that, at least in his ecclesial community, the issue was not negligible.

In order to appreciate the *Didascalia*'s forceful opposition to the practice of menstrual separation, we have to situate this church order within its larger cultural context. As a textual product of early third-century Syrian Christianity, the *Didascalia Apostolorum* is shaped by the "shared discursive space" of the

---

[27]   Origen, *Homilies on Leviticus, 1–16*, translated by Gary Wayne Barkley, The Fathers of the Church: A New Translation 83 (Washington, DC: The Catholic University of America Press, 1990).

[28]   Origen simply skips Leviticus 15 in his homilies, but does read Leviticus 12 in a quite literal sense. For more, see below, and Wendebourg, "Die alttestamentlichen Reinheitsgesetze," 155–61.

[29]   Dionysius of Alexandria, *Ep. ad Basilidem* 2; *The Epistle to Bishop Basilides*, 96.

[30]   Timothy of Alexandria, *Canonical Answers* 8; *Discipline Générale Antique* 2, 244. The particular question Timothy responds to is phrased as if the woman in question discovered her menstrual period to have begun during worship, the concern then being primarily of her receiving communion.

[31]   *Testamentum Domini* 1.23.

region, especially the vibrant interaction between different Jewish and Christian communities, "in which community boundaries remain fluid, ... and in which people experiment, even convert from one community to another and import with them their former experience."[32] One shared element of this space is the authority of the Hebrew Bible—including the Torah with its purity laws—as Scripture. In this ethnically-mixed ecclesial community of the *Didascalia Apostolorum* (which includes gentiles), the author or compiler is confronted with a group within the church "converted from the [Jewish] people"[33] who not only continue to honor the Sabbath but also to observe ritual purity laws. Addressing this group directly in his lengthy last chapter, the writer of the *Didascalia* distinguishes between the law—the Ten Commandments, ultimately identified with Christ—and the "secondary legislation," that is, all subsequent legislation, which was abrogated by Christ. With this distinction in place, the author turns his attention to "those who observe the days of menstrual flux," a practice he identifies as part of the secondary legislation. A female audience comes into view at this point:

> Now if, woman, you think that you have been deserted by the Holy Spirit in the seven days of your menstruation, and if you die during these days you will go forth empty and devoid of hope. Yet if the Holy Spirit is with you constantly there is no reason to stay away from prayer and from eucharist and from the Scriptures. Consider that prayer is taken up by the Holy Spirit, that the eucharist is sanctified by the Holy Spirit, and that the Scriptures are holy because they are the words of the Holy Spirit. For if the Holy Spirit is in you, it is pointless to try and avoid the deeds of the Holy Spirit.[34]

The writer identifies three particular practices from which the women abstain during their menses: (public?) prayer, Eucharist, and the study of Scripture. His profoundly pneumatological counterargument is consonant with what we know of Syrian Christianity: if the Holy Spirit really were to depart from a woman's body during her menses, then the unclean spirit expelled at her baptism would return and claim the empty space. Sharpening this baptismal line of argument, the author addresses his female audience directly:

> And, moreover, tell me, woman: the seven days of your menstruation or flux are unclean to you according to the secondary legislation, so are you then, as it were, unbaptized at the end of the seven days and so are cleansed, or baptized,

---

[32]  Charlotte E. Fonrobert, "The *Didascalia Apostolorum:* A Mishnah for the Disciples of Jesus," *Journal of Early Christian Studies* 9 (2001): 483–509, here 489. The notion of a "shared discursive space" is Peter Schäfer's.

[33]  *Didascalia Apostolorum* 26.1. English translation: *The Didascalia Apostolorum: An English Version*, ed. and translated by Alistair Stewart-Sykes, Studia Traditionis Theologiae 1 (Turnhout, Belgium: Brepols, 2009), 238.

[34]  *Didascalia Apostolorum* 26.2; *The Didascalia Apostolorum*, 251f.

so that you may seem to be pure and so hand yourself over to the everlasting fire as though you were not baptized (since you have not accepted the perfect cleansing of sin?).[35]

In view here seems to be the ritual immersion at the end of a woman's menstrual cycle, a practice that for the author of the *Didascalia* is part of the "secondary legislation." He depicts this postmenstrual bath as in tension with the baptismal waters. If behind his first argument one might glean the position of the women themselves—namely that the presence of the Holy Spirit is understood to follow a woman's bodily rhythm[36]—then the second argument—ritual bath after menstruation versus baptismal bath—seems too far-fetched not to be an authorial construct.

Possibly in recognition of this, the author abruptly changes audiences and now turns to the men in the group, instructing them "with regard to emissions of semen and intercourse with women."[37] The tenor is in keeping with the argument made *vis-à-vis* the women, namely against post-baptismal practices of ritual purification. Returning to the subject of menstrual separation, the author now enlists the cooperation of his male audience. Husbands are encouraged not to separate from their wives during menstruation. The point of this encouragement is a negative one, namely, to prevent women from practicing marital menstrual separation. As biblical warrant, the author cites the example of the woman with a 12-year hemorrhage who touched Jesus and was healed. His interpretation is the exact opposite of what Dionysius of Alexandria will make of the same text a few years later in Alexandria; for the author of the *Didascalia*, the woman is proof that one can indeed approach the sacred even with a severe bodily discharge. A summary statement concludes his labored argument: "And so a woman when she is menstruating, and a man who has an emission of semen, and a man and woman who come together in marriage and then get up from each other, are to pray without observance and without washing, as they are pure."[38]

How does a gender-attentive historian of liturgy read this text? Several points are important. First, despite the insistence on freedom from gender-specific ritual purity laws, the *Didascalia* itself remains deeply gendered from beginning to end. (I analyzed the gender-specific arrangement of the gathered assembly in

---

[35]   *Didascalia Apostolorum* 26.7; *The Didascalia Apostolorum*, 253f.

[36]   Charlotte E. Fonrobert argues this forcefully and at length in *Menstrual Purity: Rabbinic and Christian Reconstructions of Biblical Gender*, Contraversions: Jews and Other Differences (Stanford: Stanford University Press, 2000), 166–98. For her, the significance of the *Didascalia* lies in the fact that "this is the only document in premodern history of Judaism and Christianity in which we find women developing an argument for why they wish to practice menstrual separation." (p. 168) I myself remain less certain that we can discern actual women's voices behind the argument that the (presumably male) author of this church order mounts. Cf. *The Didascalia Apostolorum*, 254 n. 120.

[37]   *Didascalia Apostolorum* 26.7; *The Didascalia Apostolorum*, 254.

[38]   *Didascalia Apostolorum* 26.8; *The Didascalia Apostolorum*, 257.

a previous chapter, and located this within the overall gender-specific ordering of ecclesial and domestic life in this church order.) It is thus unlikely that the *Didascalia*'s stance *vis-à-vis* women who observe menstrual separation is based on an ecclesial vision of freedom from gender constraints. Second, the lengthy argument against women's practices of menstrual separation comes within a larger argument against all ritual impurities based on bodily discharges, be they female, male, or the result of sexual intercourse between spouses. Women, in other words, are not the primary concern here, nor is their liturgical freedom.[39] This recognition leads to a third point. The argument over ritual purity practices in the *Didascalia Apostolorum* has to be understood as part of a larger struggle over ecclesial identity, namely, that of an ethnically mixed community in a fluid and hybrid shared space, a space marked not least by Christian polemics against Jewish ritual practices. The *Didascalia*'s lengthy argument about practices of ritual purity followed by some Christians shows the lines of one such possible hybridity. Moreover, sharp polemics against such hybrid bodily practices become more intelligible if we take into account the (growing) ritual importance of the sexed body in Judaism at the time.[40] The *Didascalia*'s writing, after all, takes place at the same time as the textual assemblage of mishnaic traditions in rabbinic circles,[41] which codify practices of Jewish identity especially through male circumcision and female ritual immersion.[42] Finally, I note two silences in this text. First, we do not know whether in the ecclesial community depicted in the *Didascalia Apostolorum* women were baptized during their menses—or not. Certainly, bodily propriety at baptism was a concern in this community, leading to women playing an important role in the baptism of other women (although they were explicitly forbidden to baptize). Second, the author does not mention any ritual separation after childbirth.[43] Is this because such separation was not practiced by the baptized women in question (which seems unlikely, given their insistence on menstrual separation, which involved a lesser form of bodily discharge) or because the writer had no argument with the postpartum liturgical separation of women?

In summary, in the *Didascalia Apostolorum*, the non-observance of ritual purity laws becomes one marker of ecclesial identity and boundaries. It is by no means simply a Christian celebration of the natural rhythms of the body; the oppositional thrust in which the argument is embedded has to be taken seriously. That said, the

---

[39]  I emphasize this against Christian readings of the text that all too quickly claim the *Didascalia* as a liberating voice.

[40]  See Charlotte E. Fonrobert, "Gender Identity in Jewish Law," in *Jewish Women: A Comprehensive Historical Encyclopedia* (CD-Rom Edition), ed. by Paula Hyman and Dalia Ofer (Philadelphia: Jewish Publication Society, 2007), n.p.

[41]  Fonrobert, "The *Didascalia Apostolorum*," 496–8.

[42]  See Fonrobert, "The *Didascalia Apostolorum*," 496–8. It is interesting that male circumcision does not surface in the *Didascalia* as a particular problem.

[43]  The *Apostolic Constitutions*, in its reworking of the *Didascalia*, adds postpartum purification as a practice not to be followed by Christian women, see 6.27.3 and 7.

document is intriguing because we catch a glimpse of a group of baptized women who continue to observe menstrual separation in the face of ecclesial opposition. The *Didascalia*, then, speaks primarily to its own particular context, namely the perceived need to distinguish Christian communities with Jewish converts from Jewish communities themselves, especially in terms of ritual practices. Thus this church order may not be a voice in opposition to other ecclesial communities that consider it a given that Christian women should practice menstrual separation. In any case, the *Didascalia* remains a minority voice, even if it is taken up in the late fourth-century *Apostolic Constitutions*, also from Syria, which reworks the earlier church order in books 1–6. The *Apostolic Constitutions* basically repeats the arguments against women who observe menstruation separation, but adds an explanatory note about menstruation as part of the natural order, created by God. The compiler suggests that menstruation was given by God for the sake of a woman's health, because she is confined to sitting at home and does not get enough bodily exercise.[44]

It is not until almost four centuries later, and then in the West, that a text argues that women be allowed to enter church and partake of communion at the time of their menstruation. Once again, a particular situation is in view. Pope Gregory the Great (+ 604), who advocates this position, is responding at length to questions about liturgical impediments owing to bodily discharges. These questions had been raised by Augustine, sent to England in 596 to champion Roman Christianity there.[45] The pope's responses are marked by pastoral concern. To Augustine's worry about whether it is lawful for a woman "to enter the church if she is in her periods or to receive the sacrament of holy communion," Gregory answers that "a woman must not be prohibited from entering a church during her usual periods, for this natural overflowing cannot be reckoned a crime."[46] The pope substantiates his understanding of menstruation with a pointer to the biblical woman with the flow of blood:

> For we know that the woman who was suffering from the issue of blood humbly came behind the Lord's back and touched the hem of his garment and

---

[44] *Constitutiones Apostolorum* 6.28.7. Funk set the texts of both church orders in parallel: *Didascalia et Constitutiones Apostolorum* 1, ed. Franz Xaver Funk (Paderborn: Ferdinand Schöningh, 1905), here 368–81.

[45] Bede the Venerable later included the correspondence between Augustine and Gregory in his *Ecclesiastical History of the English People* (edited by Bertram Colgrave and R. A. B. Mynors, Oxford Medieval Texts [Oxford: Clarendon Press, 1991], with English translation). Gregory's answers are now judged to be authentic; see Hubertus Lutterbach, *Sexualität im Mittelalter. Eine Kulturstudie anhand von Bußbüchern des 6. bis 12. Jahrhunderts*, Beihefte zum Archiv für Kulturgeschichte 43 (Köln: Böhlau Verlag, 1999), 87 for details.

[46] Gregory's response to Augustine's ninth question, in Bede's *Ecclesiastical History of the English People*, 89, 93.

immediately her infirmity left her. So if she, when she had an issue of blood, could touch the Lord's garment and win commendation, why is it not lawful for a woman in her periods to enter the Lord's church?[47]

Anticipating a counterargument from Augustine, Gregory stresses the similarity between menstruation and the biblical woman's infirmity:

> But you will say, "She was driven by her infirmity; but these we speak of are fettered by the natural order of things." ... a woman's menstruous flow of blood is an infirmity. Therefore if that woman who, in her infirmity, touched our Lord's garment was justified in her boldness, why is it that what was permitted to one was not permitted to all women who are afflicted through the weakness of their natures? A woman ought not to be forbidden to receive the mystery of the Holy Communion at these times.[48]

That said, Gregory does explicitly praise women who abstain from the Eucharist during their menses. He leaves the final decision as to whether to attend or to abstain to the women themselves (as Dionysius of Alexandria did centuries earlier but only for men with a bodily discharge). The pope writes:

> If, out of deep reverence she does not venture to receive it, that is praiseworthy; but if she has received it she is not to be judged. ... Let women make up their own minds and if they do not venture to approach the sacrament of the Body and Blood of the Lord when in their periods, they are to be praised for their right thinking: but when as the result of the habits of a religious life, they are carried away by the love of the same mystery, they are not to be prevented, as we said before.[49]

Gregory's willingness to let women judge for themselves whether or not to abstain from communion during their menses did not become the general rule in subsequent centuries despite the fact that his text continued to be read. As many medieval penitentials show, the prohibition against women receiving the Eucharist during their menses won the day.[50] Furthermore, not only the Eucharist was affected by such menstrual prohibition. For women in religious communities, the *Institutio Sanctimonialium Aquisgranensis* of 816, a rule drawn up at the Synod of Aachen,

---

[47]    Ibid., 93.

[48]    Ibid.

[49]    Ibid., 93, 95.

[50]    For more on this, see Rob Meens, "Ritual Purity and the Influence of Gregory the Great in the Early Middle Ages," in *Unity and Diversity in the Church*, ed. R. N. Swanson, Studies in Church History 32 (Cambridge, MA: Blackwell, 1996), 31–43, and Lutterbach, *Sexualität im Mittelalter*, esp. 80–96.

prohibits nuns from participating in their community's liturgy of the hours during the time of their menstruation.[51]


## Liturgical Anxieties over Nocturnal Emissions

Like questions about the liturgical consequences of women's bodily flows, anxieties about nocturnal emissions of semen also arise in Christian sources by the third century. In the following centuries these anxieties increase, especially with regard to ascetic and priestly bodies. Since the production of most liturgical sources lay in their hands, the evidence for the particular concerns of these male writers obviously far outweighs their number among worshippers. Yet broader factors also contributed to rising anxieties over nocturnal emissions and their consequences for liturgical participation. One of these factors, mentioned already, is the reception of biblical proscriptions regarding bodily discharges. These proscriptions included emission of semen as cause for ritual impurity: "If a man has an emission of semen, he shall bathe his whole body in water, and be unclean until the evening. Everything made of cloth or of skin on which the semen falls shall be washed with water, and be unclean until the evening" (Lev 15:16–17). Regulations pertaining to warfare add to this:

> When you are encamped against your enemies you shall guard against any impropriety. If one of you becomes unclean because of a nocturnal emission, then he shall go outside the camp; he must not come within the camp. When evening comes, he shall wash himself with water, and when the sun has set, he may come back into the camp. (Deut 23:9–11)

The link made here between the male body's readiness for battle and genital abstinence understood as purity will resonate with Christians who come to see the ascetic life as warfare against demonic forces, the world, and the ascetic's own bodily desires. The growing attraction of the ascetic vision of sexual renunciation heightened negative interpretations of nocturnal emissions. Even if Christian interpretations varied—from a denial of any consequences for one's prayer life to increasing suspicion, and to strict prohibitions, especially of reception of the

---

[51]    More on this in Gisela Muschiol, "Men, Women and Liturgical Practice in the Early Medieval West," in *Gender in the Early Medieval World: East and West, 300–900*, ed. Leslie Brubaker and Julia M. H. Smith (New York: Cambridge University Press, 2004), 198–216, esp. 207f. See also her "Time and Space: Liturgy and Rite in Female Monasteries of the Middle Ages," in *Crown and Veil: Female Monasticism from the Fifth to the Fifteenth Centuries*, ed. Jeffrey F. Hamburger and Susan Marti, trans. by Dietlinde Hamburger (New York: Columbia University Press, 2008), 191–206.

Eucharist[52]—they all agreed on the issue's significance, namely whether nocturnal emissions constituted a liturgical impediment. Different answers to this question—and simply taking it seriously—speak to existing anxieties and uncertainties. These anxieties were heightened, in comparison with questions about menstruation, by the fact that while menstruation could be understood as an involuntary, "natural" part of a woman's life, nocturnal emissions of semen were more easily linked with sexual desire and willful acquiescence.

Our earliest two witnesses, both from the third century, come to divergent conclusions about the liturgical consequences of nocturnal emissions. The *Didascalia Apostolorum*, in its long argument against baptized Christians who observe purity laws, addresses the men "with regard to emissions of semen and intercourse with women."[53] This Syrian church order opposes all practices of purification: "these observances are foolish and harmful."[54] The author ridicules the man who thinks he needs to wash after an emission of semen before he can pray: "he will have the constant vexation of baptizing himself, and washing his things and his bed as well, and he will not be able to do anything else."[55] In the summary statement that follows, regarding the irrelevance of bodily discharges for prayer, nocturnal emission is explicitly named: "a woman when she is menstruating, and a man who has an emission of semen, and a man and woman who come together in marriage and then get up from each other, are to pray without observance and without washing, as they are pure."[56] As I have argued above, this chapter of the *Didascalia Apostolorum* is best understood not as championing Christian freedom from purity laws, but rather as arguing for ecclesial boundaries and self-definition by way of a denial of the relevance of ritual purity regulations as these defined another faith community. This reading is supported by the adaptations to the *Didascalia*'s position in the late fourth-century *Apostolic Constitutions*. This subsequent Syrian church order maintains the *Didascalia*'s general position with regard to bodily flows and participation in worship, yet "secondary legislation" is no longer the main threat. Instead, the sexual morality of the larger culture is now in view as that from which the lives of faithful Christians are distinguished.[57]

The other third-century source that reflects on possible liturgical consequences of nocturnal emissions is the letter of bishop Dionysius of Alexandria to his fellow bishop Basilides, who had raised this issue as a concern. Dionysius's answer is simple: "As to those who are overtaken by an involuntary flux in the night-time,

[52]  See David Brakke's important essay "The Problematization of Nocturnal Emissions in Early Christian Syria, Egypt, and Gaul," in *Journal of Early Christian Studies* 3 (1995): 419–60.

[53]  *Didascalia Apostolorum* 26.7; *The Didascalia Apostolorum*, 254.

[54]  *Didascalia Apostolorum* 26.7; *The Didascalia Apostolorum*, 254.

[55]  *Didascalia Apostolorum* 26.7; *The Didascalia Apostolorum*, 254.

[56]  *Didascalia Apostolorum* 26.8; *The Didascalia Apostolorum*, 257.

[57]  Brakke argues this in some detail in his "The Problematization of Nocturnal Emissions," 432f.

let such follow the testimony of their own conscience."[58] This advice to let each man judge for himself whether to attend worship after a nocturnal emission or not follows Dionysius's clear prohibition of women coming to worship during their menses. Women, in other words, are not accorded the freedom to follow their own consciences with regard to their bodily discharges; men are. Dionysius's position *vis-à-vis* nocturnal emissions does not seem set in stone, however. He invites Basilides to let him know what he thinks about the suggestion to allow men to judge for themselves. Dionysius acknowledges to have already advocated this position in public. We can, then, say that the question was under discussion in mid-third century ecclesial communities in Egypt and North Africa. For men, both attendance at worship after a nocturnal emission and liturgical absence were considered appropriate responses.

A century later, bishop Timothy of Alexandria will be more precise and at the same time less certain that nocturnal emissions were not a problem for attendance at worship. Timothy responds to a specific question, namely, what answer a priest should give to a layman who asks whether he can go to communion after experiencing a nocturnal emission. In his response Timothy distinguishes two different possible causes for nocturnal emissions. A man should not receive communion if his nocturnal emission was called forth by sexual desire, but if the nocturnal emission was caused by Satan's trying to keep him away from communion, then the man should commune.[59] Timothy's response is quite different from that of his third-century predecessor Dionysius. No longer are men themselves to decide whether to attend worship after a nocturnal emission or not. Neither does Timothy consider nocturnal emissions to be natural bodily discharges, with no liturgical consequences.

David Brakke has convincingly argued that in the roughly one hundred years between the episcopates of Dionysius and Timothy, Egyptian monasticism had flourished, and with it a novel focus on a believer's inner disposition. Brakke points to monastic authors who "used their [nocturnal] emissions as tools for the diagnosis of their own spiritual condition."[60] From Antony the Great through Evagrius Ponticus to Dioscorus, monks took up the question of nocturnal emissions and their liturgical consequences with increasing care and concern, generally advising abstention, especially from the Eucharist, if there was any suspicion of sexual desire in the emission. This concern must have been intense by the time of Athanasius, bishop of Alexandria from 328 to his death in 373 (with many interruptions). In a letter to an anxious monk Athanasius strongly condemns ascetics who interpret nocturnal emissions as defiling, and thus absent themselves from the church's Eucharist. The

---

[58]   Dionysius of Alexandria, *Ep. ad Basilidem* 4; *The Epistle to Bishop Basilides*, 96.

[59]   See Timothy of Alexandria, *Canonical Answers* 12; *Discipline Générale Antique* 2, 247f.

[60]   Brakke, "The Problematization of Nocturnal Emissions," 435.

bishop argues instead that nocturnal emissions, since they happen during sleep and involuntarily, are simply natural discharges of the body.[61]

Insistence on the naturalness of nocturnal emissions was short lived. The ascetic position on the liturgical consequences of nocturnal emissions gained ground even beyond male monastic communities. Timothy insisted that laymen not be admitted to communion if their nocturnal emissions related in any way to (voluntary) sexual desire. A canon attached to Timothy's pronouncement, but probably not by him,[62] takes a slightly different position: if the man in question lives in the world, he should be allowed to commune after a nocturnal emission.[63] This response renders visible a distinction still made between lay and monastic men. Since it is doubtful that this canon is Timothy's, the very repetition of the question witnesses to ongoing anxieties about nocturnal emissions and communion, at least in the Egyptian church.

The Egyptian church was not alone in this, especially as monasticism and its vision of sexual renunciation spread. Jerome (+ 420) confesses that he does not dare to enter the basilicas of the martyrs after a "nocturnal phantasm."[64] His contemporary Augustine also ponders the power of sexual dreams and nocturnal emissions in his life.[65] In Gaul, at about the same time, John Cassian (+ ca. 430) —who was familiar with Egyptian monasticism through his own experience, and also with the writings of Augustine —similarly worries about nocturnal emissions, particularly in relation to a monk's presence at communion. Anxieties about exterior and interior impurities when touching the Body of Christ are in full force here, with Cassian's ultimate goal being a monk who is found to be "the same in bed as he is at prayer."[66] In this emission-free space — both nocturnal and devotional/liturgical— the monk's gender identity has been transformed into that of a blessed eunuch. Unlike Augustine, Cassian can imagine a monk reaching such a state.[67]

Although Cassian's focus is clearly on a monastic body rather than the male body in general, suspicion about attendance at communion after a nocturnal emission deepened in the Western church. Indeed, Peter Browe has argued

---

[61]    See Athanasius, "Epistle to the Monk Ammus," in *The Seven Ecumenical Councils*, 602f. Brakke, "The Problematization of Nocturnal Emissions," 442–5, argues that Athanasius had in view not only the anxious monk's well-being but the wider congregational life of his diocese, which would have included many sexually active married men.

[62]    See the editor's note in *Discipline Générale Antique* 2, 238f.

[63]    Timothy of Alexandria, *Canonical Answers* 20; *Discipline Générale Antique* 2, 253.

[64]    Jerome, *Against Vigilantius*, 12, in NPNF series 2/6, 422. Jerome is writing against a former fellow ascetic, Vigilantius, who had criticized the intensifying devotion to the saints.

[65]    More on this in Brown, *The Body and Society*, 396–408.

[66]    John Cassian, *Collationes* 12.8, as quoted in Brakke, "The Problematization of Nocturnal Emissions," 451.

[67]    More on this in Brown, *The Body and Society*, 420–23.

that by the Middle Ages anxieties surrounding nocturnal emissions became the central concern with regard to ritual impurities.[68] The amount of evidence Browe cites for this concern is certainly remarkable, even if we take into account the predominance of monastic and priestly writers within the knowledge production at the time. Earlier on, Gregory the Great had actually offered a less anxious view. In his response to the questions of his emissary Augustine in England, the pope argues that nocturnal emissions are simply natural discharges. Augustine's question had been two-fold: "Can anyone receive the Body of the Lord after an illusion such as is wont to occur in a dream; and if he is a priest can he celebrate the holy mysteries?"[69] Gregory begins with Deuteronomy and acknowledges that it "declares him to be unclean and, unless he has washed, it does not allow him to enter the church until evening."[70] Yet, continues Gregory

> in this same illusion a very necessary distinction must be carefully made as to the reason why it enters into the sleepers' mind; sometimes it happens through gluttony, sometimes through a natural superfluity or weakness, sometimes through thoughts. And indeed when it happens through a natural superfluity or weakness, the illusion is not in any way to be feared; for though it is a matter of regret that the mind unwittingly suffered it, it did not bring it about. But when a gluttonous appetite carries one away into immoderate eating and the receptacles of the humours are overburdened, then the mind contracts some guilt but not enough to prevent him from partaking of the holy mystery or celebrating the solemn rites of the mass, when perhaps a feast day demands it or necessity compels him to administer the mystery because there is no other priest in the place. If others are present who can fulfill the ministry, an illusion caused by gluttony ought not to prevent one from receiving the sacred mystery, provided that the mind of the sleeper has not been overcome by vile imaginations. I think, however, that he ought humbly to abstain from offering the sacrifice of the holy mystery.[71]

For the sake of liturgical participation, Gregory is willing to make a number of distinctions. Even if a man bears some responsibility for a nocturnal emission, e.g. by overeating, he should still receive the Eucharist. A priest should preside at the Eucharist if there is a need, but if another is available, he should not preside but still receive the elements — unless of course the nocturnal emission was caused willfully by a sexual fantasy.

---

[68]   Browe, *Beiträge zur Sexualethik des Mittelalter*, 80. Pierre J. Payer has refined Browe's assessment in light of his analysis of the penitentials; see his *Sex and the Penitentials: The Development of a Sexual Code 550–1150* (Toronto: University of Toronto Press, 1984), 49–54.

[69]   Gregory's response to Augustine's ninth question in Bede's *Ecclesiastical History of England*, 99.

[70]   Ibid.

[71]   Ibid., 101.

As later medieval prohibitions surrounding nocturnal emissions and liturgical presence show, Gregory's position did not win the day, although his answers to Augustine's questions continued to be transmitted.[72] In the end, other voices proved stronger than the pope's.

## Sexual Relations as an Impediment to Prayer

If anxieties over both male and female bodily discharges mark much of liturgical history, so do questions about attendance at worship after sexual intercourse. In view here is marital intercourse alone; all other forms of intercourse were taken to be defiling always. Even the *Didascalia* — which understands marital intercourse to be "pure" and thus not an obstacle to prayer — declares other sexual relations to be profoundly polluting. The author (addressing this issue from the husband's position only) writes: "Whoever corrupts and defiles the wife of another after illumination, or defiles himself with a prostitute, shall not be pure when he has got up from her, even if he is washed in all the seas and all the rivers in the world."[73] The *Didascalia* insists, however, that "a man and woman who come together in marriage and then get up from each other, are to pray without observance and without washing, as they are pure."[74]

Once again, the *Didascalia*'s understanding — in this case of marital intercourse as pure and thus no impediment to worship — remains a minority voice, although it is not alone. Clement of Alexandria (c. 150–c. 215) had similarly insisted that spouses do not need to wash ritually after intercourse, since in baptism they were cleansed once for all.[75] Subsequent Christian writers, however, increasingly see sexual relations as problematic for the spouses' attendance at worship. As with other bodily discharges, here too a number of factors contribute to rising anxieties with regard to liturgical presence. To begin with, the Hebrew Bible refers explicitly to ritual impurities connected with the sexual encounter between husband and wife: "If a man lies with a woman and has an emission of semen, both of them shall bathe in water, and be unclean until the evening" (Lev 15:18). Furthermore, as mentioned above, marital intercourse during a wife's menses is considered impure: "If any man lies with her, and her impurity falls on him, he shall be unclean seven days; and every bed on which he lies shall be unclean"

---

[72]   See also Dyan Elliott, "Pollution, Illusion, and Masculine Disarray: Nocturnal Emissions and the Sexuality of the Clergy," and "Sex in Holy Places: An Exploration of a Medieval Anxiety," both in *Fallen Bodies: Pollution, Sexuality, and Demonology in the Middle Ages*, The Middle Ages Series (Philadelphia: University of Pennsylvania Press, 1999), 14–34, and 61–80.

[73]   *Didascalia Apostolorum* 26.8; *The Didascalia Apostolorum*, 257.

[74]   Ibid.

[75]   See Clement of Alexandria, *Stromateis* 3.82.6, trans. John Ferguson, The Fathers of the Church 85 (Washington, DC: Catholic University of American Press, 1991), 307–8.

(Lev 15:24; cf. Lev 18:19). The penalty for violations ends up being stark: "both of them shall be cut off from their people" (Lev 20:18).

In addition to these levitical proscriptions, one New Testament text begins to exert influence with regard to anxieties about marital intercourse and liturgical presence. In his first letter to the Corinthians, the apostle Paul admonishes married couples: "Do not deprive one another [of sexual relations] except perhaps by agreement for a set time, to devote yourselves to prayer" (1 Cor 7:5a). The *ad hoc* link Paul here makes between sexual abstinence and freedom for prayer and worship will prove powerful, especially in the context of the growing strength of stoic and ascetic themes in early Christian understandings of sexuality. A number of sources point to this developing link.[76] Thus Tertullian (+ ca. 225) insists on a connection between sexual abstinence, freedom for prayer, and the presence of the Holy Spirit in a believer. In his *De exhortatione castitatis*, written in his later, Montanist years, Tertullian seeks to discourage a widower from a second marriage; one of his arguments is the increased power of prayer that comes with sexual abstinence. Tertullian writes:

> If [a man abstaining from marital sexual relations] prays to the Lord, he comes close to Heaven. If he applies himself to reading the Scriptures, he is completely absorbed in them. If he sings a Psalm, he sings with joy in his heart. If he adjures a demon, he does so with confidence. It is for this reason that the Apostle recommends periodic abstinence, so that we may be able to pray more effectively. He wishes us to realize that a policy which is temporarily expedient ought to be made permanent, so that it may be permanently expedient. …

> It is our conscience which leads us to pray; if our conscience feels shame, we shall be ashamed to pray. It is our spirit which directs our prayer to God; if our spirit has to accuse itself because of a guilty conscience, how will it dare place our prayer on God's altar, since, when our conscience is guilty, this holy minister, our spirit, is also put to the blush?

> There is a prophecy in the Old Testament which reads: You shall be holy because God is holy; and another: With the holy Thou wilt be holy and with the innocent Thou wilt be innocent, and with the elect, elect. We must walk worthily in the discipline of the Lord, and not according to the unclean desires of the flesh.[77]

---

[76]  Elizabeth A. Clark has mapped the reading of this text in early Christianity in her *Reading Renunciation: Asceticism and Scripture in Early Christianity* (Princeton: Princeton University Press, 1999), 277–82.

[77]  Tertullian, *De Exhortatione castitatis*, 10.2–4; English translation in *Treatises on Marriage and Remarriage*, trans. William P. LeSaint, S.J., Ancient Christian Writers 13 (Westminster, MD: Newman Press, 1951), 58–9.

Tertullian quotes the Montanist leader and prophet Prisca, who links holiness/purity (understood as sexual abstinence) with liturgical ministry: "every holy minister will know how to administer things that are holy. 'For,' she says, "continence effects harmony of soul, and the pure see visions and, bowing down, hear voices speaking clearly words salutary and secret.'"[78]

What follows in *De exhortatione castitatis* is central to my purposes in the present chapter. Tertullian suggests that marital intercourse is a hindrance to prayer because it alienates [*avertit*] the Holy Spirit. And if this is true even for a legitimate first marriage, how much more in a (spiritually dubious) second one? Tertullian describes the effect of marital sexual relations on prayer as deadening or dulling [*haec obtusio*]:

> But if spiritual insensibility, which results from the use of sex in even a single marriage, repels the Holy Spirit, how much more will this be the case if the practice continues in a second marriage![79]

The incompatibility of marital intercourse with the presence of the Holy Spirit in the believer at prayer also comes into view in Origen's notion that the Holy Spirit takes a leave of absence from Christians during marital intercourse. In a lengthy discussion of the presence of the Holy Spirit in believers' lives, Origen argues that the Spirit's presence is not static but rather oscillates, depending on what activities a believer is engaged in. As his example, Origen points to marital intercourse as one of those activities "not worthy for us to think that the Holy Spirit is present in them."[80] He insists that although "lawful marriage is free from sin, nevertheless at that time when conjugal acts are being done, the presence of the Holy Spirit will not be granted, even if the one who is complying with his responsibility to reproduce seems to be a prophet [i.e., Spirit-inspired in particular depth]."[81] Origen's student Dionysius of Alexandria simply considers it proper to abstain from sexual relations in order to give oneself to prayer, citing Paul in support of his opinion.[82] Jerome supports his conviction of the incommensurability of prayer and sexual relations with yet another biblical text, 1 Thess 5:17. Writing to Eustochium, Jerome insists that since Christians are encouraged to pray without ceasing, and since prayer is interrupted during marital intercourse, ascetic virginity is infinitely preferable to marriage for a Christian committed to a life of prayer.[83]

---

[78] Tertullian, *De Exhortatione castitatis*, 10.5; *Treatises*, 59.

[79] Tertullian, *De Exhortatione castitatis*, 11.1; *Treatises*, 59.

[80] Origen*, Hom. in Num.* 6.3.7. English translation in Origen, *Homilies on Numbers*, ed. Christopher A. Hall; trans. Thomas P. Scheck, Ancient Christian Texts (Downers Grove, IL: IVP Academic, 2009), 23.

[81] Origen, *Hom. in Num.* 6.3.7; *Homilies on Numbers*, 23.

[82] Dionysius of Alexandria, *Ep. ad Basilidem* 3; *The Epistle to Bishop Basilides*, 96.

[83] See Jerome, *Ep.* 22.22.

The profound sense of the incommensurability of sexual relations and worship, which pervades these early Christian writings, could have drastic consequences. The Council of Gangra (c. 341), in canons directed against the extreme asceticism of Eustathius, bishop of Sebaste, condemned his followers for shunning liturgical assemblies that gather in the houses of married couples and for refusing to join in liturgies presided over by married presbyters.[84]

The *Didascalia Apostolorum*, as noted above, takes another position: "a man and woman who come together in marriage and then get up from each other, are to pray without observance and without washing, as they are pure."[85] This will be a minority position, although the *Didascalia* is not entirely alone. The *Apostolic Constitutions* follows its source, and the Egyptian *Canons of Hippolytus*— otherwise marked by deep anxieties about bodily discharges, especially those of women—echoes in part the position of the *Didascalia* (and/or of Clement of Alexandria) at this point. Canon 27, which deals with domestic prayer, stipulates:

> The Christian is to wash his hands each time he prays. He who is bound by marriage, even if he rises from beside his wife, he is to pray because marriage is not impure and there is no need of a bath after second birth, except for the washing of the hands only, because the Holy Spirit marks the body of the believer and purifies him completely.[86]

The *Canons* here tries to have it both ways: spouses are "not impure" after sexual relations and thus do not need to bathe before prayer—yet they should wash their hands. I note that the canon has in view the husband only. Like other early liturgical sources, the *Canons of Hippolytus* speaks androcentrically—that is, with men in view—much of the time.[87] In this case, the *Canons* follows its source, the *Apostolic Tradition*, which already expresses anxieties over sexual relations and the propriety of prayer. These anxieties lie behind some of the instructions in the horarium included in the *Apostolic Tradition*. One instruction, directed at "every faithful man and woman, when they arise early from sleeping," tells them to "wash

---

[84]   The relevant Canons of the Council of Gangra are available in English translation, *inter alia*, in *Women in Early Christianity: Translations from Greek Texts*, ed. Patricia Cox Miller (Washington, DC: Catholic University of America Press, 2005), 150f.

[85]   *Didascalia Apostolorum* 26.8; *The Didascalia Apostolorum*, 257.

[86]   *Canons of Hippolytus* 27; ibid., 29.

[87]   Marcel Metzger, "Pages féminines des *Constitutions Apostoliques*," in *Crossroad of Cultures: Studies in Liturgy and Patristics in Honor of Gabriele Winkler*, ed. Hans-Jürgen Feulner et al., *Orientalia Christiana Analecta* 260 (Rome: Pontificio Istituto Orientale, 2000), 515–41, rightly notes the largely androcentric character of the early church orders, see esp. pp. 517, 541. Wendy Mayer has demonstrated how to read such androcentric sources without prematurely concluding that mostly men were present in worship; see her "Female Participation and the Late Fourth-Century Preacher's Audience," *Augustinianum* 39 (1999): 139–47.

their hands and pray to God."[88] More important are the instructions for prayer at midnight. The *Apostolic Tradition* admonishes: "wash your hands with water and pray."[89] The next sentence clearly has a married couple in view (although once again only the husband is addressed): "if your wife is also present, pray both together."[90] What follows reveals that anxieties about sexual relations prior to prayer underlie these instructions:

> He who is bound in marriage is not defiled. For those who have washed do not have necessity to wash again because they are clean. Through consignation with moist breath and catching your spittle in your hand, your body is sanctified down to your feet. For when it is offered with a believing heart, just as from the font, the gift of the Spirit and the sprinkling of washing sanctifies him who believes.[91]

The text of the *Apostolic Tradition* in its various versions presents some difficulties here,[92] probably not least because its subject-matter is sensitive. What the horarium proposes seems to be a purificatory moment before midnight prayer after rising from the marriage bed. A theological tension becomes visible: The horarium of the *Apostolic Tradition* wants to maintain that Christian marriage does not defile and that Christians have no need of postbaptismal purificatory washings. At the same time, the text seems to think the marriage bed and its proximity to midnight prayer problematic enough to suggest a ritual buffer.[93] This ritual powerfully evokes baptism: the gift of the Spirit is stirred up through one's breath, and the baptismal font through one's spittle. The believer's body thus is sanctified, "just as from the font." The suggested ritual action, with its deep resonance with baptism, belies the *Apostolic Tradition*'s insistence that Christian marital relations are no impediment to worship.

More than midnight prayers, however, the reception of communion becomes a focal point of anxieties surrounding sexual relations. Origen had already suggested that the two are incommensurate; Jerome thinks likewise.[94] When

---

[88]   *Apostolic Tradition* 41.1, quoting from the Sahidic version; *The Apostolic Tradition: A Commentary*, 194.

[89]   *Apostolic Tradition* 41.11, quoting from the Latin version; *The Apostolic Tradition: A Commentary*, 198.

[90]   Ibid.

[91]   *Apostolic Tradition* 41.13–14; quoting from the Latin version; *The Apostolic Tradition: A Commentary*, 198–200.

[92]   See *The Apostolic Tradition: A Commentary*, 204f.

[93]   This has been pointed out by the editors of *The Apostolic Tradition: A Commentary*, 210–11. Given that Tertullian also mentions the sign of the cross and "blowing away some impurity" by a wife rising at midnight from the marriage bed to pray, one wonders whether the horarium's origins lie in North Africa?

[94]   At least in his treatise *Adversus Jovinianum*, esp. 1.7. Jerome's treatise is marked by what Elizabeth Clark describes well as an "unguarded contempt for marriage"; Clark,

Timothy of Alexandria in the late fourth century faces the question of worshippers receiving communion after marital intercourse, his answer is clear: spouses should not receive communion after sexual relations but wait awhile. In support of his position Timothy quotes Paul's injunction in 1 Cor 7:5.[95] Even Pope Gregory assumes that marital intercourse constitutes a liturgical impediment. He insists that one should not enter a church on the following day, not even after having washed. Gregory writes, once again with the husband in view:

> A man who has had intercourse with his wife ought not to enter the church unless he has washed himself; and even when washed he ought not to enter immediately. Now the law commanded the ancient people that when a man had intercourse with a woman he ought to wash himself and should not enter the church before sunset.[96]

Gregory goes on to search for a way to spiritualize these regulations, arguing that the real problem is sexual desire, not sexual intercourse as such:

> ... this can be explained in a spiritual sense. A man has intercourse with a woman when his mind is united with her in thought in the delights of illicit concupiscence, so unless the fire of concupiscence is first quenched in his mind he should not consider himself worthy of the company of his brethren while he sees himself burdened by the sinfulness of depraved desire.[97]

Gregory grants that others hold different positions on this question, but insists that Rome has "from ancient times" encouraged such a one "to seek purification by washing and reverently to abstain from entering the church for a brief period."[98] At the same time, Gregory is at pains to stress that it is not marital relations that create this liturgical impediment but rather the sexual desire and pleasure inherent in them. If a man were able to have sex only in service of procreation, he could decide for himself "both in the matter of entering the church and of receiving the mystery of the Lord's Body and Blood."[99] As to the women, Gregory manages to derive their need to be in "the purity of the flesh" when receiving the Eucharist from another commandment for men to abstain sexually before the encounter with God:

---

*Reading Renunciation*, 41. For Origen, see his reflection on 1 Cor 7:5 in the *Fragmenta e catenis in Epistulam primam ad Corinthios*, 34.123. Greek text published, by Claude Jenkins, in the *Journal of Theological Studies* 9 (1909): 500–514, here 501f.

[95]   Timothy of Alexandria, *Canonical Answers* 5; *Discipline Générale Antique* 2, 242–43.

[96]   Gregory's response to Augustine's eighth question in Bede's *Ecclesiastical History of England*, 95.

[97]   Ibid.

[98]   Ibid.

[99]   Ibid., 97.

It should be considered that when the Lord was about to speak to the people from Mount Sinai he first commanded them to abstain from women. And if such a standard of bodily purity was demanded when the Lord spoke to men through a creature as his substitute, that those who received the words of the Lord were not to approach women, how much more carefully should women who are receiving the Body of the omnipotent Lord preserve the purity of the flesh lest they be weighed down by the greatness of that inestimable Mystery?[100]

The Pope's focus, however, is clearly not on the women but on the men, to whose liturgical subject position *post coitum* he returns presently:

For this reason also the priest instructed David that if his followers had not approached women, they might receive the shewbread, which they would by no means have received if David had not first declared that they were pure in this respect. A man then who, after intercourse with his wife, has washed, is able to receive the mystery of the Holy Communion, since it is lawful for him, according to what has been said, to enter the church.[101]

Gregory's labored argument with regard to attendance at worship after sexual relations seems more ambiguous than his stance on menstruation and nocturnal emission as impediments to worship. The reason is his concurrent desire to declare marriage good while at the same time being uncertain that sexual relations can ever be free of sexual pleasure. Not surprisingly, the rite of marriage itself began to be marked by such ambivalence, which resulted in liturgical prohibitions. The *Nights of Tobit* (sexual abstention on the night or nights following the wedding, in imitation of Tobit and Sarah) and the practice of abstention from church for 30 days following one's wedding are cases in point.[102] Medieval mass texts for a mass on the thirtieth day after a wedding also have a decidedly penitential and purificatory tone.[103] Moreover, from the sixth century onwards, penitentials witness to requirements of marital sexual abstention for the night preceding Sunday, other

---

[100]  Ibid., 99.

[101]  Ibid.

[102]  See John K. Leonard, "Rites of Marriage in the Western Middle Ages," in *Medieval Liturgy: A Book of Essays*, ed. Lizette Larson-Miller, Garland Medieval Casebooks 18 (New York: Garland Publishing, 1997), 165–202, here 182f. Many of the medieval references to the *Nights of Tobit* can be found in an older study, Peter Browe's *Beiträge zur Sexualethik des Mittelalters*, Breslauer Studien zur historischen Theologie 23 (Breslau: Verlag Müller & Seiffert, 1932), 114–36.

[103]  See Leonard, "Rites of Marriage," 183; and Lutterbach, *Sexualität im Mittelalter*, 77f; 97.

times of eucharistic reception, days of the Lenten period, and before important feast days in the sanctoral cycle and other key feasts of the liturgical year.[104]

## Liturgical Prohibitions Related to Birth-giving

Upon reaching puberty, women (unless they entered monastic life) were likely to encounter a steady round of liturgical proscriptions related to three different bodily flows: those of menstruation, of sexual relations, and of birth-giving. The last of these, birth-giving, not only resulted in a prolonged period of abstention from worship but also generated an official rite, known as the "Churching of Women," to mark liturgically the end of this postpartum period of abstention from church.

As with the development of other liturgical prohibitions related to bodily discharges, one influence on Christian liturgical practices surrounding childbirth was purity regulations in the Hebrew Bible. With regard to the ritual impurity caused by birth-giving, the Book of Leviticus prescribed two different time periods, depending on whether a male or female child was born:

> If a woman conceives and bears a male child, she shall be ceremonially unclean seven days; ... Her time of blood purification shall be thirty-three days; she shall not touch any holy thing, or come into the sanctuary, until the days of her purification are completed. If she bears a female child, she shall be unclean two weeks, as in her menstruation; her time of blood purification shall be sixty-six days. ... and the priest shall make atonement on her behalf, and she shall be clean. (Lev 12:2–8)

The New Testament seems to stand in continuity with this particular purity regulation. In the Gospel according to Luke, Mary's purification after Jesus' birth (conflated here with the redemption of the firstborn) follows the stipulations of Leviticus 12 for a poor woman unable to afford a lamb for a burnt offering:

> When the time came for their purification according to the law of Moses, they brought him up to Jerusalem to present him to the Lord (as it is written in the law of the Lord, "Every firstborn male shall be designated as holy to the Lord"), and they offered a sacrifice according to what is stated in the law of the Lord, "a pair of turtledoves or two young pigeons." (Lk 2:22–4)

As an event in the life of Jesus (his first entry into the Temple, no less), Mary's purification continued to be important. In addition, the *Protoevangelium of James* noted the observation of postpartum purity laws in the birth of Mary herself. The infancy narrative describes Mary's mother Anna as following these laws: "Anna

---

[104] See Muschiol, "Men, Women and Liturgical Practice in the Early Medieval West," 208.

gave birth … When, however, the prescribed days were completed, Anna cleansed herself of the flow of blood."[105] Christians who by the second century told and retold this story were unlikely to live in faith communities hostile to such ritual observances, especially since the discharges connected to birth-giving were widely considered impure in the broader culture.[106] Certainly by the time Origen delivered his *Homilies on Leviticus* (between 238 and 244), his question is *why* (not whether) a woman who gives birth "is said to become 'unclean' not only when 'she received the seed' but also when 'she gave birth'."[107] Origen's attempts at an answer range widely—from the biblical woes about being born, and saints whose day of death (rather than their day of birth) the church celebrates, to the infant baptism that shows there is cleansing to be done even for newborns. Yet Origen proves mostly the presence only of a deep sense of the impurity of birth-giving. After all, did not even Mary, the mother of Jesus, submit to this purification?[108] Noticeably, Origen seems unable or unwilling to spiritualize a mother's defilement in giving birth, a hermeneutic strategy he otherwise uses throughout his homilies.[109]

A major feast dedicated to Mary's purification was celebrated in Jerusalem by the fourth century.[110] Its main focus was Christ's first coming into the Temple. At the same time, the appointed Gospel reading (Lk 2:22–40) kept the story of the purification of the mother of God alive for worshippers. By the seventh century, when the feast is first attested in the West, it had come to be called the "Purification of Mary." Its liturgical focus had shifted to the postpartum ritual cleansing of the Mother of God. At about the same time, early Irish penitentials mention the purification of Christian mothers after childbirth, although actual liturgical texts for a rite of "churching" are not known to exist before the eleventh century.[111]

When we look for earlier sources, we find less evidence for postpartum liturgical prohibitions than for other impediments based on bodily discharges. Silences of course are notoriously difficult to read, but a number of factors suggest that the postpartum liturgical abstention of a new mother was not a contested issue among early Christians. The practice was authorized by the Old Testament,

---

[105] *Protoevangelium of James* 5:5–9. *The Infancy Gospels of James and Thomas*, 41.

[106] See Daniel Schäfer, "Geburt" in *Antike Medizin—Ein Lexikon*, edited by Karl-Heinz Leven (München: C. H. Beck, 2005), 327–9, here 327.

[107] Origen, *Homilies on Leviticus*, 8; p. 155.

[108] Origen, *Homilies on Leviticus*, 8; p. 159f.

[109] Gerard Rouwhorst, "Leviticus 12–15 in Early Christianity," in *Purity and Holiness: The Heritage of Leviticus*, ed. M. J. H. M. Poorthuis and J. Schwartz, Jewish and Christian Perspectives Series (Boston: Brill, 2000), 181–93, here 186.

[110] For more on this feast, see Heinzgerd Brakmann, "Ἡ ὑπαπαντὴ τοῦ Κυρίου. Christi Lichtmess im frühchristlichen Jerusalem," in *Crossroad of Cultures: Studies in Liturgy and Patristics in Honor of Gabriele Winkler*, ed. Hans-Jürgen Feulner et al., Orientalia Christiana Analecta 260 (Rome: Pontificio Istituto Orientale, 2000), 151–72.

[111] See Adolph Franz, *Die kirchlichen Benediktionen im Mittelalter*, 2 (Freiburg i.B.: Herder, 1909; reprint Graz: Akademische Druck- und Verlagsanstalt, 1960), here 213–40.

observed by the Mother of God after the birth of Jesus, commemorated every year in an important liturgical feast, and supported by the medical knowledge of the day. Finally, of all the bodily discharges, postpartum discharge (i.e., lochial flow) is by far the most substantial and longest lasting bodily flow, usually continuing for four to six weeks after birth-giving.

This reading of silence as acquiescence might explain why the earliest source for contestations surrounding bodily discharges and their consequences for worship, the *Didascalia Apostolorum*, makes no reference to postpartum practices of separation, while loudly condemning all others. The author simply does not mention ritual separation after childbirth among the practices he attacks. As I indicated earlier, it seems unlikely that the baptized women the author argues with did not practice such postpartum separation, given their insistence on menstrual separation. If menstruation already demanded ritual separation, how much more would postpartum discharge! This, then, leaves the possibility that the author of the *Didascalia* did not have an argument with postpartum abstention from worship. The later *Apostolic Constitutions*, however, in its reworking of the *Didascalia*, explicitly added ritual separation after births and miscarriages to the list of practices not to be followed by Christian women.[112]

By the time a liturgical source first specifies prohibitions related to childbirth, these prohibitions are both detailed and extensive, covering not only mothers but also the midwives who assist at a birth. The fourth-century Egyptian *Canons of Hippolytus*, in a canon that jumbles together rules for catechumens (based on the *Apostolic Tradition*) and rules for postpartum separations, stipulates the following (note that the midwives are in view first):

> The midwives are not to partake of the mysteries, until they have been purified. Their purification shall be thus: if the child which they have delivered is male, twenty days; if it is female, forty days. They are not the [sic] neglect the confinements, but they are to pray to God for her who is confined. If she goes to the house of God before being purified, she is to pray with the catechumens.[113]

It is not immediately obvious whether the woman in the last sentence who is to pray with the catechumens until she is purified is one of the midwives addressed earlier (in the plural) or the woman who has given birth. The canon later repeats the same regulation for a new mother: "If she enters the church, she is to pray with the catechumens."[114] The prohibition of attendance at worship for the mother, however, is worded in accordance with Leviticus 12, and more strictly than that for

---

[112] See *Constitutiones Apostolorum* 6.27.3 and 6.27.7; *Didascalia et Constitutiones Apostolorum* 1, 368–81.

[113] *Canons of Hippolytus* 18. English translation, by Carol Bebawi, in *The Canons of Hippolytus*, edited by Paul F. Bradshaw, Alcuin/GROW Liturgical Study 2; Grove Liturgical Study 50 (Nottingham: Grove Books Limited, 1987), here 20.

[114] *Canons of Hippolytus* 18; ibid.

the midwives: "The woman who has given birth stays outside the holy place forty days if the child which she has born is male, and if it is female, eighty days."[115] The midwives were only instructed not to "partake of the mysteries" and that for a shorter period of time; the mothers are not to enter a church at all. The canon also ends on a pastoral note for the midwives whose professional labor entails a liturgical hazard: "The midwives are to be numerous so that they may not be outside all their lives."[116] That birth-giving was indeed considered liturgically problematic in the communities of the *Canons of Hippolytus*, and not only for mothers, is evident in canon 8, which finds it necessary to clarify: "A presbyter, when his wife has given birth, is not to be excluded" (i.e., suspended from his priestly ministry).[117] The particular statement is *Sondergut* as are all the other regulations regarding birth-giving and women's attendance at worship.[118] None of these regulations is found in the *Apostolic Tradition*, on which the *Canons* draws for much of its material.

In the Western church, it is once again Pope Gregory who responds at length to his emissary Augustine's anxiety, in this case about a mother's attendance at worship after having given birth. Gregory's response is pastorally motivated. He writes:

When a woman has been delivered, after how many days ought she to enter the church? You know by the teaching of the Old Testament that she should keep away for thirty-three days if the child is a boy and sixty-six days if it is a girl. This, however, must be understood figuratively. For if she enters the church even at the very hour of her delivery, for the purpose of giving thanks, she is not guilty of any sin: it is the pleasure of the flesh, not its pain, which is at fault. But it is in the intercourse of the flesh that the pleasure lies; for in bringing forth the infant there is pain. That is why it was said to the first mother of all: "In sorrow thou shalt bring forth children." So if we forbid a woman who has been delivered to enter the church, we reckon her punishment as a sin.

But there is nothing to hinder you from baptizing a woman who has been delivered or her infant either, if there is danger of death, even at the very hour when one is delivered and the other born. For while the grace of the holy mystery is to be discreetly provided for those who are still alive and have understanding, let it be administered without delay to those who are on the point of death for fear that while we are waiting for a suitable time to administer the mystery of

---

[115]  Ibid.

[116]  Ibid.

[117]  *Canons of Hippolytus* 8; ibid., 16.

[118]  The latter includes such detailed instructions as "She is not to wear fringes on the head when she wishes to partake of the holy mysteries." *Canons of Hippolytus* 17; ibid., 19.

redemption, if there should be even a very small interval of delay, the person to be redeemed could no longer be found.[119]

In keeping with his position on the liturgical consequences of other bodily discharges, Gregory seeks to honor the biblical purity regulations, while at the same time being clear about the roots of a particular liturgical impediment. In this case, it is not the birth as such that renders impure, but the sexual desire that preceded it.

The observance of a time of abstention from worship after birth-giving, and especially of its ending, also lead to a particular rite marking the mother's re-entry into the church, the so-called Churching of Women.[120] Although the development of this rite lies beyond the scope of this chapter, it is a rite clearly born out of the subject analyzed here, namely impediments to liturgical presence based on bodily discharge.

## Conclusions

This inquiry has shown the increase of liturgical anxieties surrounding bodily flows in the early centuries of Christian liturgy. These anxieties not only affected both women and men but also cut across the lines dividing lay, monastic, and clerical bodies. Liturgical prohibitions based on bodily flows thus regularly affected the shape of an assembly gathered for worship, and that in a number of ways. The impact could be in the form of absences, namely of worshippers who had experienced discharges, be they nocturnal emission, menstruation, or childbirth. Liturgical prohibitions could also shape the kind of attendance at worship, for example by prohibiting worshippers from receiving communion if they had engaged in marital intercourse or experienced a nocturnal emission the night before. Finally, liturgical prohibitions around bodily discharges engendered their own rituals, as was the case with the rituals before midnight prayers and the churching of women.

Individual worshippers confronted bodily discharges as impediments to worship in accordance with their own gender identities and status. If monastic

---

[119] Gregory's response to Augustine's eighth question, in Bede's *Ecclesiastical History of the English People*, 91.

[120] For more, see Joanne M. Pierce, "'Green Women' and Blood Pollution: Some Medieval Rituals for the Churching of Women after Childbirth," in *Studia Liturgica* 29 (1999): 191–215; Susan Roll, "The Churching of Women after Childbirth: An Old Rite Raising New Issues," *Questions Liturgiques* 76 (1995): 206–29; and chapter 9 on "Churching" in David Cressy, *Birth, Marriage, and Death: Ritual, Religion, and the Life-Cycle in Tudor and Stuart England* (New York: Oxford University Press, 1997). See also Paula Rieder, *On the Purification of Women: Churching in Northern France, 1100–1500*, The New Middle Ages (New York: Palgrave Macmillan, 2006).

women confronted the effects of menstrual taboos in their liturgical lives, monks and priests were faced with liturgical consequences of nocturnal emissions. Married men and women lived with liturgical prohibitions surrounding sexual relations, and a woman who had given birth with liturgical impediments surrounding childbirth. One only has to think about a married layman like Thomas More, or a Carmelite nun like Teresa of Avila, or a laywoman like the mother of Catherine of Siena, who birthed 25 children, to realize the intricate web of constraints woven into their liturgical lives by prohibitions related to bodily discharges. Even if we take into account that liturgical prohibitions point not only to what was never allowed to happen, but also to existing practices that the prohibitions seek to control, the historical witnesses to liturgical anxieties surrounding bodily discharges remain. Gradations of such anxiety obviously existed, with communion, the reception of the Body of Christ into one's own body, becoming central. Not only had a heightened sense of awe developed around eucharistic reception since the fourth century, but the embodied reality of communion—believers receiving and ingesting the very Body of Christ—intensified the need for the worshippers to be worthy and pure.

Given the wide-ranging impact of liturgical prohibitions surrounding bodily discharges on the lives of worshippers, we must acknowledge that some bodies were not affected by what has been described here, e.g. those whose gender had been manipulated (eunuchs); those who because of deprivations, whether owing to rigorous asceticism, poverty, or disease, did not menstruate or discharge semen; and the bodies of children and of many of the aged. This, however, does not mean that these worshippers were not subject to liturgical prohibitions of their own, or that there were not slippages in the gender-specific constraints described above. One only has to think of the liturgical lives of transvestite nuns—the Christian tradition knows a surprising number of them—to realize that liturgical prohibitions *vis-à-vis* particular bodily discharges were sometimes lived in quite complicated environments, e.g., that of a female monastic living under cover in a male monastic house.[121]

In all the complicated ways in which gender identities and liturgical lives intersect, one basic fact remains constant, namely, that gender marked liturgy in both basic and intricate ways. If in the past liturgical historiography treated as marginal these fundamental markers of liturgical life, this was due in large part to the focus of liturgical history. This focus was on the development of liturgical prayers and ritual structures. These seldom are the sites of liturgical anxieties surrounding bodily flows. This site is human bodies—and whenever human bodies come into liturgical view, gender is there, in their midst.

---

[121] My colleague Vasileios Marinis has recently published the Greek text, with an English translation, of the *vita* of such a Byzantine nun disguised as a monk: *The Life of St. Anna/Euphemianos*, in *Journal of Modern Hellenism* 27 (2009/2010): 53–69.

# Chapter 6

# Liturgical Leadership: Gender-Troubled

It was November 22, 1903, the feast day of Saint Cecilia, patron saint of musicians and church music. In the Vatican, the newly elected Pope Pius X promulgated his Instruction on Sacred Music, *Tra le Sollecitudini*. Because of its insistence on the "active participation" of the faithful in the liturgy, the document would later be seen as heralding the twentieth-century liturgical movement. Less acclaimed are some of the gender-specific constraints on liturgical ministry embedded in *Tra le Sollecitudini*. Among these is the insistence that since "singers in church have a real liturgical office, ... women, therefore, being incapable of such office, cannot be admitted to the choir."[1] This insistence is only a prelude to a quite different gender-specific constraint in the document, one that will lead to a decisive change in the Sistine Chapel Choir's membership. The pope writes: "If high voices, such as treble and alto, are wanted, these parts must be sung by boys, according to the ancient custom of the Church."[2] What is implied but not stated here is the discontinuation of castrati voices, which had been heard in the Sistine Chapel since the sixteenth century. These castrati had taken the soprano parts required by polyphonic music.[3] In 1903 the voice of the then best known castrato of the Sistine Chapel, Alessandro Moreschi (1858–1922), had just been captured on a recording. His voice was considered angelic; and he continued singing in the papal chapel well beyond 1903.[4]

## Introduction

*Tra le Sollecitudini* opens this chapter because the famous papal Instruction reveals some of the complexities of liturgical ministry (in this case the ministry of music). For one thing, the range of active participation in ministry here envisioned is clearly related to gender. For Pius X, women simply were "incapable" of a

---

[1]    Pius X, *Tra le Sollecitudini*, 13. English translation in Robert F. Hayburn, *Papal Legislation on Sacred Music: 95 A.D. to 1977 A.D.* (Collegeville: Liturgical Press, 1979), 228.

[2]    Ibid.

[3]    The historiography of the origins of castrati singers in the Sistine Chapel has recently been reconfigured by Giuseppe Gerbino's compelling essay, "The Quest for the Soprano Voice: Castrati in Renaissance Italy," *Studi Musicali* 33 (2004): 303–57.

[4]    For more on this, see Nicholas Clapton's biography *Moreschi: The Last Castrato* (London: Haus Publishing, 2004).

liturgical office, singing included (women could of course sing in worship, but this singing would not be a "real liturgical office," Saint Cecilia not withstanding). The pope here presupposes the longstanding historical link between masculinity and liturgical office, a link that deserves to be studied. Furthermore, *Tra le Sollecitudini*, with all its insistence on active participation, spelled the end of active participation for the Vatican's castrati singers. Not that one would wish for the practice of castration to have continued, but for centuries, the aesthetics of liturgical singing were created in part by this form of gender-bending.[5] Liturgical history cannot simply ignore these bodies at worship. Finally, *Tra le Sollecitudini* did not leave male singers unmarked but described in detail the kind of masculinity needed for this liturgical office:

> only men of known piety and integrity who, by their modest and reverent demeanor during the service, show themselves worthy of the sacred duty they perform, may be allowed to sing in the choir. It would also be more suitable if the singers, while they are in choir, were to wear cassocks and surplices; and if their place be too much exposed to the gaze of the people, it should be guarded by a grating.[6]

Here, a man's ecclesial standing ("known piety"), bodily bearing at worship ("modest and reverent demeanor"), clothing ("cassocks and surplices"), and place (hidden) together shape the kind of masculinity needed for the liturgical ministry of singing. With all these gender-specific contours to liturgical ministry, *Tra le Sollecitudini* provides a fitting starting point for the present chapter, which traces various gender troubles that accompany the emergence of an authoritative pattern of liturgical leadership in the church. In particular, I am interested in the emerging link between masculinity and liturgical leadership.

## Liturgical Leadership and the Politics of Gender

A prominent gender particularity running through much of liturgical history has remained largely unmarked in scholarly writings, namely the link between liturgical presidency and masculinity. This link deserves attention not least because it confirms—in so basic and unquestionable a way—the power of gender in the history of worship. To date, scholarly inquiry into gender and liturgical leadership has focused almost exclusively on women and the questions surrounding their liturgical ministries. The literature on this subject, which is substantial by now, has contributed to changing the traditional image in regard to women's liturgical leadership. This traditional image still governed, for example, the Vatican's

---

[5]    For castrati singers in the Eastern church, see Neil Moran, "Byzantine Castrati," *Plainsong and Medieval Music* 11 (2002): 99-112. For Rome, see Gerbino, "The Quest."

[6]    Pius X, *Tra le Sollecitudini*, 14; *Papal Legislation on Sacred Music*, 228.

1976 declaration *Inter Insigniores, On the Question of the Admission of Women to the Ministerial Priesthood*. This declaration grounds its negative response to the possibility of women's ordination in "the church's *constant* tradition" of calling "only men to the priestly Order and ministry."[7] Since the writing of *Inter Insigniores*, however, scholarly inquiry has considerably lessened the authorizing power of this claim by revealing that the past is much less "constant" about having "only men" exercise liturgical offices than had previously been imagined. Today many scholars acknowledge not only the presence of women office holders in early Christianity but also a centuries-old tradition of ordaining women, at least until the twelfth century.[8]

As important as these scholarly revisions to the imagined past are, what has remained largely unmarked—and therefore seemingly natural—is the link between masculinity and liturgical presidency. This link should be interrogated, however, for two reasons. One of these is the relationship between the emerging insistence on maleness in the exercise of liturgical ministry and contestations around women's leadership, two developments not unrelated to each other. A second reason why the link between masculinity and liturgical presidency deserves a closer look is the fact that priestly masculinity (understood as the meanings surrounding a person with a male body who comes to exercise priestly ministry[9]) develops into a particular kind of masculinity. This masculinity comes to be distinguished from other

---

[7] Congregation for the Doctrine of the Faith, Declaration *Inter Insigniores, On the Question of the Admission of Women to the Ministerial Priesthood* (October 15, 1976), # 6. Emphasis mine. English text in *The Order of Priesthood: Nine Commentaries on the Vatican Decree "Inter insigniores"* (Huntingdon, IN: Our Sunday Visitor, 1978), 1–20, here p. 3f. John Paul II's Apostolic Letter *Ordinatio Sacerdotalis, on Reserving Priestly Ordination to Men Alone* of 1994 repeats the same claim: "Priestly ordination ... has in the Catholic Church *from the beginning always* been reserved to men alone" (# 1). Emphasis mine. The English text is available on the Vatican's website at http://www.vatican.va/ holy_father/john_paul_ii/apost_letters/documents/hf_jp-ii_apl_22051994_ordinatio-sacerdotalis_en.html.

[8] I mention only three of the most important here: Karen Jo Torjesen, *When Women Were Priests: Women's Leadership in the Early Church and the Scandal of their Subordination in the Rise of Christianity* (San Francisco, CA: HarperCollins, 1993); Ute E. Eisen, *Women Officeholders in Early Christianity: Epigraphical and Literary Studies*, trans. Linda M. Maloney (Collegeville: Liturgical Press, 2000); and Gary Macy, *The Hidden History of Women's Ordination: Female Clergy in the Medieval West* (New York: Oxford University Press, 2008); the latter has an extended survey of recent scholarship in Chapter 1.

[9] I note here a thoughtful reflection, by a contemporary priest and scholar, on this construction of priestly masculinity in his own life: Johannes Pock, "Der Priester als 'Mann Gottes'. Die Bedeutung des Geschlechts für das katholische Priesterverständnis," in *Geschlecht quer gedacht. Widerstandspotentiale und Gestaltungsmöglichkeiten in kirchlicher Praxis*, ed. M. E. Aigner and J. Pock, Werkstatt Theologie 13 (Wien: LIT, 2009), 227–40.

masculinities (e.g., that of marriage and fatherhood, and of political or military power). How priestly masculinity is constituted—and develops into a privileged form of masculinity, in the church and beyond—is a question worth asking.

*Early Liturgical Presiding: Gender Troubled?*

I begin with two observations that may seem obvious, but that deserve to be stated in order to create some distance from what otherwise might be considered simply a "natural" historical development. First, we have no evidence that maleness—as a gender identity—was ever considered an impediment to liturgical leadership. The second observation refines the first: the kind of masculinity considered appropriate for liturgical presidency becomes particularized early on. In contradistinction, questions about the liturgical leadership of women that emerge in early Christian communities focus on female gender as such as an obstacle to liturgical leadership. To some degree, these questions are already visible in New Testament writings, e.g., in differing accounts of the post-resurrection role of Mary of Magdala, and in regulations pertaining to women's active participation. Among other things, women in Pauline churches were counseled not to abandon female attire during prayer and prophecy (1 Cor 11:2–16) and to keep silent in church (1 Tim 2:9–12). The kind of leadership women exercised in various Christian communities continues to be debated, not least because the evidence is scant, and interpretive strategies on how to read this evidence are contested. Much unfortunately will have to be left to speculation. For example, would a woman who was the head of a household automatically have taken a leadership role when the faithful gathered in her house? What seems clear enough is that contestations about women's liturgical leadership arose early, and cannot safely be distanced from some supposedly pristine egalitarian Christian origins.

With regard to forms of liturgical leadership in the earliest Christian communities, scholars nowadays assume a degree of diversity and independence in how different communities organized themselves. At least three patterns are in evidence: charismatic leadership by those with the authority of Spirit-inspired gifts; leadership by the host and patron of the household in which the community gathered; and some (loosely) structured ways of selecting and authorizing appropriate leadership for the community.[10] These three patterns were not mutually exclusive. The head of a household, for example, might also be the bearer of Spirit-inspired gifts.

Among these three patterns, the first—of charismatic, prophetic leadership— clearly was not limited by gender. The Spirit was poured out on all; both "sons and daughters" prophesied (Joel 2:28; Acts 2:17). The *Didache* witnesses to the link between prophet and presider in that it allows prophets to eucharistize, that is, pray

---

[10]    Paul Bradshaw describes these in *The Search for the Origins of Christian Worship: Sources and Methods for the Study of Early Liturgy*, 2d ed. (New York: Oxford University Press, 2002), 194f.

in thanksgiving, "as much as they wish."[11] At least for this earliest church order, eucharistic praying and presiding could be authorized by the charism of prophecy, a charism that was not gender-constrained. If anything, prophetic inspiration and the Spirit's freedom to empower whomever the Spirit chose were particularly open to women's claims to leadership.[12] Not surprisingly, "in the first centuries the majority of the clear cases of women's leadership based their legitimacy on claims to prophetic experience."[13] Examples are the New Testament women prophets, among them Philip's four daughters (Acts 21:9); key leaders of the Montanist movement, including Maximilla, Priscilla/Prisca, and Quintilla; and the unnamed prophet mentioned in the correspondence between Cyprian, bishop of Carthage, and Firmilian, bishop of Caesarea in Cappadocia. Firmilian, in a letter written around 256, describes a woman who, more than 20 years earlier, had prophesied, baptized, and celebrated the Eucharist in his region, using the Church's own liturgical materials:

> There rose up suddenly then a certain woman who, in a state of ecstasy, presented herself as a prophet and acted as if filled with the Holy Spirit … But that woman, … had also often dared … to sanctify the bread and to pretend to confect the eucharist and make the sacrifice to the Lord … and she also baptized many, usurping the usual and legitimate mode of questioning, so that nothing might seem to deviate from ecclesiastical rule.[14]

Firmilian does not accuse this woman of belonging to a heterodox group. On the contrary, he explicitly situates her liturgical leadership within "usual and legitimate" forms and "ecclesiastical rule." As Reinhard Messner has noted, if by the third century for a woman to baptize and to preside at the eucharistic meal century would have been unthinkable, this female prophet would hardly have

---

[11] *Didache* 10.7. English translation in Aaron Milavec, *The Didache: Text, Translation, Analysis, and Commentary* (Collegeville: Liturgical Press, 2003), 25.

[12] See also Reinhard Messner, "Grundlinien der Entwicklung des eucharistischen Gebets in der frühen Kirche," in *Prex Eucharistica* 3/1, ed. Albert Gerhards et al., Spicilegium Friburgense 42 (Freiburg, Schweiz: Academic Press Fribourg, 2005), 3–40, here 36, who argues that in the first two centuries, eucharistic presiding was most closely linked to the charism of prophecy, and thus open to women.

[13] Karen L. King, "Prophetic Power and Women's Authority," in *Women Preachers and Prophets through Two Millennia of Christianity*, ed. Beverly Mayne Kienzle and Pamela J. Walker (Berkeley: University of California Press, 1998), 21–41, here 21. See also Eisen's chapter on women prophets in *Women Officeholders in Early Christianity*, 63–87.

[14] Cyprian of Carthage, *Ep.* 75 (from Firmilian). English translation in *Ordained Women in the Early Church: A Documentary History*, ed. Kevin Madigan and Carolyn Osiek (Baltimore: The Johns Hopkins University Press, 2005), 182.

been able to minister in an ecclesial community.[15] Moreover, Firmilian's primary objection to her ministry does not seem to be her gender, but the fact that her prophetic spirit was revealed by an exorcist to be an evil spirit. This mid-third century letter thus renders it plausible that liturgical authority rooted in prophetic inspiration continued in some Christian communities for some time, and did so irrespective of the gender of the one empowered by the Spirit.[16]

The second pattern, ecclesial leadership by the head of the household in whose home the community gathered, also was not gender-constrained *per se*. As we have already noted, men as well as women presided over households; and these heads of households may well have exercised ministerial leadership in the assembly that gathered in their homes. This pattern of ecclesial leadership, though, did not last. By the time ecclesial communities moved into the public sphere and rising basilicas, liturgical leadership was mostly in the hands of the bishop, and we have no unambiguous evidence of a woman appointed to that office. Some epigraphical evidence for women with the title *episcopa* does exist,[17] but its interpretation remains debated. In particular, arguments over whether the title *episcopa* denotes a bishop who happens to be a woman, or the wife of a bishop, continue.

With the leadership of bishops we have arrived at the center of the third pattern of ecclesial leadership, namely by some structured (even if initially largely informal) way of authorizing appropriate persons. This pattern will come to dominate as Christianity grows and spreads. In the early centuries, evidence points to men and also women being so authorized to liturgical ministry.[18] Here too, however, the reading of the evidence continues to shift. Albert Harrill has recently argued, for example, that the female slaves whom Christians called "*ministrae*," according to Pliny's famous letter to Trajan, did not in fact hold a position of ministerial leadership, i.e., as deacons. Rather, Harrill argues that *ministrae*, in Pliny's letter, must be understood as slave assistants.[19]

However we weigh the historical evidence for women's liturgical leadership, maleness never is seen as an impediment to such leadership. Given that Christianity

---

[15]   See Messner, "Grundlinien der Entwicklung des eucharistischen Gebets in der frühen Kirche," 38.

[16]   Eisen, *Women Officeholders in Early Christianity*, 63f, lists a tomb epigraph from Asia Minor, dating probably to the fourth century, for the "prophet Nanas, daughter of Hermogenes."

[17]   Eisen, *Women Officeholders in Early Christianity,* 199–216, surveys the epigraphical evidence.

[18]   All known evidence for women deacons and presbyters, in both the Greek- and Latin-speaking parts of the church, is collected, in English translation, in Madigan and Osiek, eds, *Ordained Women in the Early Church*.

[19]   In Roman domestic religion, the term *minister* denoted the slave assistant in ritual practices. See J. Albert Harrill, "Servile Functionaries or Priestly Leaders? Roman Domestic Religion, Narrative Intertextuality, and Pliny's Reference to Slave Christian *Ministrae* (Ep. 10,96,8)," *Zeitschrift für die neutestamentliche Wissenschaft* 97 (2006): 111–30.

emerged and grew in a cultural context that understood gender differences hierarchically—with men as superior, women as inferior, and no woman equal to a man of her status—this assumption of the "natural" connection between masculinity and leadership is not surprising. The assumption of such a natural connection does however point to the power of a particular gender construction in the life of the church. Furthermore, if masculinity and leadership are seemingly natural fits for early Christianity, questions about what kind of man should preside over the community and its worship soon emerge. The detailed list of qualifications in 1 Timothy 3:2–7, for example, includes the proper ordering of episcopal marriages, here by stipulating that a bishop must be "married only once." Sexuality, marriage, and its renunciations will soon become a crucial marker of priestly masculinity. Another constraint on the particular kind of maleness a leader needed to embody is age. Ecclesial leadership would not have been entrusted to boys, but rather to mature men. The *Didascalia Apostolorum*, for example, stipulates that a bishop must be "a man not less than fifty years old."[20] The reason given is moral maturity: "for so it will be evident that he has put aside youthful manners and devilish vices."[21] Yet in its long list of additional qualifications for a bishop, the *Didascalia Apostolorum* also confronts the possibility that there may be communities so small that nobody "of advanced years" or even "of age" can be found.[22] The *Didascalia* clearly has in view the possibility of an underage boy as a last resort: if "there is a youth ... worthy of the episcopate," he ought to be tested and appointed.[23] This unusual act is legitimized through biblical precedents: "For Solomon likewise was king over Israel at the age of twelve years, and Josiah reigned in righteousness at the age of eight years, and Joash likewise reigned when he was seven years old."[24]

*Eunuchs: Liturgical Presence and Presiding*

Before I attend in more details to how priestly masculinity comes to be circumscribed, another particular form of male embodiment needs to be added. I have so far concentrated, in my gender-specific analysis of early patterns of leadership in Christian communities, on the question of what pattern might have enabled both men and women to exercise liturgical leadership. One particular form

---

[20]   *Didascalia Apostolorum* 4.2. English translation: *The Didascalia Apostolorum: An English Version*, ed. and translated by Alistair Stewart-Sykes, Studia Traditionis Theologiae 1 (Turnhout, Belgium: Brepols, 2009), 117.

[21]   Ibid.

[22]   *Didascalia Apostolorum* 4.2–3; *The Didascalia Apostolorum*, 118. The markers of such coming of age were not unequivocally clear at the time; they could include the onset of puberty, the first sprouting of a beard, or, for Romans, the donning of a *toga virilis*; see Marie-Luise Deißmann, "Jugend," in *Antike Medizin—Ein Lexikon*, edited by Karl-Heinz Leven (München: C. H. Beck, 2005), 475f.

[23]   *Didascalia Apostolorum* 4.3; *The Didascalia Apostolorum*, 118.

[24]   Ibid.

of male embodiment, however, is occluded from the picture when the question is asked in that way, namely men who were considered "eunuchs" in antiquity. Their numbers were more significant and their liturgical presence more complex than liturgical historiography to date has shown.

In order to attend to the subject of eunuchs in early Christian worship meaningfully, a number of issues need to be addressed first. To begin with, we have to acknowledge that eunuchs are almost invisible in liturgical historiography to date, probably not least because of a (unacknowledged) modern unease with ancient practices of castration.[25] Such invisibility is true even in places where the subject of castration should be present, e.g., in scholarly indices to editions of the *Apostolic Tradition* and the *Apostolic Constitutions.* Both church orders, after all, deal with issues arising over the ecclesial participation of castrated men. In order to undo the longstanding invisibility of eunuchs in liturgical historiography, the recent vibrant scholarship on eunuchs is indispensable. I draw on this scholarship for what follows.[26]

A second subject also demands attention. When attempting to think through the presence of eunuchs in liturgical assemblies, we have to acknowledge, first of all, that "eunuch" covered a number of quite dissimilar and unrelated embodiments in antiquity, some of which we perceive very differently today. For early Christianity, any of the embodiments that were then thought to make someone a eunuch could well be present in a sizeable liturgical assembly, but they need to be distinguished because they were linked to very different lives and social status. Someone might, for example, be a eunuch "by nature," that is have gender-indefinite genitalia from birth. In antiquity, such persons would be understood to be eunuchs; today, they are included under the umbrella term "intersexed." In recent years, the culture of silence surrounding the births of intersexed persons has begun to break, and figures for such births are now more readily available.[27] If we assume that birth rates

---

[25]    The latter is the suggestion of Walter Stevenson; see his "Eunuchs and Early Christianity," in *Eunuchs in Antiquity and Beyond,* ed. Shaun Tougher (London: The Classical Press of Wales and Duckworth, 2002), 123–42, here 123.

[26]    Especially important are Robert Muth, "Kastration," *Reallexikon für Antike und Christentum* 20 (Stuttgart: Anton Hiersemann, 2004), 285–342, and Shaun Tougher, *The Eunuch in Byzantine History and Society* (New York: Routledge, 2008). See also Kathryn M. Ringrose, *The Perfect Servant: Eunuchs and the Social Construction of Gender in Byzantium* (Chicago: The University of Chicago Press, 2003), esp. 166–74; *Eunuchs in Antiquity and Beyond,* ed. Shaun Tougher (London: The Classical Press of Wales and Duckworth, 2002); and *Women, Men, and Eunuchs: Gender in Byzantium,* ed. Liz James (New York: Routledge, 1997). I note that Peter Browe treated the subject much earlier in his *Die Geschichte der Entmannung. Eine religions- und rechtsgeschichtliche Studie,* Breslauer Studien zur historischen Theologie Neue Folge 1 (Breslau: Verlag Müller & Seiffert, 1936).

[27]    The Intersex Society of North America notes that experts at medical centers, when asked how often a child is born so noticeably atypical in terms of genitalia that a specialist in sex differentiation is called in, report the number to be about one in 1500 to 2000 births;

remain relatively stable over time, then at least some early Christian assemblies included intersexed persons or "eunuchs by nature," and by the fourth century intersexed Christians would have numbered in the thousands.[28]

These eunuchs by nature, however, were only one embodiment among many that made someone a eunuch. That is to say, there will have been significantly more worshippers who were eunuchs in the fourth-century church than the number of intersexed persons alone suggests. A second embodiment that qualified someone as a eunuch was voluntary castration for health reasons, an operation typically done by a physician. Since castration was considered a remedy for a range of ailments, among them something as basic as a hernia,[29] men who had undergone castration for medical reasons (numbers here are near impossible to come by) would have existed among Christians too.

A third cause for someone's status as a eunuch was involuntary, forced castration, either for the purposes of creating eunuch slaves, or as a form of punishment and vengeance. These castrations, illegal in the Roman Empire, were forced mostly on foreigners and on enemies. Eunuch slaves, traded as a luxury commodity, were found mostly in elite contexts, serving at the imperial court and in aristocratic and affluent households. In particular, eunuchs as servants attended to elite women.[30] The Ethiopian eunuch in the Book of Acts, a "court official of the Candace, queen of the Ethiopians" (Acts 8:27), is a case in point. At least in this particular case, a court eunuch was welcomed into the Christian faith, and baptized. By the time the Roman aristocracy and the imperial court turned to the Christian faith, eunuch servants will have entered churches in growing numbers, not least as chaperons of their women owners. From the letters of Jerome, for example, we know that aristocratic women in Rome came to church accompanied by their eunuchs—indeed the entourage of eunuchs who accompanied their mistresses in public was one of the markers of ostentatious luxury for which he berated women![31]

---

for more information, see its website http://www.isna.org/faq/frequency. More people than that are born with subtler forms of sex anatomy variations. Anne Fausto-Sterling's groundbreaking book, *Sexing the Body: Gender Politics and the Construction of Sexuality* (New York: Basic Books, 2000), analyzed the medical data on human sex differentiation for contemporary gender theory.

[28]   If we take statistics of intersexed births and match them, simply for the sake of a rough estimate, to a Christian presence of around five million faithful by the year A.D. 312 (a number suggested by Ramsay MacMullen, *Christianizing the Roman Empire (A.D. 100–400)* [New Haven: Yale University Press, 1984], 85), there could have been around three thousand intersexed Christians by that time. MacMullen's number—like all the others that have been suggested—is questionable of course, but for my purpose here, namely some basic sense of the numbers of "eunuchs by birth" in the fourth century church, MacMullen's estimate will do.

[29]   Cf. Jacqueline König, "Kastration," in *Antike Medizin—Ein Lexikon*, 484–6, here 485.

[30]   They could also serve as the passive sexual partners of men.

[31]   See, for example, Jerome, *Ep.* 22.16; 22.32; 54.13; 130.4.

Yet another kind of eunuch familiar to the world of early Christianity was the self-castrated religious devotee. The most famous examples of this phenomenon were the *galli*, religious eunuchs devoted to the mother goddess Cybele (as she is known from the Phrygian version of this cult of the great goddess). Christians in Asia Minor would have been familiar with these religious eunuchs.

If we take all these different forms of male embodiment that are designated "eunuch" together, it is obvious that this designation covered a range far exceeding what in contemporary common parlance is understood by the term "eunuch," namely a castrated servant. For late antiquity, an additional distinction needs to be born in mind, which pertains to those eunuchs who were "made" rather than born. The effects of castration were quite different in prepubertal and postpubertal eunuchs. Prepubertal castration, mostly of foreigners captured in military expeditions or raids, was for the purpose of creating eunuch slaves.[32] The social status of these eunuchs was correspondingly low, although they lived in an elite context, being owned by the affluent few, and could rise to quite powerful positions, both at the imperial court and in households of the elite. The distinction between prepubertal and postpubertal castration is significant because someone castrated before puberty would be recognizable as such, in public, and in worship. Prepubertal eunuchs were beardless, and spoke with unbroken, prepubertal voices; they were also considered androgynous or effeminate in appearance.[33] Postpubertal eunuchs on the other hand, e.g., men castrated for medical reasons or by ascetic choice long after puberty, would have been much harder to recognize.

With these distinctions in place, what can be gleaned of eunuchs in early Christian assemblies? Most fundamentally, the historian of liturgy needs to acknowledge that eunuchs were present in worship. And given the broad range of what made someone be counted as a eunuch, their numbers will not have been marginal. As the Jesus logion in Matthew 19:12 makes clear ("there are eunuchs who have been so from birth, and there are eunuchs who have been made eunuchs by others, and there are eunuchs who have made themselves eunuchs for the sake of the kingdom of heaven"), not only eunuchs themselves but also their disparate origins were not strange to earliest Christian communities. In addition, the account of the baptism of the Ethiopian eunuch in Acts 8 demonstrates that eunuchs were received into the community of faith. The narrative in fact stresses the Ethiopian's gender identity, mentioning no fewer than five times that he is a eunuch. Furthermore, we have no evidence whatsoever that "eunuchs from birth" and adult men castrated for medical reasons would have been excluded from earliest Christian assemblies. And why should they? Their identities as eunuchs, in any case, were not readily discernable. As to eunuchs who were recognizable as such – for the most part the specific social group of (prepubertal) eunuch slaves –

---

[32]   Even for this group, however, complete castration (by removal of penis and testicles) was rare and the survival rate slim. This in turn made these eunuchs especially valuable.

[33]   For references, see Muth, "Kastration," 309.

Christian funerary inscriptions with the descriptor *eunuchus* in early Roman burial sites bear witness to their presence among the faithful.[34]

The evidence is too limited for us to speculate whether being a eunuch was considered an impediment to leadership in the earliest communities of faith. If we take the three major patterns of ecclesial leadership identified above, we may say the following: being a eunuch in all likelihood did not mean exclusion from charismatic gifts, and thus from leadership based on prophetic inspiration. The coming of the Spirit at Pentecost was linked explicitly not only to prophesying by "sons and daughters" but also by "slaves" (Acts 2:17f). This suggests that neither gender nor status (nor age: both young men and old men will prophecy) were important when the Spirit empowered a person. Acts 8 substantiates this in that it is precisely the Holy Spirit who compels Philip to evangelize the eunuch on the desert route; the same Spirit snatches Philip away after the eunuch's baptism. Moreover, Galatians 3:28, if read with slave eunuchs in mind, suggests that none of their particular markers of difference—their gender identity as castrated males, their social status as servants, their ethnicity as foreigners—was an impediment to ecclesial belonging.

As to the other two pattern of leadership identified above, much will have depended on what type of eunuch a Christian believer was, i.e., how he had come to be a eunuch. A male head of a household with a family, who had undergone a medical castration long after puberty, might well have functioned as an ecclesial leader in the assembly that gathered in his home. A prepubertal foreign eunuch slave in the same household may not have functioned in a leadership role so easily. The main issue here, however, would have been social status rather than gendered embodiment. The two of course cannot neatly be separated; eunuch slaves are a prime example of what gender theory means by intersectionality, i.e., the way in which gender and other markers of difference belong together. As to the third main pattern of organizing liturgical leadership in earliest Christian communities, namely through some (loosely) structured way of selecting and authorizing leaders, we simply do not have enough evidence to speculate what being a eunuch might mean for such authorization. Presumably what I have claimed about the first two patterns—namely that the authority of the Spirit's gifts was not limited by gender or status, yet that status and gender mattered especially in ecclesial assemblies that followed the pattern of domestic leadership—would also have influenced the more structured ways that developed of authorizing ecclesial leaders.

Certainly by the third and fourth centuries we know of presbyters who were "eunuchs by nature," that is, who were born intersexed. Dorotheus, a learned presbyter in Antioch whom Eusebius (c. 260–c. 340) heard expounding the Scriptures in church, is an example.[35] Similarly, there is mention of a presbyter

---

[34]   See Muth, "Kastration," 334.

[35]   See Eusebius, *Church History*, 32.2. For more, see Tougher, *The Eunuch in Byzantine History*, Appendix 2, which lists the known late Roman and Byzantine eunuchs in alphabetical order.

who was a (freed) eunuch slave in Constantinople at the time of John Chrysostom. And a patriarch, Macedonius (496–511), was discovered to be a eunuch (what kind remains unclear) when accused of sexual misconduct.[36] These cases show that eunuchs not only were members of early Christian assemblies, but that they could rise to positions of ecclesial, and that means liturgical, leadership. Moreover, with the growth of the ascetic movement, connotations of the term "eunuch" also change in a more positive direction. Rather than meaning a defective male (whether through birth, force, or choice), "eunuch" becomes a descriptor of an ideal Christian masculinity, namely of a man who had mastered his sexual desires and lived in continence. Jerome puts it pithily in a letter to Eustochium: "Some men may be eunuchs of necessity; I am one by choice."[37]

Jerome brings us to a world beyond earliest Christianity however; I will have to return to his world, and that of eunuchs and their liturgical leadership, later in this chapter. For now, I need to trace the movement from an initial variety of patterns of leadership to one dominant pattern with a view to what this meant for women's liturgical ministries. For the most part, the move meant trouble.

*Troubling Women's Liturgical Ministries*

In the course of the second century the initial variety of patterns of leadership was superseded by the emergence of one model as authoritative: the three-fold order of ministry. Liturgical presidency came to focus on the bishop, surrounded by presbyters and deacons. As Paul Bradshaw has stressed, this pattern of liturgical leadership is a *corporate* liturgical presidency, at least in its early stages.[38] This does not, however, mean that such collegial presidency was non-hierarchical. Within the corporate frame of this presidency women as well as men exercised liturgical ministry, at least in some communities. Besides women deacons, a group of female office holders existed in the canonical widows. Tertullian indicates that penitents seeking reconciliation prostrated themselves in the center of the assembly "before the widows, before the presbyters."[39] In Carthage at least, both the place of the widows with the presbyters, and their role in reconciliation suggest that these women were more than merely recipients of ecclesial charity.[40] Three hundred years later, the *Testamentum Domini* placed its canonical widows

---

[36]   More details on these and other eunuchs in Tougher, *The Eunuch in Byzantine History*, Appendix 2, especially nos. 124, 125, 226. See also Muth, "Kastration," 336.

[37]   *"Alium eunuchum necessitas faciat, me voluntas."* Jerome, *Ep.* 22:19; Latin original and English translation from *Select Letters of St. Jerome*, trans. F. A. Wright, Loeb Classical Library (Cambridge, MA: Harvard University Press, 1975), 93.

[38]   See Paul F. Bradshaw, *Liturgical Presidency in the Early Church*, Grove Liturgical Study 36 (Bramcote: Grove Books, 1983), 21f.

[39]   Tertullian, *De Pudicitia* 13.7. English translation in *Ordained Women in the Early Church*, 180.

[40]   See ibid.

in close proximity to the bishop in the gathered assembly. This Syrian church order envisioned widows receiving an ordination, and sitting "in front."[41] At the celebration of the Eucharist, these widows stood within the veil along with the bishop, presbyters, and other ministers.

These examples of a collegial liturgical presidency that included women are dwarfed by texts that make visible considerable contestations surrounding women's leadership in worship. Being female begins to appear as a distinct liturgical impediment. Contributing to the heightened visibility of this issue were accusations of heresy combined with women's liturgical leadership. One marker of heresy, in other words, comes to be the liturgical roles of women in the accused group.[42] The power of this accusation rested in part on the image of women as potent practitioners of magic, a negative image that was widespread.[43] In Christian sources these accusations created a distinct "topography of heresy," which was linked to the persistence of an earlier pattern of household gatherings, some of them headed by women.[44] The combination of accusations of heresy, with both the household as a liturgical site, and women in positions of leadership, had a specific subtext, namely the strengthening of the bishop and his church as the center of the church's worship.

The troubling of women's liturgical ministries also becomes visible in texts other than those written "against heresies." One particular text, from a literary genre important for liturgical scholarship, is worth highlighting, even if I otherwise bypass the already richly mapped field of women's ministries in the early church.[45] The *Apostolic Church Order* is remarkable among early church orders for the deep anxieties it evidences with regard to women's liturgical ministries. This composite text dates from the third century, but draws on earlier sources; its provenance remains unclear.[46] In its second part, the *Apostolic Church Order* focuses on the proper organization of ecclesial ministries. Among these is the appointment of three widows, whose tasks are defined as constant prayer, "revelations," and care of women who are sick.[47] These widows notwithstanding, a key concern of the

[41] *Testamentum Domini*, 2.4. English translation from Paul F. Bradshaw et al., *The Apostolic Tradition: A Commentary*, Hermeneia (Minneapolis: Fortress Press, 2002), 101.

[42] For more on this, see Harry O. Maier, "Heresy, Households, and the Disciplining of Diversity," in *Late Ancient Christianity*, ed. Virginia Burrus, A People's History of Christianity 2 (Minneapolis: Fortress Press, 2005), 213–33.

[43] See Kim Bowes, *Private Worship, Public Values, and Religious Change in Late Antiquity* (New York: Cambridge University Press, 2008), 213.

[44] Maier, "Heresy, Households, and the Disciplining of Diversity," especially 214, 219.

[45] See notes 8, 12, and 13 in this present chapter.

[46] Alistair Stewart-Sykes dates the text earlier than most scholars, namely to ca. 200–235; see Alistair Stewart-Sykes, *The Apostolic Church Order: The Greek Text with Introduction, Translation, and Annotations*, Early Christian Studies 10 (Strathfield: St. Pauls [sic] Publications, 2006), here 78.

[47] *Apostolic Church Order* 21; Stewart-Sykes, *Apostolic Church Order*, 112.

remainder of the *Apostolic Church Order* is the explicit rejection of any liturgical role for women, most decisively at the celebration of the Eucharist. This rejection is construed as an apostolic charge, being put in the mouth of the apostles Andrew, Peter, and John. The three apostles attribute this rejection to Christ himself, claiming that "when the teacher requested the bread and the cup and blessed them saying: This is my Body and Blood, he did not permit the women to stand alongside us."[48] The reason given for this exclusion, interestingly, is a momentary bodily impropriety of one of the women present, not female gender as such: "Martha said it [the rejection] was on account of Mary because he [Christ] saw her smiling."[49] Mary, however, is quoted as denying the charge: "I did not laugh at this."[50] The apostles then advance another reason for the exclusion of women from eucharistic ministry: Christ taught that "the weak would be saved through the strong."[51] This teaching presumably is taken to support women's exclusion from eucharistic leadership: women are to gain access to the eucharistic table only through male leadership.

Whatever the particular arguments (and their origins and weaknesses),[52] one point is clear. The stakes in the struggle over women's liturgical leadership have become high indeed in this third-century compilation. Christ himself is depicted as authorizing the exclusion of women from leadership. What remains for women, in the *Apostolic Church Order,* is a charitable ministry, and that toward other women only: "the ministry of supporting women in need."[53] With that, the *Apostolic Church Order* foreshadows the later gender-specific pattern of ministry in the church.

### Circumscribing Priestly Masculinity

By the time of the *Apostolic Church Order*, the pattern of a threefold ministry of bishop, presbyters, and deacons had emerged as the authoritative form of ecclesial leadership. Priestly language accrues to that pattern of leadership at roughly the same time, a shift from an earlier insistence on the priestly nature of the whole Christian community.[54] Clear contours of a Christian ideal of masculinity also become visible now. When joined with the pattern of a threefold "priestly" ministry, a particular construal of ecclesial authority—in the form of priestly masculinity—emerges. This development was aided by the contemporaneous

---

[48]   *Apostolic Church Order* 26; Stewart-Sykes, *Apostolic Church Order*, 113.

[49]   Ibid.

[50]   Ibid.

[51]   Ibid.

[52]   Stewart-Sykes, *Apostolic Church Order*, 45–8, argues that behind these paragraphs in the *Apostolic Church Order* lie second-century debates with Gnostic groups.

[53]   *Apostolic Church Order* 28; Stewart-Sykes, *Apostolic Church Order*, 114.

[54]   Cf. Paul F. Bradshaw, *Eucharistic Origins*, An Alcuin Club Publication (New York: Oxford University Press, 2004), 85–7.

weakening of traditional markers of Roman masculinity such as political power, military prowess, and the authority of the *pater familias*. As Mathew Kuefler has argued in his study of the subject, a number of Christian markers of masculinity begin to take the place of the traditional Roman ones. Among these are heroic endurance (as in martyrdom[55]), renunciation of sexuality and family (as in the ascetic life), and civic, public authority, as in the ministry of the bishop.[56] Within the larger shifts in understandings of masculinity, the particulars of ecclesial authority and liturgical leadership also are defined. Two of these particulars are explicitly gender-related. One has to do with sexuality and various modes of its renunciation; the other has to do with the kind of eunuchs to admit to ordination and thus to liturgical leadership. Both issues are clearly in view in conciliar legislation by the early fourth century. The two issues might appear unrelated, yet both of them have to do with male (genital) embodiment and its proper relation to ecclesial ministry. I attend to these issues in turn.

*Disciplining Priestly Sexuality*

A crucial marker of masculinity in relation to the exercise of authority and leadership has been the proper ordering of sexuality. This holds true also for liturgical leadership. As we saw in the previous chapter, for example, both marital sex and nocturnal emissions gave rise to anxieties in relation to worship early on, and became problematic especially for those authorized to preside at the Eucharist. As far as nocturnal emissions are concerned, a number of rules and regulations emerged with regard to liturgical presiding; I have described those in the previous chapter. As for marital sexual relations, anxieties over their bearing on liturgical leadership developed from an earlier insistence of marriage to one wife only, through the suggestion of sexual abstention before worship and the requirement of marital continence, to—in the Latin West at least—mandatory celibacy as the one proper ordering of priestly masculinity and sexuality.

Appreciation of sexual renunciation in those ordained to ministerial leadership initially focused on abstention from sexual activity, but not from marriage. Thus, for example, the *Apostolic Church Order* discussed above advocates not only a rejection of women's liturgical ministry but also an explicit appreciation of leadership either by an unmarried man, or by the husband of one wife (rather than a widower who remarried). This preference is put in the mouth of the Apostle

---

[55]  When female martyrs display heroic endurance, they are typically appreciated for their "manly" faith. For more on this, see, most recently, L. Stephanie Cobb, *Dying to Be Men: Gender and Language in Early Christian Martyr Texts*, Gender, Theory, and Religion (New York: Columbia University Press, 2008).

[56]  See Mathew Kuefler, *The Manly Eunuch: Masculinity, Gender Ambiguity, and Christian Ideology in Late Antiquity*, The Chicago Series in Sexuality, History, and Society (Chicago: University of Chicago Press, 2001).

Peter no less: "It is good should he [the one to be elected bishop] be unmarried, otherwise he should be of one wife."[57]

Soon, however, sexual activity within clerical marriage comes to be judged negatively. If married, those ordained should live in sexual continence, i.e., abstinence within marriage. The appreciation of male continence in evidence here was not invented by Christians but circulated in the wider culture. Importantly, it was one possible reading of masculine power. In this reading, virility was expressed not in sexual prowess but in masculine control over sexual desire. Furthermore, loss of semen meant not only a loss of control but also a loss of male bodily vitality. Consequently, the "most virile man was the man who had kept most of his vital spirit—the one, that is, who lost little or no seed."[58] What is important here for the developing image of priestly masculinity is that sexual renunciation could be linked to vigor and authority rather than coded as an emasculated way of life.[59]

The earliest evidence for the *requirement* of marital continence for the ordained is a canon from a local council held in Spain at the beginning of the fourth century, later known as the Council of Elvira.[60] In canon 33, the council—whose canons throughout are marked by rigorous sexual constraints—stipulates:

> Bishops, presbyters, and deacons and all other clerics having a position in the ministry are ordered to abstain completely from their wives and not to have children. Whoever, in fact, does this, shall be expelled from the dignity of the clerical state.[61]

This canon enjoins marital continence on all the ordained, that is, abstention from sexual relations with their wives. The canon does not prescribe abstention from marriage, but assumes that bishops, presbyters, and deacons are indeed married. Should they, however, not live a life of marital continence—a pregnancy would be obvious proof—the consequences for their ecclesial status are decisive: these men

[57]   *Apostolic Church Order* 16.2; Stewart-Sykes, *Apostolic Church Order*, 109.

[58]   Peter Brown, *The Body and Society: Men, Women and Sexual Renunciation in Early Christianity*, Columbia Classics in Religion (New York: Columbia University Press, 1988; 20th anniversary ed. 2008), 19.

[59]   The subject of ascetic renunciation in early Christianity is a vast and vibrant field of scholarly inquiry. I have to limit myself strictly here to the effects of the increasing appreciation of sexual renunciation on constructions of masculinity in liturgical leadership. A concise overview over the field and its recent shifts can be found in Elizabeth A. Clark, *Reading Renunciation: Asceticism and Scripture in Early Christianity* (Princeton: Princeton University Press, 1999), 18–27.

[60]   The exact dating of this synod continues to be debated.

[61]   Synod of Elvira, can. 33; English translation of the synodal decrees in Samuel Laeuchli, *Power and Sexuality: The Emergence of Canon Law at the Synod of Elvira* (Philadelphia: Temple University Press, 1972), 126–35, here 130.

are to be "expelled from the dignity of the clerical state." Marital sex and priestly masculinity, in other words, cannot cohabit. From this, however, it is not far to the insistence that marriage itself cannot coexist with priestly masculinity. The Council of Elvira stands at the beginning of ecclesial legislation that increasingly tightens the rules of sexual propriety, and indeed renunciations, associated with priestly masculinity, until clerical celibacy becomes normative, at least in the Latin West.[62]

At the end of the fourth century one of the North African Councils interpreted marital continence and priestly ordination as belonging together since apostolic times:

> When at the past council the matter on continency and chastity was considered, those three grades, which by a sort of bond are joined to chastity by their consecration, to wit bishops, presbyters, and deacons, so it seemed that it was becoming that the sacred rulers and priests of God as well as the Levites, or those who served at the divine sacraments, should be continent altogether, by which they would be able with singleness of heart to ask what they sought from the Lord: so that what the apostles taught and antiquity kept, that we might also keep.[63]

The canon links priestly authority to sexual renunciation, and understands this link to be ancient and apostolic. Such a reading of the authorization for priestly continence was not uncontested, however. This is clear from a letter written in 385 by Siricius, bishop of Rome, to Himerius, bishop of Tarragona in Spain. This letter is of significance for a number of reasons, not least because it allows a glimpse of the priestly opponents of marital continence, and of their argument that the Scriptures themselves authorize priestly marriages that are not lived continently. Siricius writes:

> We have learned that very many priests and levites of Christ, after long periods of their consecration, have begotten offspring from their wives as well as by shameful intercourse, and that they defend their crime by this excuse, that in

---

[62]    In the East, the development followed somewhat different lines. At the Council of Nicaea, for example, the regulations on priestly sexuality display other anxieties than those in the West. Thus, the council deliberates about which eunuchs to admit to ordination, and objects to priests cohabiting in spiritual marriage with an ascetic virgin. Western legislation focuses on continence in marriage. Spiritual marriages and continent marriages may seem similar in that both result in the same sexual practice, namely abstinence, but their starting point is distinctly different. Spiritual marriage follows ascetic renunciation, when a male and a female ascetic decide to cohabit in sexual abstinence; in a continent marriage, a wife and/or a husband choose to embrace sexual renunciation after having entered into marriage.

[63]    Canon 33; English text in *The Seven Ecumenical Councils of the Undivided Church, Their Canons and Dogmatic Decrees, Together with the Canons of All the Local Synods Which Have Received Ecumenical Acceptance*, ed. Henry R. Percival, NPNF 2.14, 444.

the Old Testament it is read that the faculty of procreating was given to the priests and the ministers. Whoever that follower of sensual desires is let him tell me now: ... Why does [the Lord] forewarn those to whom the holies of holies were to be entrusted saying; Be ye holy, because I your Lord God am holy [Lev. 20:7; 1 Pet. 1:16]? Why also were the priests ordered to dwell in the temple at a distance from their homes in the year of their turn? Evidently for this reason that they might not be able to practice carnal intercourse with their wives, so that shining with purity of conscience they might offer an acceptable gift to God. ... All priests and levites are bound by the indissoluble law of these sanctions, so that from the day of our ordination, we give up both our hearts and our bodies to continence and chastity.[64]

Siricius's letter reveals several things. For one, he knows of "very many priests" who at the time continued to live non-continently in marriage. These priests argued for their way of life based on biblical precedent, namely the priests of the Old Testament. Siricius's counterargument links sexual abstinence to priestly authority, God's own holiness, and the power of purity (understood as sexual renunciation) in prayer. His emphasis on the necessity of sexual continence in the ordained is underlined by the strictures Siricius envisions for offenders, who

should know that by the authority of the Apostolic See they have been cast out of every ecclesiastical office, which they have used unworthily, nor can they ever touch the sacred mysteries, of which they themselves have deprived themselves, so long as they give heed to impure desires.[65]

Siricius's line of argument will prevail in the following centuries. Priestly masculinity comes to be circumscribed as a particular kind of masculinity: pure and powerful, not least for the sake of presiding at liturgy. This of course does not mean that women never exercised priestly functions, nor that priests always and everywhere lived lives of sexual renunciation. What it does mean is that the public face of liturgical leadership became that of a male, celibate presider. Such a "Father" is anything but gender-less. On the contrary, priestly masculinity came to carry its own specific gender particularity, clearly distinguished from worldly masculinities. Here, gender is writ very large indeed into liturgical life.

---

[64]    Siricius, *Ep. ad Himerium*, 7–8. English translation from Heinrich Denziger's *Enchiridion Symbolorum: The Sources of Catholic Dogma*, transl. Roy J. Deferrari (St. Louis: B. Herder Book Co., 1955), no. 89. For background to Siricius's exegesis, see Clark, *Reading Renunciation*, 204–32.

[65]    Siricius, *Ep. ad Himerium*, 10; *Enchiridion Symbolorum*, no. 89.

*Problems with "Eunuchs for the Sake of the Kingdom of Heaven"*

A second way in which priestly masculinity came to be circumscribed in the fourth century involved a more drastic intervention in male embodiment than the practice of continence, namely castration. Here we need to remember the distinctions made above regarding the diverse meanings of the term eunuch. In fourth-century debates about the ordination of eunuchs one kind only was a problem: the self-castrated. In early Christianity, the reasons for such castration by choice were a combination of ascetics and apologetics, fueled by a literal interpretation of Jesus' reference to "eunuchs who have made themselves eunuchs for the sake of the kingdom of heaven" (Mt 19:12). Justin Martyr, in seeking to defend Christianity against charges of sexual promiscuity, points to a Christian youth in Alexandria who had sought out physicians to castrate him in order to prove his desire for a life of sexual abstinence. The physicians had objected to such a medically unnecessary castration unless the governor approved the procedure. When the governor refused, the Christian youth was left to demonstrate his commitment to continence without surgical support.[66] Origen, on the other hand, was widely believed to have been successful in his youthful quest for self-castration.[67] His reason for becoming a eunuch was said to be proof of his own continence, especially in relation to women in his spiritual circle of friends.[68] The practice of self-castration among Christian men is documented— beyond the two cases mentioned—mostly among rigorous ascetics. Documentation for ascetic self-castration comes, not least, from ecclesial sources criticizing the practice (e.g., Origen in his later years, Basil of Ancyra, Chrysostom, Epiphanius, Ambrose, Cyril of Alexandria).[69] The number of authors attending to this subject is surprisingly large, an indication that self-castration was indeed practiced among Christians. The *Apostolic Tradition*, in its Sahidic version, names self-castration in a catalogue of practices and occupations prohibited to Christians.[70]

Seen in this context, the opening canon of the first Ecumenical Council of Nicaea in 325 appears less tangential to the contemporaneous discussions of priestly leadership and masculinity than might be imagined. The canon requires that priests who had self-castrated "should cease" from priestly ministry, and that no such self-castrated men should in future be ordained. The canon specifies:

---

[66]   See Justin Martyr, *First Apology*, 29.2.

[67]   Walter Stevenson analyses the broader context of Alexandrian exegesis for Origen's assumed self-castration in his "Eunuchs and Early Christianity," 123–42, esp. 129–38.

[68]   Virginia Burrus offers an intriguing analysis of the tensions in Eusebius's account of Origen's self-castration; see her *"Begotten, Not Made": Conceiving Manhood in Late Antiquity*, Figurae: Reading Medieval Culture (Stanford: Stanford University Press, 2000), 25–8.

[69]   More in Muth, "Kastration," 323–6.

[70]   *Apostolic Tradition* 16.12, Sahidic version. English translation in Paul F. Bradshaw et al., *The Apostolic Tradition: A Commentary*, Hermeneia (Minneapolis: Fortress Press, 2002), 90.

> If any one in sickness has been subjected by physicians to a surgical operation, or if he has been castrated by barbarians, let him remain among the clergy; but, if any one in sound health has castrated himself, it behoves that such an one, if [already] enrolled among the clergy, should cease [from his ministry], and that from henceforth no such person should be promoted. But, as it is evident that this is said of those who willfully do the thing and presume to castrate themselves, so if any have been made eunuchs by barbarians, or by their masters, and should otherwise be found worthy, such men the Canon admits to the clergy.[71]

The council goes to some length to clarify that only those eunuchs who had self-castrated should be excluded from ordination. Others, who might have become eunuchs for medical reasons or through force, are explicitly declared admissable to the priesthood.

Toward the end of the fourth century, the *Apostolic Constitutions* advances a theological reason, grounded in the doctrine of creation, for the exclusion from the priesthood of those who had self-castrated: These men had laid hands on themselves and thus were enemies of God's creation.[72] Therefore, such eunuchs "by choice" should not be admitted to ordination. If a priest should decide to self-castrate, he was to be deposed.[73] The penalty for laymen who self-castrated is noticeably different from that for the ordained: laymen should be excluded from the church for three years in that they showed themselves to be enemies of their own lives.[74] With these canons on castrated Christian men, the *Apostolic Constitutions* not only provides more detail about self-castrated men and their status in the church than earlier church orders, but also broadens the list of those eunuchs explicitly admitted to ordination.[75] The *Apostolic Constitutions* adds to the non-problematic, ordainable eunuchs—i.e., those who had been castrated by force—those eunuchs deprived of their virility in a persecution, and those born as eunuchs.[76]

Some cases display tension over prohibitions against self-castration. An example is the presbyter Leontius. Not long after the Council of Nicaea he seems to have castrated himself in order to prove that his spiritual marriage with the ascetic virgin Eustolia was, indeed, continent. In accordance with the canons of the Council of Nicaea (which had forbidden not only self-castration, but also spiritual marriages of priests), Leontius was initially removed from the priesthood. He was, however, later reinstated, and even consecrated bishop of Antioch in 339, a consecration that remained contested.[77] Clarifying which eunuchs to ordain and which to expel from

---

[71]   Canon 1, Council of Nicaea 325. English text in *The Seven Ecumenical Councils*, 8.

[72]   *Constitutiones Apostolorum* 8.47.22. English translation in ANF 7, 501.

[73]   *Constitutiones Apostolorum* 8.47.22–3; *Constitutions of the Holy Apostles*, 501.

[74]   *Constitutiones Apostolorum* 8.47.24; *Constitutions of the Holy Apostles*, 501.

[75]   The relevant canon speaks specifically to *episcopal* ordination.

[76]   *Constitutiones Apostolorum* 8.47.21; *Constitutions of the Holy Apostles*, 501.

[77]   For more on Leontius, see Tougher, *The Eunuch in Byzantine History*, 71, 154; and Muth, "Kastration," 319f.

the priesthood (as noted earlier, postpubertal self-castration did not have the same profound effect as prepubertal castration) was made more difficult by a linguistic development. "Eunuch" had become a title of honor among Christian men living continently, whether monastic, priestly, or both. Thus, Jerome's claim that he was a eunuch "of free will" was open to both literal and spiritualizing interpretations. Short of a physical exam, both interpretations were possible.

Why is a close look at eunuchs imperative for the theorizing of priestly masculinity? Most importantly, fourth-century struggles over which castrated bodies to admit to ordination display the other side of the emphasis on sexual renunciation in priestly masculinity. If one side of that emphasis is a requirement of continence and, in the end, celibacy, then the other side is the exclusion of self-castrating men. This exclusion prevents the high value placed on continence from leading to genital self-mutilation.

In between these two different ways of disciplining the male priestly body, the spectrum of early priestly masculinities could incorporate a number of quite different embodiments. These included intersexed persons ("eunuchs by nature"), eunuchs who had been castrated by others than themselves, single men, married men (some of whom lived continently, some of whom did not), ascetics living in sexual renunciation, and those cohabiting in a spiritual marriage with an ascetic virgin. Moreover, especially in relation to God, priests could be understood as embodying a quintessentially female subject position: with regard to their divine Master and Lord they were called to be meek, receptive, submissive, and obedient.[78]

In addition, even when celibate priestly masculinity became the norm in the life of the Western church, the tradition continued to carry forward elements somewhat different from this exclusionary norm. One of these is the theme of Mary as priest. I turn to this theme as a way of concluding the present chapter with something other than normative priestly masculinity. In order to display the longevity of the theme of Mary as priest, I will have to treat the subject summarily.

## A Priestly Womb and Priestly Breasts: Mary, the Mother of God

The realization that there were priestly and eucharistic connotations to Mary's "hosting" the body of Christ in her womb emerged early. One strand in early eucharistic thinking, as we saw in a previous chapter, strongly linked the presence of Christ in the Eucharist to his real bodily presence in the incarnation. Justin Martyr, for example, in his lengthy *Dialogue with Trypho, a Jew*, insists that the eucharistic bread is offered "in remembrance of the Body which He assumed for the sake of

---

[78] For more on this, see for example, Christopher C. Craun, "Matronly Monks: Theodoret of Cyrrhus' Sexual Imagery in the *Historia Religiosa*," in *Holiness and Masculinity in the Middle Ages*, ed. P. H. Cullum and Katherine J. Lewis (Toronto: University of Toronto Press, 2005), 43–57; and Carolyn Diskant Muir, "Bride or Bridegroom? Masculine Identity in Mystic Marriages," in *Holiness and Masculinity in the Middle Ages*, 58–78.

those who believe, for whom He also suffered."[79] Eucharistic remembrance here is, first and foremost, remembrance of the incarnation: having been made flesh, Jesus gives his flesh. In Justin's description of a eucharistic assembly in his *First Apology* he similarly insists that "the food which has been made the Eucharist … is both the flesh and blood of that Jesus who was made flesh."[80] The incarnational theme of this eucharistic thinking is rooted in the language of the Fourth Gospel: the Word is made flesh, and then gives his flesh and blood to be eaten, for the life of the world (see esp. Jn 1:14 in conjunction with 6:51–6).[81] Other writers after Justin Martyr similarly connected incarnation and Eucharist, among them Irenaeus and Augustine; I discussed the metaphor of Jesus giving his body and blood as nourishment in the form of milk in a previous chapter.[82]

From this link between incarnation and Eucharist to imagining Mary in a priestly role is a small step. She is the one who first gave to the world the gift of Jesus' body and blood. This theme appears, in Greek homilies, in the fourth century.[83] A homily commonly attributed to Epiphanius of Salamis but from a later date, explicitly affirms Mary's priestly role in the incarnation.[84] Epiphanius himself (+ 403) had earlier legitimated women's exclusion from priestly office with reference to the Virgin.[85] The author of this Pseudo-Epiphanian homily in Mary's honor takes a different and unguarded approach. In a lengthy poetic praise of Mary's pure womb, in which "the Word became flesh," he acknowledges the Virgin Mother's priestly, eucharistic role: "'Priest' he calls the virgin [ἱερέα καλεῖ τὴν παρθένον] and also 'altar.' As a table carrying, she has given us the heavenly bread, Christ, for the forgiveness of sins."[86]

Both positions—women cannot receive priestly ordination, since even Mary was not ordained a priest; and, Mary was a priest in that she first offered to the world the body of Christ—become part of the theological repertoire of the following centuries. In the Greek-speaking East, Mary's incarnational, priestly role is inscribed into the iconographic scheme of post-iconoclastic churches,

[79] Justin Martyr, *Dialogue with Trypho, a Jew*, 70.4; English translation in *Writings of Saint Justin Martyr*, trans. Thomas B. Falls, The Fathers of the Church 6 (New York: Christian Heritage, Inc. 1948), 262.

[80] Justin Martyr, *First Apology*, 66.2; English translation in *Writings of Saint Justin Martyr*, 105f.

[81] See Bradshaw, *Eucharistic Origins*, 87, 89.

[82] See Chapter 4.

[83] René Laurentin amassed many of these texts in his *Maria, Ecclesia, Sacerdotium: Essai sur le développement d'une idée religieuse* 1 (Paris: Nouvelles Éditions latines, 1952), 19–95.

[84] Suggested dates range from the fifth to the eight centuries; more in Laurentin, *Maria, Ecclesia, Sacerdotium* 1:26–32.

[85] See Epiphanius, *Panarion*, 79.3.

[86] [Ps-]Epiphanius, "Hom. 5 in Laudes Sanctae Mariae Deiparae," PG 43:497. Translation mine.

which depicts the Theotokos in the conch of the sanctuary apse. This Theotokos, rising over the altar with arms outstretched in prayer, carries the Christ in the nimbus of her womb, thus linking Christ's incarnation with Christ's eucharistic body. In the Western church, an insistence on Mary's priestly role can be found, for example, in theologians such as Bonaventure, Albert the Great, and John Gerson.[87] Yet the danger of linking too closely priestly ministry—by then authoritatively connected with masculinity—to the body of a woman (even if one forever virginal) was not lost. Thus a number of voices also painstakingly distanced Mary from priestly ministry.[88] If Mary was seen to exercise a priesthood at all, it had to be distinguished from the ministerial priesthood exercised exclusively by men. One of the ways in which this distinction was safeguarded was by shifting too unguarded a language of Mary's priesthood to a broader eucharistic discourse. By the thirteenth century a growing number of spiritual writers spoke of Mary "eucharistically," for example as host iron (i.e., a baking mould for host making), or as tabernacle. In one of the most widely-read texts of the Middle Ages, the poet Konrad of Würzburg (ca. 1235–87) describes Mary as the "host iron of the living bread of heaven" [*oblatisen des lebenden himelbrotes*] and as "God's tabernacle" [*gotes tabernackel*].[89] Yet some spiritual writers continued to emphasize more direct parallels between Mary's life and priestly ministry: as Mary offered Jesus at the presentation in the temple, so the priest offers the mass; as Mary made possible the presence of Christ in her womb with her word (*fiat*), so the priest makes possible the presence of Christ in the Eucharist with the words of institution. The latter theme dominates one of the visions of the great Benedictine monastic leader, writer, composer, and preacher Hildegard of Bingen (1098–1179). Hildegard, a visionary since childhood, felt called to write down her visions, and Pope Eugene III himself had approved her writing (the as-yet incomplete *Scivias*) in 1147–48 at a synod in Trier. In the "eucharistic" vision of the second part of the *Scivias*, Hildegard ponders the analogy between the mystery of the incarnation and the mystery of the Eucharist. The analogy is explained to her by God's voice:

> as Divinity displayed its wonders in the womb of the Virgin, it shows its secrets also in this [eucharistic] oblation. How? Because here are manifested the body and blood of the Son of God. … For, as the body of my Son came about in the womb of the Virgin, so now the body of My Only-Begotten arises from the sanctification of the altar.[90]

---

[87]  See Laurentin, *Maria, Ecclesia, Sacerdotium*, 1:97–207.

[88]  Ibid. See also see Gregor Martin Lechner, "Priestertum," in *Marienlexikon* 5, ed. Remigius Bäumer and Leo Scheffcyzk (St. Ottilien: EOS Verlag, 1993), 314–18.

[89]  Konrad von Würzburg, *Die Goldene Schmiede*, ed. Edward Schröder (Göttingen: Vandenhoeck & Ruprecht, 1926), ll. 495 and 1274.

[90]  Hildegard of Bingen, *Scivias*, 2.6.12–14. English translation by Mother Columba Hart and Jane Bishop, The Classics of Western Spirituality (New York: Paulist Press, 1990), here 244–5.

This strong link between incarnation and Eucharist reappears when Hildegard ponders how the eucharistic elements become Christ's body and blood. She envisions an analogy between Mary's *fiat* and the priest's eucharistic prayer: both enable God's real presence. Hildegard writes: "As My Son miraculously received humanity in the Virgin, so now this oblation miraculously becomes his body and blood on the altar."[91] She brings an additional analogy into play. Both Mary and the priest enable this real presence of Christ through their virginity, chastity, and purity, necessitating purity in those who receive: "As she bore Him in her virginity to be pure and stainless, now the bread that is truly consecrated as His flesh and is pure in its integrity should be received by the faithful in purity of heart."[92]

In Hildegard's vision, God interprets the connection between the incarnation and the Eucharist to her in the following way: "when the priest does his office as is appointed him, invoking Me in sacred words, I am there in power, just as I was there when My Only-Begotten, without discord or stain, became incarnate."[93] Interestingly, Hildegard develops in depth the analogy between incarnation and Eucharist while also stressing, toward the end of this eucharistic vision, that women cannot be ordained. Or is it that her close linking of a woman's body (the site of God's incarnation in Mary's womb) and Christ's eucharistic presence on the altar raised anxieties about what the theological consequences for the link between masculinity and ordination might be? Whatever the reasons, Hildegard repeatedly stresses that "those of female sex should not approach the office of My altar."[94] She authorizes her insistence of women's exclusion from ordained ministry not by pointing to Mary's lack of ordination, but with a specific understanding of what takes place in human reproduction. A gender-specific understanding of the reproductive process that sees men as active and women as passive is crucial for Hildegard's argument:

> A woman conceives a child not by herself but through a man, as the ground is plowed not by itself but by a farmer. Therefore, just as the earth cannot plow itself, a woman must not be a priest and do the work of consecrating the body and blood of My Son; though she can sing the praise of her creator, as the earth can receive rain to water its fruits.[95]

This argument against women's ordination is based on the conviction that women are the passive part in sexual intercourse and conception. Eucharistic consecration, in contradistinction, is seen as active, and thus the work of men, akin to insemination. Hildegard here draws on a particular understanding of priestly bodies

---

91    Hildegard of Bingen, *Scivias*, 2.6.15; p. 246.
92    Hildegard of Bingen, *Scivias*, 2.6.26; p. 254.
93    Hildegard of Bingen, *Scivias*, 2.6.34; p. 259.
94    Hildegard of Bingen, *Scivias*, 2.6.76; repeated verbatim 2.6.77; both p. 278.
95    Ibid.

as assertively male, in the sense of being liturgically active and generative. Such an understanding of priestly masculinity as spiritually fecund and inseminating was in place centuries before Hildegard, especially in Benedictine exegesis,[96] with which the learned Benedictine abbess would have been familiar. In this exegesis, the spiritually reproductive powers of priestly men were linked especially to sacred words, whose speaking was interpreted as a generative discharge of the mouth, analogous to the discharge of semen.[97] (This interpretation is not as far-fetched as it might initially seem since the Latin *"semen"* can mean both "seed" and "semen"; the Vulgate thus renders Jesus' explanation of the parable of the sower as *"semen est verbum Domini"* [Lk 8:11].) This image of priestly, generative masculinity seems to underlie Hildegard's argument against the ordination of women. As passive receivers by nature, women are in no position to discharge the seminal, generative words of consecration at the altar. The "ritually reproducing priest"[98] needs to be male, and a chaste male no less, so that his reproductive powers are not wasted on anything less than the divine. Priestly masculinity here is understood as potent precisely because it does not engage in mere human sexual practices.[99]

For consecrated virgins, as opposed to women in general, Hildegard does envision "the priesthood and all the ministry of My altar" despite their passivity. The reason is that consecrated virgins receive "the High Priest as Bridegroom."[100] Female virginity, in other words, receives a form of priestly ordination in that the virgin's body is penetrated by the High Priest.[101] Yet aside from the way in which Hildegard lays claim to a specific virginal priesthood of female monastics, the clear distinction she makes between Mary's priestly role on the one hand, and

---

[96]  See Lynda Coon, "'What is the Word if not Semen?' Priestly Bodies in Carolingian Exegesis," in *Gender in the Early Medieval World: East and West, 300–900*, ed. Leslie Brubaker and Julia M. H. Smith (New York: Cambridge University Press, 2004), 278–300. Cf. also Jacqueline Murray, "Masculinizing Religious Life: Sexual Prowess, the Battle for Chastity and Monastic Identity," in *Holiness and Masculinity in the Middle Ages*, ed. P. H. Cullum and Katherine J. Lewis (Toronto: University of Toronto Press, 2004), 24–42.

[97]  Cf. Coon, "What is the Word if not Semen?," 296.

[98]  Ibid., 299. For a fascinating example of how celibate priestly masculinity can be linked, ritually, with marriage, see Sharon T. Strocchia, "When the Bishop Married the Abbess: Masculinity and Power in Florentine Episcopal Entry Rites, 1300–1600," *Gender & History* 19 (2007), 346–68. The essay describes one element of espiscopal installation in Florence, namely the symbolic, ritual marriage of the incoming bishop with the most powerful abbess of his diocese. The ritual included a ring ceremony in front of witnesses, a wedding banquet, and the bishop's overnight stay in an elaborate nuptial bed prepared for him in the convent.

[99]  For an interesting case study, see Jennifer D. Thibodeaux, "Man of the Church, or Man of the Village? Gender and the Parish Clergy in Medieval Normandy," *Gender & History* 18 (2006): 380–99, esp. 384.

[100]  Hildegard of Bingen, *Scivias*, 2.6.76; p. 278.

[101]  One wonders what liturgical consequences this priestly office of the virgins might have had in Hildegard's monasteries.

women's exclusion from priestly office on the other, is not without tensions.[102] These tensions demonstrate that insistence on the priestly role of Mary does not fit easily with the exclusion of women from priestly office. The unease produced by this tension marks many theological writings on the priestly role of Mary, but does not often appear in a text as visibly as it does in Hildegard's.

It is not only theological texts that imagine Mary as priest. Artistic representations of Mary also understand the Mother of God eucharistically. The Lucca Madonna of Jan van Eyck is a case in point.[103] In this painting of 1436 the artist depicts a *Maria lactans* on whose (unusually flat) lap an infant Christ rests. Mary's lap evokes a eucharistic table; a niche with a bowl, suggesting the priestly washing of hands, is on the right, and the room as a whole resembles a small chapel. In this painting, maternal womb and eucharistic altar belong together, as do maternal nursing and the eucharistic feeding of the Body of Christ, both gifts of the mother's own body as nourishment. As Caroline Walker Bynum has put it succinctly: "Late medieval art emphasized Mary both as provider of food to her son and as provider of Jesus-as-food to all Christians."[104]

Artistic representations of Mary in liturgical vestments also exist.[105] A particularly striking example can be found in the Evangeliary of the Benedictine monastery of Gengenbach, which dates from the twelfth century. The illumination for the feast of the Annunciation shows Mary wearing eucharistic vestments and a stole, her arms extended in prayer, and the Spirit descending on her.[106] The Blessed Virgin, with the angel next to her, is clearly styled analogously to the priest at the moment of consecration. Mary also appears in priestly vestments in a number of visions of medieval mystics. Elisabeth of Schönau, a contemporary of Hildegard of Bingen, had a vision of Mary wearing a priestly chasuble and standing beside the altar during a Mass in her honor.[107] The Blessed Benvenuta (+ 1292), a Dominican tertiary and mystic, in a vision saw Mary as the celebrant

---

[102] I agree with Anne L. Clark's reading of Hildegard's vision as exhibiting this tension; see her essay "The Priesthood of the Virgin Mary: Gender Trouble in the Twelfth Century," *Journal of Feminist Studies in Religion* 18 (2002): 5–24, here 15f.

[103] The Lucca Madonna is on display at the Städelsches Kunstinstitut, Frankfurt am Main, Germany.

[104] Caroline Walker Bynum, "The Body of Christ in the Later Middle Ages," in *Fragmentation and Redemption: Essays on Gender and the Human Body in Medieval Religion* (New York: Zone Books, 1992), 79–117, here 103f.

[105] Examples in Paul Y. Cardile, "Mary as Priest: Mary's Sacerdotal Position in the Visual Arts," *Arte Cristiana* 72 (1984): 199–208. Curiously, the author does not seem to know the twelfth-century depiction of Mary in priestly vestments in the Evangeliary of Gengenbach.

[106] Württembergische Landesbibliothek Stuttgart, Cod. Bibl. fol. 28.

[107] For more, see Clark's interpretation of Elisabeth's visions, in "Priesthood of the Virgin Mary," 18–21.

of the Mass; the beguine Mechthild of Magdeburg (+ ca. 1282) witnessed Mary choreographing the celebration of the Mass.[108]

Eucharistic images of Mary are also embodied in a number of tabernacles, especially in the so-called tabernacle madonnas.[109] The origins of these madonnas, which represent Mary as a eucharistic vessel, most likely lie in the so-called shrine madonnas, wooden statues of Mary that open up, usually on two hinges in front.[110] When opened, such statues transform themselves into altarpieces. Inside these madonnas can be found either representations of the life of Christ, or a representation of the Trinity; these latter came to be suppressed by church authorities who worried about their dogmatic propriety. Other shrine madonnas fared better, such as madonnas that opened in the back to be used as reliquaries, tabernacles, and monstrances. Sometimes a piece of transparent crystal was placed in the madonna's body to let the faithful see the host inside her womb.

Not surprisingly, shrine madonnas began to multiply in the thirteenth century, a time that saw heightened interest in the Eucharist. Women's religiosity in particular found expression in intense eucharistic devotion.[111] The feast of Corpus Christi, at whose origin stands the vision of a woman, Juliana of Mount Cornillon, began to be observed in the middle of the thirteenth century. A century later, its observance had become obligatory in the Western church, and monstrances, that is, vessels for showing the Blessed Sacrament (from the Latin *monstrare*, to show), proliferated. Madonna monstrances were among these; they reached their zenith in the seventeenth century.[112] Together with madonna monstrances, another eucharistic representation of Mary had emerged in the fourteenth century, the so-called *"Ährenkleid"*-Madonnas ("Our Lady of the Grains"). In these images, Mary stands in prayer, hands folded; often she is depicted as pregnant. On the length of her gown, a plethora of full ears of wheat is imprinted. The visual link between the incarnation, Mary's womb, and the bread of life in these images is both subtle and exquisite.

---

[108] See Peter Dinzelbacher, "Rollenverweigerung, religiöser Aufbruch und mystisches Erleben mittelalterlicher Frauen," in *Religiöse Frauenbewegung und mystische Frömmigkeit im Mittelalter*, ed. Peter Dinzelbacher and D. R. Bauer (Köln: Bohlau, 1988), 1–58, here 43–4.

[109] There is no accepted English translation, other than the literal "shrine madonna," for the German *Schreinmadonna* (French: *vièrge ouvrante*), and the more particular type of the *Platyteramonstranz* (French: *vièrge-tabernacle*).

[110] The definitive study of the shrine madonnas is still that by Christoph Baumer, "Die Schreinmadonna," *Marian Library Studies* 9 (1977): 239–72.

[111] See Caroline Walker Bynum, "Women Mystics and Eucharistic Devotion," in *Fragmentation and Redemption*, 119–50.

[112] See Gregor Martin Lechner, *Maria Gravida: Zum Schwangerschaftsmotiv in der bildenden Kunst*, Münchner kunsthistorische Abhandlungen (München: Verlag Schnell & Steiner, 1981), 149–55; and idem, "Platyteramonstranzen," in *Marienlexikon* 5:253.

Even if these madonnas played a minor role in the overall development of Marian and eucharistic spirituality, they display, in material culture, what theologians had pointed to since the early centuries. The body of Christ, received in the Eucharist, first came to be "real presence" in the body of Mary. The first altar, in this reading, was a womb. A hint of this theological conviction is also embedded in the eucharistic prayer *Ave Verum Corpus*, made famous by Mozart's musical setting for it. The medieval text was prayed, privately, at the moment of the elevation of the host; it greets the eucharistic body of Christ—*Ave Verum Corpus*—as the body born of Mary: *natum de Maria Virgine*.

Even if Madonna monstrances did not flourish beyond the seventeenth century, the devotion to Mary as *Virgo Sacerdos* gained ground in the eighteenth and nineteenth centuries. The title was invoked, not least, by Pope Pius IX; and Pope Pius X (the same pope who earlier in his pontificate had declared women to be "incapable" of a real liturgical office) in 1906 approved a prayer that explicitly addressed Mary as *Maria Virgo Sacerdos*.[113] The Superior General of the Daughters of the Sacred Heart of Jesus had requested permission to use this title in prayer in the houses of her congregation. Official approval of devotion to Mary as Virgin Priest, however, was short-lived. In 1913 images of Mary in priestly vestments were forbidden, invocations of the *Virgo Sacerdos* soon followed. All devotions to Mary as *Virgo Sacerdos* also were prohibited, and the officially-approved prayer was withdrawn.[114] One reason for this turn in events was surely the fact that by then questions were being raised within the Women's Movement about the exclusion of women from priestly ordination.[115] Invoking a woman as *sacerdos* must have seemed dangerously ambiguous.

With that, the present chapter on gender and liturgical leadership has come full circle, namely to gender contestations surrounding liturgical leadership. As the present chapter has shown, these contestations emerged early on, only to be answered (or muted) by a decisive linking of masculinity and priestly presiding. Yet this decisive link constantly had to be re-asserted and re-narrated, "requiring, as does any tradition, ongoing repetition to naturalize it and endow it with seeming inevitability."[116]

---

[113] See Laurentin, *Maria, Ecclesia, Sacerdotium*, 1:522–6; Lechner, "Priestertum," 315f.

[114] See Laurentin, *Maria, Ecclesia, Sacerdotium*, 1:527–31.

[115] For more on this, see my *"Liturgie und Frauenseele." Die Liturgische Bewegung aus der Sicht der Frauenforschung*, Praktische Theologie Heute 10 (Stuttgart: Kohlhammer Verlag, 1993), 73–83.

[116] The felicitous description is Anne Clark's, "Priesthood of the Virgin Mary," 11 n. 22.

# PART III
# Gender, History, and Liturgical Tradition

The historiographic work of Part II gestures toward a theological argument about liturgical history as it grounds authorizing claims to the past. The question is this: what happens with authorizing claims to liturgy's past when a new liturgical historiography reconfigures the contours of what this past has been perceived to be? I attend to this question in the last part of *Gender Differences and the Making of Liturgical History*, in the form of a concluding chapter (Chapter 7). The task here is three-fold. First, I highlight the consequences, for liturgical historiography, of the findings of the previous chapters. Second, I attend to the theological question underlying the historiographic work of this book, namely: what happens to authorizing claims to the past when historical knowledge comes to be reconfigured in gender-attentive ways? Finally, I turn to contemporary discussions around gender and liturgy in order to ask: what happens to the many ways in which liturgy continues to be shaped by gender when these ways are understood to have a history—that is, when contemporary realities come to be seen as part of a long history of Christian worship that has never been devoid of gender processes as basic, potent, and troubling ingredients of all liturgical life and practice.

# Chapter 7
# The Lasting Presence of Liturgy's Past

July 22. In the calendars of both Eastern and Western churches this day is the memorial of Saint Mary Magdalene. Yet depending on when and where in history this saint was honored on her feast day, very different women, with quite divergent pasts and paths, have been recalled. The biblical figure of Mary of Magdala—key disciple of Jesus and first witness to the resurrection—was remembered in early centuries as the "apostle to the apostles" (*apostola apostolorum*).[1] Much of the liturgical tradition that followed, however, knew her best as the "great sinner." In the proper of saints she was listed, until the reforms of Vatican II, as "Saint Mary Magdalene, Penitent." How a first witness to the resurrection became, in the church's liturgical memory, primarily a repentant prostitute is a complex story, involving divergent traditions among the earliest Christian communities, struggles over authority, apostolicity, and gender, and a reception history that conflated different biblical women into a "Magdalene."

One way to map this complex history is to imagine a set of veils covering the historical Mary of Magdala. The biblical writings themselves lift the textual veil on this woman in only a few places, all of them in the four Gospels. What can be glimpsed there is far less than later stories of Mary's life would have us believe, but the little there is proves intriguing.[2] Mary, in contradistinction to most other biblical women, is not identified as a daughter, wife, or mother of a male figure, but rather through her native city, Magdala. This identification with a city rather than the

---

[1]   Hippolytus first described Mary of Magdala as someone who is like an apostle to the apostles in his *Commentary on the Song of Songs*, 25.6–7. Others—from Rhabanus Maurus in the ninth century, Abelard and Bernard of Clairvaux in the twelfth century, and Thomas Aquinas in the thirteenth century, to Pope John Paul II in the twentieth century—have followed Hippolytus in this. See John Paul II, *Mulieris Dignitatem, On the Dignity and Vocation of Women*, # 16 n. 38. The English text of this Apostolic Letter is available on the Vatican's website: http://www.vatican.va/-holy_father/john_paul_ii/apost_letters/documents/hf_jp-ii_apl_15081988_mulieris-dignitatem_en.html (accessed July 22, 2010).

[2]   The scholarly literature on Mary of Magdala is vast; suffice it here to point to the recent weighty monograph by Andrea Taschl-Erber, *Maria von Magdala—Erste Apostolin? Joh 20,1–18: Tradition und Relecture*, Herder's Biblical Studies 51 (New York: Herder, 2007), and to the literature in the following footnotes. A succinct overview of the historical development is presented by Katherine Ludwig Jansen, "Maria Magdalena: *Apostolorum Apostola*," in *Women Preachers and Prophets through Two Millennia of Christianity*, ed. Beverly Mayne Kienzle and Pamela J. Walker (Berkeley: University of California Press, 1998), 57–96.

usual male figure probably means that Mary was both independent and wealthy, a privileged subject position for a woman of her time. The Gospel according to Luke recounts that Mary suffered a profound illness and was healed in her encounter with Jesus, whose disciple she became (Lk 8:2). Mary of Magdala is mentioned as one among several women on whom the Jesus movement depended for financial support. She is distinguished by her presence at Jesus' crucifixion, burial, and resurrection, and also as the first to encounter the risen Lord—as least this is what the Gospel according to John knows. There, Jesus charges Mary with proclaiming the good news of the resurrection to the other disciples,[3] and her subsequent proclamation "I have seen the Lord" (John 20:18) becomes the foundational witness to the risen Christ. Not surprisingly, Mary's name routinely leads the list of women disciples in the gospels, much as Peter's heads the list of male disciples. One of the noncanonical gospels even bears Mary's name and describes her as Jesus' closest disciple.[4] Lifting the earliest textual veil on the historical Mary of Magdala thus reveals a woman leader among Jesus' followers, one to whom the risen Christ appeared, authorizing her to proclaim his resurrection.

This glimpse of the historical figure of Mary of Magdala is soon shrouded in layers of veils, one of them so elaborate that several women found room to hide under it. In fact, the New Testament itself does not speak with one voice about Mary of Magdala. The Gospel according to Luke, for example, passes over any apostolic charge given to her by the risen Christ; the apostle Paul does not list her among the first witnesses to the resurrection (1 Cor 15:5f); and her name is conspicuously absent from the Acts of the Apostles and from all the epistles.[5]

As centuries passed, the slim figure of the biblical Mary of Magdala expanded in quite different directions. A number of separate Gospel stories involving different women came to be read together, leading to the composite image of a "Magdalene." The biblical Mary of Magdala was identified not only with the unnamed woman who anoints Jesus in Mark's Gospel (Mk 14:3–9, par. Matt 26:6–13) and with Mary of Bethany (Jn 12:1–8), but also with an unnamed woman Luke describes as a public sinner, that is, a prostitute (Lk 7:36–50). This conflation invited a further one when the unnamed woman caught in adultery (Jn 8) joined the other women already under the veil of the "Magdalene."

The voluptuous veils now covering the historical figure, Mary of Magdala, continued to make room for additional elements. By the time of Jacobus de

---

[3]    For more on the Johannine Mary of Magdala, see Susanne Ruschmann, *Maria von Magdala im Johannesevangelium: Jüngerin—Zeugin—Lebensbotin*, Neutestamentliche Abhandlungen n.F. 40 (Münster: Aschendorff, 2002).

[4]    See Karen L. King, *The Gospel of Mary of Magdala: Jesus and the First Woman Apostle* (Santa Rosa, CA: Polebridge, 2003).

[5]    For more on these divergent narratives—and the divergent claims to apostolic authority that undergird them—see Ann Graham Brock, *Mary Magdalene, The First Apostle: The Struggle for Authority*, Harvard Theological Studies 51 (Cambridge, MA: Harvard University Press, 2003).

Voragine's *Legenda Aurea*, a widely read thirteenth-century collection of saints' lives, Mary was not only a repentant prostitute but also of royal lineage; she had sailed to southern France and preached the Gospel there, converting the ruling family and its peoples. The memory of her apostolic work lingered in the story of her preaching; and the veneration of an apostolic Mary Magdalene gained strength, for example, in the twelfth century.[6] A number of artistic representations testify to this. The St. Albans Psalter, probably commissioned by the anchoress and then prioress Christina of Markyate, depicts Mary authoritatively proclaiming the resurrection to the eleven remaining apostles. This illumination invites viewers to imagine Mary as the twelfth apostle.[7] Nevertheless, in popular memory Mary Magdalene is primarily the repentant prostitute, that is, the great sinner who became the quintessential penitent.

The complex history of the liturgical memory of Mary Magdalene opens this final chapter of *Gender Differences and the Making of Liturgical History* for several reasons. To begin with, the story illustrates how, when it comes to liturgical memory, we often find more than one veil to lift, even over a single subject. Furthermore, lifting a veil on the past rarely yields simple, straightforward representations. In the case of Mary Magdalene, pitching her image in "Scripture" against that of "Tradition"—which is how much recent scholarship has proceeded—proves to be not so simple. The scriptural witness to Mary of Magdala itself, after all, is inconsistent. Only the Gospel according to John knows her as the first to encounter the risen Christ; other New Testament writings tell a different story. Neither is the Tradition uniform in framing Mary Magdalene as only a repentant prostitute; stories, sermons, images, and liturgical practices also kept alive the memory of the apostolic Mary, the preacher of the good news of the resurrection.[8] To complicate matters even further, after Vatican II, the criterion of liturgical reform that led to the removal of the (historically non-sustainable) title "penitent" from Mary's memorial in the calendar of saints also led to a disproportionately greater decline in female than male saints. The criterion of reform—namely, greater historical accuracy and verifiability—affected the *vitae* of women disproportionally, since

---

[6] See Katherine Ludwig Jansen's study, *The Making of the Magdalen: Preaching and Popular Devotion in the Later Middle Ages* (Princeton, NJ: Princeton University Press, 2000), and her "Maria Magdalena: *Apostolorum Apostola*," 60–80.

[7] This iconographic theme is rare in Western art before the twelfth century, but appears in Byzantine cycles of Gospel illustration. See *The St. Albans Psalter*, Studies of the Warburg Institute 25 (Leiden: E. J. Brill, 1960), 62.

[8] Josef Andreas Jungmann pointed out that in the Middle Ages the feast of Mary Magdalene was among only a few saints' days on which the *Credo* might be recited at Mass; see Joseph [sic] A. Jungmann, *The Mass of the Roman Rite* 1, trans. Francis A. Brunner from the rev. German ed. of 1949 (New York: Benziger Brothers, 1950), 470 n. 55. Mary Magdalene, so the argument went at the time, took part in an event mentioned in the Creed (this was the key criterion for when to recite the *Credo* in a Mass) and thus deserved that honor.

their histories are less well documented than those of men.[9] This disproportionate loss of female saints in the calendar surely was not what the postconciliar liturgical reforms intended, but it serves as a sobering reminder of the side effects that may occur when well-intended liturgical work is inattentive to the realities of gender history. Last and not least, the preconciliar liturgical past is officially present again in the church since Pope Benedict XVI resanctioned use of the "Roman Missal promulgated by Blessed John XXIII in 1962" as an "extraordinary form of the Liturgy of the Church" in 2007.[10] Those who honor the memorial of Saint Mary Magdalene according to this preconcilar liturgy will, once again, know Mary of Magdala by the title "*poenitens*."

In this concluding chapter, I will concentrate on the consequences of having lifted a veil on liturgy's past. This does *not* imply that the explorations in liturgical history as gender history presented in the previous chapters are in any way complete; they are not. I hope to have demonstrated in the previous chapters, in sufficient depth, what a gender-attentive liturgical historiography can accomplish so as to convince other scholars to consider and engage this field of inquiry. In what follows here, I attend to a question that grows out of the kind of liturgical history writing I have advocated in the previous chapters: what happens when the imagined past—the image of the past as we knew it—changes? What are the consequences of a re-envisioned history?

The first and most basic level for responding to this question lies within the scholarly field of liturgical historiography. A second level is related to the theological use to which liturgical history is put, that is, the recourse to liturgical tradition; a specific case of such theological recourse to the *lex orandi* is ecclesially authoritative, authorizing claims to the liturgical past. A third and final level is that of contemporary liturgical life and gender differences as these are present in worship. What happens when struggles involving gender in liturgical life are seen to have a genealogy? I take these topics up in turn.

## The Challenge: Writing Liturgical History without Veiling Gender

The preceding chapters have sought to display how liturgical history is also a history of gender, or, more precisely, how gender differences shaped liturgical life in multiple ways. As we have seen, many of the traditional sources for the writing of liturgical history readily speak of gender differences and their importance in

---

[9]     Gisela Muschiol first brought this to my attention in her short essay, "Wer braucht den Drachentöter noch? Heiligenlegenden nach der Revision des römischen Kalenders," *Diakonia* 31 (2000): 127–31.

[10]     See Benedict XVI, Motu Proprio *Summorum Pontificum*, on the "Roman liturgy prior to the reform of 1970," # 1. An (unofficial) English translation is available on the website of the United States Conference of Catholic Bishops: http://www.usccb.org/liturgy/VISEnglishSummPont.pdf.

lived liturgical life. These traditional, much-studied sources have to be read afresh, with the veil over gender lifted from our interpretive lenses. Gender differences and their bearing on liturgical life become clearer still when the traditional canon of sources is broadened to include other sources, among them architectural, musical, visual, and medical witnesses. An expanded set of sources strengthens our initial observation that gender as a subject is present in liturgy's past, just as judgments on gender differences were present in the larger cultural context in which Christian liturgy arose.[11] Traditional liturgical historiography, focused on liturgical texts, and without critical scholarly tools to theorize gender differences, failed to probe this fundamental marker of liturgical life.

Once the veil over gender differences has been lifted, I hope that such failure will be more difficult to justify and to sustain in the future. To put this point more positively, I hope that the ongoing writing of liturgical history will be deepened and energized by attention to the many ways in which gender differences impressed liturgy's past. This attention is not about inscribing the fascinating details of "male embodiment" or of "birthgiving"—not to mention "sex"—in the writing (and the occasionally tedious reading) of liturgical historiography. Rather, gendered realities are of principal importance for a history of liturgy because they display worship as a lived, embodied, corporal, and corporate practice. The study of this practice of worship is not exhausted by an analysis of rites alone. Even the most traditional liturgical historiography, with its keen focus on official texts, ultimately sought to be not a history of texts alone, but a history of liturgical life. Official liturgical texts simply seemed the best way to enter the worship life of the past. Yet when bodies at worship are concerned, every imaginable way into the past—from the visual arts to musical scores, from medical treatises to remnants of clothing, from architectural particularities to relics of the saints—bears relevance.

Once liturgical history is read as (also) a history of gender differences, an image of liturgy's past emerges that is somewhat at variance with previous histories. The emphasis shifts to lived liturgical life, to every gendered body present or absent from the gathered assembly, to bodily propriety, posture, and place, to gendered embodiment and liturgical role, and to liturgy as part of a larger world whose particular gender arrangements influence, shape, conflict with, or control what takes place in the sanctuary. From the liturgical lives of eunuchs and intersexed persons to the ways in which bodily flows controlled liturgical presence and absence, new knowledges emerge about ancient realities. With these new knowledges, intriguing new questions also emerge, a sure sign of an interpretive tool that functions well.

I am not under the false impression that the interpretive tools of gender history will be the last in revisionist history writing. As John Baldovin has rightly noted,

---

[11] The term "gender" as used in this book obviously reflects contemporary theorizing, yet what the term describes is readily discernible in early Christian writings, even if under a different nomenclature. In this regard, the use of the term "gender" is not dissimilar from the term "liturgy"; see Chapter 1.

"every good historical investigation is at least to some extent revisionist," or it is "mere repetition of what has already been written."[12] Liturgical historiography must be *semper reformanda*, and ever new ways of studying the past will emerge as long as this scholarly endeavor has vibrancy. That said, I emphasize that we have only begun to scratch the surface of what a gender-attentive reading of liturgical sources can accomplish. My hope is that this book's lifting of a veil on liturgy's past will encourage further sustained work in this area rather than becoming the one "gender"-book cited in future writings of liturgical history. Gender analysis must not become simply one more add-on to all the other scholarly tools that have recently been suggested for historians of liturgy to yield. Gender differences are as fundamental an ingredient in past liturgical life as are the ancient languages of Christian liturgy; without some familiarity with their workings, how can one adequately engage the past?

When it comes to gender-attentive readings of liturgy's past, vast areas await further study. A quick look at several subjects barely glimpsed in *Gender Differences and the Making of Liturgical History* will make this clear. First, there are the many liturgical choreographies that developed along gender-specific lines. In previous chapters, we saw hints of these choreographies in concern over the proper sequencing of adult baptisms (women after the men), over the baptism of menstruants (to be postponed), and in the rite of churching mothers (after birthgiving). Such gender-specific choreographies are evident in many other rites. One example is the choreography of prebaptismal exorcisms described in Cyril of Jerusalem's *Procatechesis*.[13] Cyril instructs those who have come to church for exorcism—during which they would be veiled—to assemble in gender-separate groups and to engage in devotional exercises that are also gender-specific. The men are encouraged to read to one another or to pray. The women, who are divided between young and married women, are encouraged to sing, pray, or read—all without being heard. Women were to engage in these devotions silently, moving their lips alone. Cyril points to Paul's injunction in 1 Cor 14:34—"women should be silent in the churches"—in explanation. The slightly different choreographies surrounding this exorcism signal gender-specific forms of liturgical presence: only men's voices should be heard in church.

Here is a liturgical fundamental that is deeply gendered, namely the worshippers' voices, a key element in active participation. This subject too deserves heightened attention. The voices of women in worship, after all, were a problem from the very beginning; that explicit injunction in a Pauline letter had made them so. Yet voices, and silence, in worship did not follow a traditional male-female divide alone.

---

[12]     John F. Baldovin, "The Uses of Liturgical History," in his *Reforming the Liturgy: A Response to the Critics* (Collegeville: Liturgical Press, 2008), 158–73, here 160.

[13]     Cyril of Jerusalem, *Procatechesis* 14; English translation, together with the Greek text, in *St. Cyril of Jerusalem's Lectures on the Christian Sacraments*, ed. F. L. Cross (reprint: Crestwood, NY: St Vladimir's Seminary Press, 1986), 48f. Veiling at exorcism is mentioned in *Procatechsis* 9.

Liturgical gender history is far more complex than that, as women's voices in convent liturgies, and the voices of castrati singers in the Sistine Chapel, illustrate.

Clothing is also an essential element of presence at worship, and a prominent marker of gender identity. Many liturgical sources through the centuries reflect concern over appropriate attire in worship, both for those in the pews and those at the altar.[14] In the Liturgical Movement of the twentieth-century, for example, some leaders criticized the breadth of "effeminate" lace in priestly vestments, while others—in an attempt to return to the earliest centuries of Christian liturgy— encouraged women to veil themselves when at worship.[15] Clothing conventions in liturgical life are always linked to broader cultural trends, but clothing—whether in the sanctuary, the marketplace, or the household—is always a marker of both gender and of status. In liturgical life (gender-specific) attire came to be inscribed in liturgical rituals themselves, from veilings and vestments to tonsures and monastic habits. Conversely, the transgression of gender-specific dress codes, for example through cross-dressing, was frowned on, from the Book of Leviticus through the Council of Gangra, to Hildegard of Bingen, and up to modern times.

Attire in worship leads to another subject that deserves scholarly attention. In cultural contexts where the sexes did not mix freely in public, mixed-gender gatherings for worship could be perceived as dangerous. Once again, this is not simply a male-female issue. Chrysostom, to name but one writer, chastizes some men for coming to church "to gape at the beauty of the women" and others for being "curious to see the blooming youth of the boys."[16]

A final subject to highlight is gendered representations of the Holy One. The issue here is not a lack of gendered images for God. Official liturgical texts routinely address God the *Father*, through his *Son*, who for our sake became *man*—making use of gendered terms throughout.[17] In other words, it was by no means feminist theologians who first forced gender into liturgical God talk in the late 1960s. God as male (e.g., as king, lord, father, shepherd) is a dominant image

---

[14]   In the summer of 2010 the Vatican made news by applying the dress code previously enforced only for those visiting Saint Peter's Basilica to all who entered Vatican City. Men in shorts, and women with bare shoulders or knees, were stopped by the Swiss guards. More at http://www.upi.com/Top_News/International/2010/07/28/Shorts-bare-shoulders-banned-in-Vatican/UPI-36851280289657/.

[15]   I documented this *in Liturgie und Frauenseele. Die Liturgische Bewegung aus der Sicht der Frauenforschung*, Praktische Theologie Heute 10 (Stuttgart: Kohlhammer Verlag, 1993), see esp. 82, 103.

[16]   John Chrysostom, *In Matthaeum homiliae* 73 (PG 58:677). Chrysostom does not stop there; the whole passage is well worth reading, especially in the forthright English translation offered by Robert Taft in "St. John Chrysostom, Preacher Committed to the Seriousness of Worship," in *The Serious Business of Worship: Essays in Honour of Bryan D. Spinks*, ed. Melanie Ross and Simon Jones (New York: Continuum, 2010), 13–21, here 16f.

[17]   As for the last of these, the Greek and Latin really demand an English translation that stresses the incarnation as God taking on human, not only male, flesh.

throughout liturgical history; yet it is not the only gendered image known in the past, and in prayers. The liturgical tradition is full of diversely gendered images for God. Rupert of Deutz (+ 1129/30), author of an allegorical exposition of the liturgy, writes of the Holy Spirit as both masculine—powerfully penetrating the soul and bringing it to ecstasy—and as feminine, hovering over the baptismal waters like a mother bird.[18] Rupert claims that the Holy Spirit as "mother" will even descend and spread her wings over those "outside of the nest of baptismal waters" if only they so desire.[19] In using both male and female images for the Holy Spirit's presence, Rupert is part of a tradition that has a broad repertoire of gendered images for God. Besides the use of both male and female metaphors, there are gender-bending ones, for example when Jesus is seen as birthing new life on the cross, or as giving his body as nourishment as a mother nurses her infant. A study of the gender-specific ways of signifying God in the liturgical tradition would also need to look at liturgy as a practice of encounter, adoration, and reverence.

My hope at this point is that the necessity for gender-attentive work in the writing of liturgical history is clear. One can summarize this necessity in the form of twin prohibitions, that is, twin commandments in a negative voice.[20] These twin commandments are:

> First, Thou shalt not write liturgical history without paying attention to gender differences. This is the first and great commandment. The second is this, Thou shalt not dishonor the diversity of gendered lives in worship.

Much would be accomplished if those writing liturgical history in the future heeded these twin commandments.

The scholarly writing of liturgy's past is part of a larger context of history-, memory-, and meaning-making in ecclesial life. In the church, a historian's voice is one among others that lay claim to the past. Among these others are theologians, the *magisterium*, i.e., the teaching authority of the church, and the liturgy itself.[21] These distinct voices do not necessarily speak the same language about the (same)

---

[18]   Rupert of Deutz, *Liber de divinis officiis*, 10.11, 7.4. No English translation of Rupert's work is available. I use the critical edition of the *Liber de divinis officiis* edited by Helmut and Ilse Deutz in the series Fontes Christiani: Zweisprachige Neuausgabe christlicher Quellentexte 33:1–4 (Freiburg i.B.: Herder, 1999).

[19]   Rupert of Deutz, *Liber de divinis officiis*, 7.4. Translation mine.

[20]   I owe this idea to Terrence Tilley's presentation at the Annual Meeting of the American Theological Society in Princeton, April 2010.

[21]   How the liturgy itself is a way of making history has been demonstrated brilliantly in Margot E. Fassler's *The Virgin of Chartres: Making History through Liturgy and the Arts* (New Haven, CT: Yale University Press, 2010).

past; neither do they claim the same authority when they speak.[22] Each is bound by slightly different authorizing audiences. Historians, as scholarly and professional "experts," are bound, *inter alia*, by the possibilities and constraints of the scholarly field they inhabit. Theologians and the teaching authority of the church are bound, *inter alia*, by the sources of the faith, especially Scripture, and the larger whole within which it is embedded, i.e., Tradition. The Spirit breathes, so Catholics are taught to hope, through them all.

The different voices (and their differing authorizing powers in the church) that lay claim to the past make scholarly inquiry into liturgy's past a challenging task. Mark Jordan, in his essay titled "Arguing Liturgical Genealogies," pointed to one such challenge by asking about the power of historiographic work in contemporary gender issues in the church. He writes, "why fret about a more exact history when the real fight is over the institutions that will determine what counts as church history—and who gets to be counted in?"[23] Unquestioningly, this is a vexing issue. So is the question of the authorizing power of "a more exact history." Even at its most "exact," such history after all never maps neatly onto the reality of the past but remains on the level of representation and interpretation. Granted that Jordan is primarily concerned with institutional power here (and rightly so), the implied division of labor—namely the struggle for a more "exact" history, and the struggle over the meaning of the past—deserves to be questioned. The two struggles are more intertwined than an unambiguous division—history to the historians, theology to the theologians, authoritative definitions to the *magisterium*—allows for, even if such an unambiguous division holds explanatory power. For historians of liturgy, Paul Bradshaw formulated this division of labor thus: "The task of the liturgical historian … is only to show how and why practices have changed: it is for the church to determine whether and how they should do so again."[24] In reality, this precise division of labor does not function quite so precisely. Behind Bradshaw's own booklet on liturgical presiding, in which he made this claim, stood not only his scholarly curiosity but also larger ecclesial questions about liturgical presidency that had become virulent. Conversely, if the *magisterium* builds an argument for a particular practice on an image of the past that historical research proves to be inadequate, then this research creates a degree of pressure.

---

[22] On this important subject see Terrence W. Tilley, *History, Theology, and Faith: Dissolving the Modern Problematic* (Maryknoll, NY: Orbis Books, 2004), esp. 142–91; and the essays in *Historiographie und Theologie: Kirchen- und Theologiegeschichte im Spannungsfeld von geschichtswissenschaftlicher Methode und theologischem Anspruch*, eds. Wolfram Kinzig et al., Arbeiten zur Kirchen- und Theologiegeschichte 15 (Leipzig: Evangelische Verlagsanstalt, 2004).

[23] See his essay "Arguing Liturgical Genealogies, or the Ghost of Weddings Past," in *Canon, Tradition, and Critique in the Blessing of Same-Sex Unions,* ed. Mark D. Jordan et al. (Princeton: Princeton University Press, 2006), 102–20, here 112.

[24] Paul F. Bradshaw, *Liturgical Presidency in the Early Church*, Grove Liturgical Study 36 (Bramcote: Grove Books, 1983), 28.

Such pressure does not have to be interpreted negatively, i.e., as challenging the teaching authority of the church, but can be seen as creating freedom, space, and impetus for movement and change.

There is a way to elucidate the intertwining of these two struggles—for a more "exact" history, and over the meaning of the past—in relation to the present book. Arguably, *Gender Differences and the Making of Liturgical History*, by insisting that gender differences are critically important issues for liturgical historiography, is not about the interpretive power of gender history alone. Using the tools of gender history, as I have maintained throughout this book, is also about liturgical and theological commitments that happen to be well served by this historiographic work. An example is the importance, in liturgy, of truthful ἀνάμνησις. Such *anamnesis*—i.e., the presence, in retelling, of God's redemptive power in history— plays a fundamental role in the liturgical assembly. Narrating the past was always a fundamental liturgical act, long before it became the scholarly focus of professional historians. Psalms in the Hebrew Bible that retell the history of Israel (e.g., Ps 78) are an early example of this intertwining of liturgy and historical memory. A contemporary example comes in a song by John L. Bell of the Iona Community titled "God It Was." In this song Bell remembers God's collaborators in the past, and names them in evenly divided pairs of men and women (which they are not in Scripture). Thus, Abraham is paired with Sarah, Moses with Miriam, Joseph with Mary, and Matthew with Martha.[25] Bell here re-reads and re-shapes the biblical memory in light of the theological conviction that God does not really privilege male collaborators in the workings of redemption even if the Scriptures mostly remember their side of the story. (That gender is not so clearly and simply balanced in real lived life, and that there are human beings who are intersexed, is occluded in this seemingly inclusive vision of salvation history.)

The theological question underneath all this is the following: what if liturgical memory, and with it the *anamnesis* of God's life-giving presence in this world, happens to be shrouded, for example in a pointedly androcentric narrative? To be more precise, what if the narrative is flawed beyond what any human attempt at retelling God's redemptive presence in time must be? One response to this question is to interpret the historiographic inquiry of the present book as positive liturgical work. The labor of interrogating narratives of the past, of identifying flaws, and of striving for the most truthful narrative possible is not only a historian's scholarly responsibility but also an important part of liturgical reflection and practice. At the same time, a more nuanced retelling of the past, even with its dual historiographical and liturgical commitments, is only one of the consequences of lifting a veil on liturgy's past. The second consequence is of equal importance, and of even deeper dispute. It concerns what comes to be construed as tradition in the life of the church.

---

[25]     Bell's text "God It Was" can be found in *RitualSong: A Hymnal and Service Book for Roman Catholics* (Chicago: GIA Publications, 1996), # 818.

## Liturgical Tradition: What Happens When *Lex Orandi* and Gender History Meet?

In a wide-ranging essay titled "The Apostolic Tradition" Maxwell Johnson traces the worship practices of early Christian communities. Over and against the scholarship of a previous generation, Johnson stresses the fragmentary and disparate nature of the evidence, and insists on a non-unified and non-linear narrative of early Christian liturgical practices. Where previous scholars had sketched a history of increasing diversity from a unified "apostolic" beginning, Johnson begins from an irreducible diversity of local practices, and identifies the formative fourth century as a time when disparate local practices were increasingly brought into conformity with larger ecclesial structures and practices, a process that had both unifying and cross-fertilizing consequences. At the end of his essay Johnson turns to a fundamental theological question raised by this revisionist historiography: what happens to conventional theological appeals to liturgical tradition (especially in that tradition's earliest apostolic contours) when the historiographic ground shifts and fragments under the theologian's feet? As Johnson acknowledges: "It has become extraordinarily difficult in the light of contemporary scholarship to say clearly from within this formative period of the first three centuries what [the tradition] actually is."[26]

Johnson's concern over what happens with theological appeals to liturgical tradition when the very image of the past—on whose basis we ascertain the tradition in the first place—is rewritten also underlies *Gender Differences and the Making of Liturgical History*. My concern, however, is not so much with one particular historical period, e.g., early Christianity, but with the whole of liturgy's past, and with the way gender has been occluded as a fundamental part of that history. The stakes are thus high indeed in *Gender Differences and the Making of Liturgical History* since basic contours of the historical narrative are in question. In addition to the sheer historiographic reach of this issue, the very understanding of tradition, in the sense of authorizing claims on the past, demands attention. And the nature of tradition has been fiercely argued in the past decades, in both constructive theology and in ecclesial life more generally.[27]

In order to clear a path for my concern here – namely authorizing claims to liturgical tradition when these claims are confronted with gender-attentive reconfigurations of the past—I begin with a look at conventional appeals to a seemingly un-gendered liturgical tradition. This analysis will demonstrate that

---

[26]    Maxwell E. Johnson, "The Apostolic Tradition," in *The Oxford History of Christian Worship*, ed. Geoffrey Wainwright and Karen B. Westerfield Tucker (New York: Oxford University Press, 2006), 2–75, here 67.

[27]    The literature on the subject is extensive; a helpful entry into the field is *Tradition and Tradition Theories: An International Discussion*, ed. Thorsten Larbig and Siegfried Wiedenhofer (Berlin: LIT Verlag, 2006), especially the essays by Kathryn Tanner and Terrence Tilley (both with substantial bibliographies).

re-writing liturgical history in gender-attentive ways responds to a distinct problem that has become more pressing since liturgy was rediscovered as a theological source in the course of the twentieth century.

*The Recovery of Liturgical Tradition as a Theological Source*

During the second half of the twentieth century theologians from quite different ecclesial traditions began to reclaim liturgy as a fundamental site for understanding and interpreting the Christian faith. These "liturgical" theologians often validated their turn to liturgy by a shorthand version of a Patristic axiom, *lex orandi, lex credendi*.[28] The terse Latin can be translated in a number of ways: The law of praying is the law of believing. Or, worship shapes faith. Or, as you pray, so you believe. Most theologians, in their rediscovery of liturgy as a theological site, drew on an image of liturgy's past as they knew (or imagined) it, leaving aside important questions surfacing in liturgical historiography at the time. Not surprisingly, theological appeals to the liturgical past continued to occlude the prayers and practices of women, which were being rediscovered at the time.[29]

The reigning consensus among these theologians that gender differences were marginal—a consensus established largely through silence—thus marked the theological recourse to "liturgical tradition" or *lex orandi*. The reasons for this occlusion of gender are manifold, but three factors stand out. First, since in most liturgical historiography, the "facts" continued to be gender-devoid—with little recognition that what comes to be counted as "fact" is always theory-specific[30]—theological claims to liturgical tradition carried forward this occlusion. Theologians who base their appeal to liturgical tradition on a (seemingly) gender-less history cannot help but reproduce the weaknesses and misrepresentations of this problematic construal of the past.

In a second step, gender occlusion is sharpened by the theological claims based on liturgical tradition. On the whole, appeals to liturgical tradition have authorized traditionalist arguments, i.e., arguments based on a very narrow recourse to the past.[31] In a satirical essay, Ronald Grimes remarked that the theological recourse

---

[28]   I have dealt with this in more detail in my *Theology in Hymns? A Study of the Relationship of Doxology and Theology according to "A Collection of Hymns for the Use of the People called Methodists" (1780)* (Nashville, TN: Abingdon, 1995), ch. 2.

[29]   For important exceptions to the wide-spread occlusion of gender in liturgical theologies see, for example, Gordon Lathrop, *Holy People: A Liturgical Ecclesiology* (Minneapolis: Fortress Press, 1999), esp. 36f, 128f, 179; a longer list would have to include the writings of Louis-Marie Chauvet, Bruce T. Morrill, and Susan A. Ross.

[30]   This concise formulation is Linda McDowell's in *Gender, Identity and Place: Understanding Feminist Geographies* (Minneapolis: University of Minnesota Press, 1999), 227.

[31]   See Rebecca Lyman, "Lex orandi: Heresy, Orthodoxy, and Popular Religion," in *The Making and Remaking of Christian Doctrine*, ed. Sarah Coakley and David A. Pailin

to liturgical tradition has primarily engendered forms of "liturgical erectitude."[32] Conversely, one does not usually encounter the liturgical tradition as an authorizing source in appeals for the ordination of women or of noncelibate gay men. Yet even the traditionalist version of the past is anything but gender-devoid, as the strong insistence on priestly masculinity and celibacy shows.

This recognition leads to a third point. Despite a seemingly gender-free recourse to liturgical tradition, the claim to liturgy as a theological site cannot but produce its own forms of gendered discourse. The *norma patrum,* the "ancient norm of the *fathers,*"[33] is inherently gendered. In a more recent example, Aidan Kavanagh's reflections on the distinction between *lex orandi* as a form of "primary" theology, and *lex credendi* as a form of "secondary" theology, invoke a "Mrs. Murphy" in the pew as the one who engages in primary theology.[34] The secondary theologian was tacitly coded as male. It does not take a gender historian to realize that most Mrs. Murphy analogies involved gender stereotypes.[35] With these gendered metaphors at the heart of a theological claim, a seemingly natural alliance was established between, on the one-hand, women, *lex orandi,* and non-scholarly "liturgical experience," and, on the other, men, *lex credendi,* and scholarly reflection on liturgy. As with other forms of traditional epistemology, theological recourse to the liturgy was gendered, with the privileged aspects of knowledge coded as masculine, while the non-reflective emotions and the body were gendered feminine.

*Glimpses of Lex Orandi, with a Lifted Veil*

My critical account of theological claims to *lex orandi* should not be understood as a rejection of liturgical tradition as a fundamental theological site. Quite the opposite is true. Especially with recent work on a theology of tradition, understood

---

(Oxford: Clarendon Press, 1993), 131–41, here 138f.

[32]   Ronald L. Grimes, "Liturgical Supinity, Liturgical Erectitude: On the Embodiment of Ritual Authority," *Studia Liturgica* 23 (1993): 51–69.

[33]   In the Bull promulgating the 1570 *Missale Romanum,* Pope Pius V invoked a return to the "norm of the fathers" as the principle of reform (*"ad pristinam Missale ipsum sanctorum Patrum normam ac ritum restituerunt"*).

[34]   See Aidan Kavanagh, *On Liturgical Theology* (New York: Pueblo, 1984), 146f. That describing Mrs. Murphy as a "primary theologian" was meant positively, as a way of empowering women in the pews, becomes clearer if one takes into account that "little old ladies praying the rosary in the pews" routinely served as a stereotype for what the Liturgical Movement sought to overcome, namely individualized prayer during Mass rather than praying the Mass. Against that backdrop Kavanagh's turn to a "Mrs. Murphy" who practiced "primary theology" was startling.

[35]   See Paul V. Marshall, "Reconsidering 'Liturgical Theology': Is there a *Lex Orandi* for all Christians?," *Studia Liturgica* 25 (1995): 129–51, here 147. For a feminist analysis, see Ninna Edgardh Beckman, "Mrs Murphy's Arising from the Pew: Ecclesiological Implications," *The Ecumenical Review* 53 (2001): 5–13.

as a set of practices rather than a list of presuppositions to be repeated, liturgy is a key site for this construal of tradition. Moreover, if bodily practices are crucial to how communities remember, as Paul Connerton has argued, then the age-old bodily practice of liturgical assembly is, indeed, a key feature both of the past and of authorizing claims to it.[36]

Once liturgy as bodily practice comes to the fore, gender differences invariably come into view.[37] This raises a theological question, left unanswered by a deepened historical vision alone: What does a gender-attentive narrative of the past have to offer with regard to theological appeals to liturgical tradition? Three key contributions stand out.

First, a gender-attentive—and thereby fuller—historiography should prevent future recourse to seemingly ungendered "facts" of the past. This historiography thus contributes to unmasking half-truths, especially if those half-truths are created by resounding silence about other truths. Liturgy's past is both richly diverse and deeply gendered; truthful theological recourse to it dare not veil this. As Maxwell Johnson's essay on the first three centuries of Christian liturgy illustrates so well, the origins of the liturgical tradition lie in an irreducible diversity of local practices. A stable, unified apostolic tradition in the form of a material deposit of "liturgy" is simply not available. Johnson notes that this historical insight renders it difficult "to say clearly from within this formative period of the first three centuries what [the tradition] actually is."[38] Yet if tradition is above all a set of practices, then an apostolic, irreducible diversity of local practices might well *be* the normative shape of the liturgical tradition in this, its earliest stage. What can be identified as *constant* in this liturgical tradition is its constant change of contours. Eamon Duffy's description of tradition as a "living and liberating testimony to the multiple and unending transformations of [the church] in its journey through times and cultures" expresses well both the dawn and the unfolding of liturgy's past.[39]

A second contribution of a gender-attentive narrative of the past lies in the depiction of gender-specific constraints as well as gender-based sites of power and agency in worship. That is to say, neither a one-dimensional narrative of liturgy's past as "oppressive" (e.g., to women, or to gay men), nor of liturgy as

---

[36]   See Paul Connerton's influential book, *How Societies Remember*, Themes in the Social Sciences (New York: Cambridge University Press, 1989). Connerton's notion of bodily practices as a key ingredient in memory and thus in tradition has become theologically fruitful in, for example, the work of Terrence W. Tilley, *Inventing Catholic Tradition* (Maryknoll, NY: Orbis Books, 2000), and of Mary McClintock Fulkerson, *Places of Redemption: Theology for a Worldly Church* (New York: Oxford University Press, 2007).

[37]   See several of the essays in *Bodies of Worship: Explorations in Theory and Practice*, ed. Bruce T. Morrill (Collegeville: Liturgical Press, 1999).

[38]   Johnson, "Apostolic Tradition," 67.

[39]   Eamon Duffy, *Faith of Our Fathers: Reflections on Catholic Tradition* (New York: Continuum, 2004), 179. I have substituted "church" for Duffy's "Catholicism" in order that his description will not seem anachronistic for the earliest centuries.

nothing but "communion in the divine life,"[40] is easily sustainable on the basis of this historiography. Liturgy's past is too messy, too unevenly gendered, and too idiosyncratic for such narratives. Even if one grants that the heart of liturgical tradition is not its messiness but its "inner side" (Hugo Rahner), an insistent haunting will have to be inscribed into all appeals to this site. Such an insistent haunting is present in all Christian faith claims that speak of a God who entrusts the witness to the Word of Life to such very earthen vessels: ancient (mostly androcentric) Hebrew stories of deliverance; the body of a young girl pregnant with Holiness beyond all telling; bread and wine produced by human labor which is always marked by inequalities, be they of gender, status, ethnicity, ability, or age. We might say that deeply inscribed into the doing of theology—and especially the move from historical narrative to the authority of tradition—needs to be a profound and continuing restlessness.

We do well to acknowledge and bless such continuing restlessness, because what liturgy's past offers—for the construal of the church's *lex orandi*—is not without its own deeply gendered problems. The voices of the past are mostly male, elite male. To put it in musical language, professionally-trained tenor and bass dominate. The liturgical tradition as we know it took shape in centuries when women, in worship, were to be mostly passive and receptive, especially to the seminal pronouncements of priestly men. Eunuchs and *castrati* were all but forgotten in the construal of liturgy's past, although they died as martyrs, served as bishops and archbishops, lived saintly lives, and sang in the Sistine Chapel Choir until just a hundred years ago.

Of course the Holy Spirit can work through such a messily gendered past. The Spirit's workings ultimately cannot be fettered by past or present gender systems. Yet the same Spirit also calls the church into an ever-deeper understanding of life and truth. Why not understand scholarly work on liturgy's past as part of that larger movement? We might then calmly claim the rich diversity of liturgy's past and of the liturgical tradition in all its complexity, oddity, and strangeness as veiling the presence of the Holy Spirit in the church on its journey through time.

This claim and its necessary twin, the continuing restlessness in appeals to liturgy's past, also yield an important insight into the nature of liturgical tradition. What becomes visible and authorized as *lex orandi* in the life of the church is not only the result of a gathering of fragments, a *bricolage*.[41] The church's *lex orandi*, moreover, is living and expanding, rather than fixed once for all, and thus is open

[40]　Thus the *Catechism of the Catholic Church* (Vatican City: Libreria Editrice Vaticana; Washington, DC: United States Catholic Conference, 2nd rev. edition 2000), # 1324f.

[41]　Vincent Miller takes up the notion of *bricolage* from Michel de Certeau in his *Consuming Religion: Christian Faith and Practice in a Consumer Culture* (New York: Continuum, 2005), esp. 174–6.

to rereadings and new understandings.[42] The activity of "traditioning," then, is an ongoing, situated, and interested mode of knowing that selects, orders, and interprets.[43] In this light, we might argue that rescuing the liturgical tradition in all its richness and ambiguity from traditionalist shortcuts is a form of profound faithfulness to the tradition.

To recapitulate: out of what is visible of the past, the church continues to lay claim to a particular construal of its past, that is, tradition, understood as Spirit-inspired and Spirit-sustained. Such a tradition cannot safely rest in accounts of the past that themselves are not safe, for example because they are based on gender-oblivious—and therefore by default androcentric—memories. Even if we acknowledge that fully knowing "the truth" about the past is an impossibility, the unmasking of half-truths that pretend (if only through silence) to be all that needs to be said remains of fundamental importance. Peter Jeffery has demonstrated this in a piercing reading of the Vatican's Instruction *Liturgiam Authenticam*. It is hard to imagine a more devastating assessment of a document that appeals to the Roman liturgical tradition than that its historical claims are "parahistorical" and even "positively fanciful."[44] Jeffery hints at the positive point of his critique when he insists: "the people who wrote [*Liturgiam Authenticam*] are seriously misinformed about the historical development of *the tradition they call on us to preserve*."[45] That is to say, appeals for the preservation of liturgical tradition cannot be grounded in historical deception. Why, then, not think of such unmasking of historically deceptive appeals to liturgical tradition as Spirit-inspired? Not least the display of the messy ways in which gender differences shaped liturgy's past may well be a part of vibrant ecclesial discernment today.

### The Past's Presence, or Offering a History of Gender Trouble to Liturgical Life Today

Just as the writing of church history is never merely about the past, so also theological claims are never merely about theology. Both of these interested modes of knowing usually involve struggles in ecclesial life. Gary Macy has put this point well: "Every single history that historians write exists in the present. Every history that is still read, is read in the present. ... history exists because

---

[42]    For a more detailed account of tradition in this vein see Kathryn Tanner, *Theories of Culture: A New Agenda for Theology*, Guides to Theological Inquiry Series (Minneapolis: Fortress Press, 1997), 128–38.

[43]    Cf. Susan Stanford Friedman, *Mappings: Feminism and the Cultural Geographies of Encounter* (Princeton, NJ: Princeton University Press, 1998), 200f.

[44]    Peter Jeffery, *Translating Tradition: A Chant Historian Reads* Liturgiam Authenticam (Collegeville: Liturgical Press, 2005), 65.

[45]    Ibid., 17. Emphasis mine.

of present interests."[46] This is true also of *Gender Differences and the Making of Liturgical History*. In the context in which this book has taken shape, issues of gender and liturgical practice are not safely in the past. In fact, if my sense of the fundamental importance of gendered embodiment in liturgical practice is right, gender will never be an issue of liturgy's past only.

Given the sustained crisis of traditional gender systems over the past century, it is not surprising that gender-specific struggles related to liturgical life and practice continue to make headlines. Among these struggles are questions over the ordination of women (whether to the diaconate, priesthood, or episcopate) and the ordination of noncelibate gays, as well as over the blessing of same-sex unions and marriages. And these are only the most public issues involving gender and liturgical practice in the churches today.[47] Some churches also continue to struggle over inclusive language, others over gender-separate seating, women's headcoverings, and liturgical taboos related to bodily fluids. Some churches are concerned about their own feminization and explore a more "muscular" spirituality. In short, in contemporary liturgical life gender concerns are present in a multitude of configurations. One would have to wear a very thick veil indeed not to see this.

What I wish to highlight here are not the public, and hotly debated, issues of the day but rather those where gender deeply shapes liturgical practice, mostly without being recognized. Highlighting these areas demonstrates how gender continues to be embedded in the basics of what we know as liturgy, not only in specific contemporary contestations. Furthermore, this gendering of the church's liturgy will remain even when contemporary struggles over specific issues have become part of the church's past. This continuous deep gendering (a "constant tradition") can, however, be named and acknowledged. In what follows, I illustrate this with two examples: the gendered nature of what we encounter as the Word of God in worship, and the nature of the communion of saints as it is enshrined in the liturgical calendar.

*The Word in Worship, Marked by Gender*

A profound gender-specific asymmetry is embedded in how most liturgical assemblies encounter and hear the Word of God in worship. This asymmetry is rooted in the Scriptures and heightened by the other voices that condition an assembly's hearing of the biblical word. Simply put, the Bible—the most important liturgical book—privileges male actors and voices in telling the story of God's redemptive presence in history. For example, of the nearly three hundred instances of actual prayers or allusions to prayer in the Hebrew Bible, only about ten are

---

[46]   Gary Macy, "The Future of the Past: What Can the [sic] History Say about Symbol and Ritual?," in *Practicing Catholic: Ritual, Body, and Contestation in Catholic Faith*, ed. Bruce T. Morrill (Gordonsville, VA: Palgrave Macmillan, 2006), 29–41, here 29f.

[47]   One might also include the sexual abuse of minors by priests here, but the central site of this scandal is not really the liturgical realm.

clearly those of women.[48] Must we assume that women in times past invoked the Holy One less frequently than did their male counterparts?

The irrevocably androcentric voice of the biblical witness is heightened by the choice of passages for reading in worship. Thus, the lectionary for Sunday Masses in the Roman Catholic Church does not attend carefully enough to biblical stories about women.[49] One example of the omission of biblical women's stories in this lectionary must suffice. The story of the two Hebrew midwives, Shiphrah and Puah, who set the scene for the Exodus by defying pharaoh, is simply cut out of the liturgical reading of Exod 1:8–22. As a result, a liturgical assembly will not hear the story or the names of these two women—although, in an irony of history, the biblical writer mentioned both women by name while obliterating the name of "the pharaoh." The lectionary reading lets worshippers know about this pharaoh while hiding the two Hebrew women who defied him.

A third way in which gender shapes the hearing of the Word of God in worship involves the translations of the biblical texts. Translation is no innocent or gender-neutral enterprise. A biblical woman "lost in translation" is the apostle Junia. This Junia, according to Paul (Rom 16:7), was "prominent among the apostles" and "in Christ" before he himself embraced the faith. Commentators initially praised this Junia as a female apostle, but later interpreted the Greek name to refer to a male Junias, although such a male name is unknown in Greek.[50] Only recently have interpreters come to acknowledge the name, once again, as that of a woman apostle, Junia.

A fourth way in which gender shapes the Word of God heard in the liturgical assembly is tied to the gender of the one who expounds the Scriptures in the homily. The homilist, for much of the past and still today, has been male, because the authority to preach was routinely linked with liturgical, priestly, male office. This link continues to mark the majority of Christian communities today.

So much for the example of the Word of God heard in worship. The following example substantiates the finding that today, as in the past, liturgical practice is deeply affected by gender differences and their historical asymmetries.

---

[48] See Patrick D. Miller, "Things Too Wonderful: Prayers of Women in the Old Testament," in *Biblische Theologie und gesellschaftlicher Wandel*, ed. Georg Braulik et al. (Freiburg: Herder, 1993) 237–51, here 237.

[49] I am using the table of readings from Sundays, Solemnities, Feasts of the Lord and the Saints, vol. 1 of *Lectionary for Mass for Use in the Dioceses of the United States of America*, Second Typical Edition (Collegeville: Liturgical Press, 1998). The issue of women and the word in worship is covered in more detail in my *Fragments of Real Presence: Liturgical Traditions in the Hands of Women* (New York: Crossroad, 2005), 26–36.

[50] Bernadette J. Brooten, "Junia," in *Women in Scripture: A Dictionary of Named and Unnamed Women in the Hebrew Bible, the Apocryphal/Deuterocanonical Books, and the New Testament*, ed. Carol Meyers, Toni Craven, and Ross Shepard Kraemer (Boston: Houghton Mifflin Company, 2000), 107.

## Liturgical Memory, Saints, and Sexual Difference

That liturgical memory is deeply affected by gender differences and their historical asymmetries was evident in the sanctoral cycle long before gender scholarship itself took shape. Even with the increasing diversity of models of sanctity evident in recent canonizations, we continue to find a numerical imbalance between men and women officially recognized as saints. The sanctoral cycle, quite simply, privileges male versions of the holy life.[51] This privileging of male saints is particularized, with a disproportionate number of male saints being priests and/or religious. This means that dominant in the communion of saints encountered in the liturgy is priestly and religious masculinity. This observation is substantiated by the liturgical ranking of days in the sanctoral cycle. The highest rank in the liturgical calendar for a female saint (leaving aside Mary, the Mother of God) is that of a memorial; no feasts or solemnities are associated with a woman saint.[52] Feasts and solemnities of male saints abound: Saint Joseph, Saints Peter and Paul, as well as the Nativity of Saint John the Baptist are celebrated as solemnities, as are all feast days of the apostles. At stake in these rankings is not only the status of a feast day within the liturgical calendar, but the richness of its celebration (including prayer texts, readings, and vigils), which differs according to rank.

A further indicator that gender shapes the liturgical memory of the saints comes in the official titles added to saints' names. The prevalence of the descriptor "virgin" for women saints (and not only religious women[53]) and its absence as a title for male saints is a case in point.[54] The liturgical memory of holy women routinely ties

---

[51]  I focus on the Roman Catholic sanctoral cycle here. On this, see Michael D. Whalen, "In the Company of Women? The Politics of Memory in the Liturgical Commemoration of Saints—Male and Female," *Worship* 73 (1999): 482–504; Ruth Fox, "Women in the Bible and the Lectionary," in *Remembering the Women: Women's Stories from Scripture for Sundays and Festivals*, comp. and annot. J. Frank Henderson (Chicago: LTP, 1999), 359–67; and Irmgard Pahl, "'Eine starke Frau, wer wird sie finden?' Aspekte des Frauenbildes in den Meßformularen der Heiligenfeste," in *Liturgie und Frauenfrage: Ein Beitrag zur Frauenforschung aus liturgiewissenschaftlicher Sicht*, ed. Teresa Berger and Albert Gerhards, Pietas Liturgica 7 (St. Ottilien: EOS-Verlag, 1990), 433–52.

[52]  Exceptions are women saints who are principal patronesses of a place or a religious order, in which case their memorials may be celebrated as feasts or solemnities. I am grateful to Karl Liam Saur for pointing this out.

[53]  Saint Martha of Bethany (memorial on July 29) and Saint Maria Goretti (optional memorial on July 6) are examples of this. Saint Bridget of Sweden (optional memorial on July 23), on the other hand, is named "religious" rather than "virgin" since she followed a religious vocation after marriage and motherhood.

[54]  This holds true even if we acknowledge that the understanding of virginity, as of all gendered identities, is ever-changing. Thus, "the concept of virginity encompassed a range of meanings well beyond the simple inviolate female body, the sealed vessel." See Samantha J. E. Riches, "St. George as a Male Virgin Martyr," in *Gender and Holiness: Men, Women, and Saints in Late Medieval Europe*, ed. Samantha J. E. Riches and Sarah

their sanctity to an "intact" virginal body. The title *doctor ecclesiae*, on the other hand, is given mostly to male saints, among whom bishops predominate (20 out of the 30 male *doctores ecclesiae* were bishops). Only after Vatican II were women accorded that rank; currently three out of the 33 official "teachers of the church" are women, all of them religious, who are also recognized as "virgins" (Teresa of Avila, Catherine of Siena, and Thérèse of Lisieux).[55]

Other virtues displayed in holy lives are also gender-specific. Men typically are depicted as embodying spiritual authority, active self-mastery, heroic faith, and theological learning. Women, besides safeguarding their virginal bodies, are more often revered for embodying longsuffering, compassion, obedience, and humility. Furthermore, female bodies are the site of the struggle for holiness in ways male bodies are not.[56] Thus, narratives of women saints in general are more focused on the body—on hair, bleeding, illness, wounds, stigmata, scars, and extra-ordinary bodily postures such as swooning, swelling, levitating, and "seeing." Even where the body becomes the site of holy struggle for both male and female saints, this struggle takes gender-specific forms. Saint Francis of Assisi, for example, renounced the world by undressing in broad daylight and in public; Saint Clare of Assisi renounced the world by having her hair shorn by Francis at night, in a little chapel at the outskirts of the city.

Gender-specific devotional practices are also evident in the making of holy lives. Living by eucharistic bread alone is a practice rarely found in the lives of male saints.[57] Since the majority of these male saints were priests (including holy bishops and popes), the equivalent devotional practice is a life marked by reverent, frequent presiding at Mass.

The liturgical tradition as we know it privileges the lives of priestly and religious men. Can we assume that the struggle for holiness was so unevenly and gender-specifically successful? Presumably, reasons for the gendered particularities and

---

Salih, Routledge Studies in Medieval Religion and Culture 1 (New York: Routledge, 2002), 65–85, here 68.

[55] Important in the addition of these women to the *doctores ecclesiae* was the implicit acknowledgement that the teaching charism specific to doctors is independent of ordination and hierarchical position. For more on this, see Bernard McGinn, *The Doctors of the Church: Thirty-Three Men and Women Who Shaped Christianity* (New York: Crossroad, 1999), esp. 3, 18–20.

[56] See Catherine M. Mooney, "Voice, Gender, and the Portrayal of Sanctity," in *Gendered Voices: Medieval Saints and Their Interpreters*, ed. Catherine M. Mooney, The Middle Ages Series (Philadelphia: University of Pennsylvania Press, 1999), 1–15, esp. 7.

[57] For more on this, see Caroline Walker Bynum, "Women Mystics and Eucharistic Devotion in the Thirteenth Century," in *Fragmentation and Redemption: Essays on Gender and the Human Body in Medieval Religion*, 3rd ed. (New York: Zone Books, 1994), 119–50; and Peter Browe, "Die Kommunion der Heiligen im Mittelalter," in *Die Eucharistie im Mittelalter: Liturgiehistorische Forschungen in kulturwissenschaftlicher Absicht*, ed. Hubertus Lutterbach and Thomas Flammer, Vergessene Theologen 1 (Münster: LIT Verlag, 2003), 199–209.

imbalances of the sanctoral cycle must be located elsewhere than in men's greater success at holy living. A primary location is the formation of the liturgical memory of the saints. The authors of authenticating narratives of holiness, especially the *vitae* of the saints, are overwhelmingly men, and priestly men for that matter. This is the case even for the *vitae* of holy women; a priestly male gaze usually controls the textualization of female lives of holiness.[58] Rare is the saint's life in which a female "voice" can actually be heard, at least before modern times.[59]

How gender differences shape the textualization of holy lives is a complex question. One line of inquiry has argued that male saints are more likely to have a story of sudden conversion and renunciation of power, status, and sexuality than female saints because, historically, men had more power to determine the shape of their own lives than women, who, for the most part, controlled neither property nor their own sexuality.[60] Caroline Walker Bynum has put this succinctly for medieval lives of holiness: "each gender renounced and distributed what it most effectively controlled: men gave up money, property, and progeny; women gave up food."[61]

A weakness of this approach is its reliance on the traditional gender binary, when other gender constructions such as eunuch saints need to be taken into account.[62] In addition, a focus on the traditional gender binary can occlude both the differences among men themselves (as also those between women) as well as the complex interplay between men and women in constructing lives of holiness.[63] Finally, there is the importance of intersectionality, that is, of the recognition that gender always intersects with other markers of difference. Scholars so far have primarily concentrated on status and class in the study of hagiography, but

---

[58] The difficult subject of the differences between women saints' own voices (that is, where we have access to them) and the representation by their male interpreters has received attention in recent years. See John W. Coakley, *Women, Men, and Spiritual Power: Female Saints and Their Male Collaborators* (New York: Columbia University Press, 2006); and Catherine M. Mooney, "Voice, Gender, and the Portrayal of Sanctity," 1–15.

[59] For an exception see Jocelyn Wogan-Browne, *Saints' Lives and Women's Literary Culture, c. 1150–1300: Virginity and its Authorizations* (New York: Oxford University Press, 2001), 227–45.

[60] See Sarah Salih, "Staging Conversion: The Digby Saint Plays and *The Book of Margery Kempe*," in *Gender and Holiness*, 121–34, for a glimpse of this theory and a partial exception to it.

[61] Caroline Walker Bynum, *Holy Feast and Holy Fast: The Religious Significance of Food to Medieval Women* (Berkeley: University of California Press, 1987), 193.

[62] On this, see Shaun Tougher, "Holy Eunuchs! Masculinity and Eunuch Saints in Byzantium," in *Holiness and Masculinity in the Middle Ages*, ed. P. H. Cullum and Katherine J. Lewis (Toronto: University of Toronto Press, 2005), 93–108.

[63] See esp. Coakley, *Women, Men, and Spiritual Power*, and the essays in *Gender and Holiness*.

ethnicity and colonial subject positions must also have shaped the making of saints and their memories.[64]

Recent scholarship agrees that scripts of sanctity are influenced by broader cultural gender constructions.[65] For much of the history of Christianity, "woman" was seen as the weaker sex, and her body "lacking" in comparison with the male body—a culturally longstanding, prominent gender theory. Thus in the liturgy, women's lives of holiness merited special praise, because women had to overcome a weaker, more sensual, and less rational nature than did their male counterparts. The peculiar challenges for women meant that the making of a woman into a saint testified in a particularly convincing way to the power of divine grace—and even more so if the woman was a repentant prostitute, a "magdalene." Yet representations of sanctity are not stable. They have shifted significantly through the centuries; and saints' lives have been read and reread in new ways by successive generations.[66]

Granted that the grammar of sanctity is often shaped by broader cultural gender constructions, we must also acknowledge the opposite. The call to a life of holiness can function as a powerful challenge to established gender identities and their cultural codes. In fact, "sainthood often works by breaking with normal social values, and gendered identity may be amongst these: constructing one's gender identity differently may be a marker of holiness."[67] The liturgical memory of the saints knows such moments of gender-bending, gender-crossing, and gender slippage, for example early Syrian male ascetics who were rendered as

---

[64]    For a glimpse of this subject, see *Colonial Saints: Discovering the Holy in the Americas, 1500–1800*, ed. Allan Greer and Jodi Bilinkoff (New York: Routledge, 2003).

[65]    For more on this, see Susan Ashbrook Harvey, "Women in Early Byzantine Hagiography: Reversing the Story," in *That Gentle Strength: Historical Perspectives on Women in Christianity*, ed. Lynda L. Coon, Katherine J. Haldane, and Elisabeth W. Sommer (Charlottesville: University Press of Virginia, 1990), 36–59; Lynda L. Coon, *Sacred Fictions: Holy Women and Hagiography in Late Antiquity*, The Middle Ages Series (Philadelphia: University of Pennsylvania Press, 1997), 71–94; and Elizabeth Castelli, "'I Will Make Mary Male': Pieties of the Body and Gender Transformation of Christian Women in Late Antiquity," in *Body Guards: The Cultural Politics of Gender Ambiguity*, ed. Julia Epstein and Kristina Straub (New York: Routledge, 1991), 29–49.

[66]    See Diane L. Mockridge, "Marital Imagery in Six Late Twelfth- and Early Thirteenth-Century Vitae of Female Saints," in *That Gentle Strength*, 60–78, and Carolyn Muessig, "Paradigms of Sanctity for Thirteenth-Century Women," in *Models of Holiness in Medieval Sermons: Proceedings of the International Symposium* (*Kalamazoo, 4–7 May 1995*), ed. Beverly Mayne Kienzle et al., Textes et études du Moyen Age 5 (Louvain-la-Neuve: Fédération internationale des instituts d'études médiévales, 1996), 85–102.

[67]    Samantha J. E. Riches and Sarah Salih, introduction to *Gender and Holiness*, 5. The cover of their book puts it succinctly: "the pursuit of holiness can destabilize a binary conception of gender. Though saints may be classified as masculine or feminine, holiness may also cut across gender divisions and demand a break from normally gendered behavior."

insatiable, receptive, passionate bridal lovers of God,[68] transvestite saints, and men who submitted to the spiritual powers of holy women. Holy lives, in other words, with all their traditionally gendered scripts, also embodied their own profound challenges to the living of gendered identity.

I have here inquired in some detail into how gender shaped the sanctoral cycle because the church's memory of the saints is an important part of liturgical tradition. In addition, the liturgical veneration of the saints shows so very clearly the impact of gender constructions on the formation of this tradition. From the uneven number of sources for male and female saints, to representations of women's lives through a priestly male gaze, to questions of power in the making of saints and their acceptance into the liturgical calendar, to how saints come to be remembered, the communion of saints, as the church constitutes it in its liturgical life, is available to us only via gender-specific lenses, asymmetries, and blindspots. Simply accepting this liturgical tradition as given, without attending to how gender has shaped it in the first place, and thereby ignoring its gender-specific contours, will only reinforce the past's gender asymmetries and stereotypes.

In conclusion, I hope to have demonstrated that the liturgical tradition encountered today in the life of the church does not come untouched by gender. Nor did an evil "modern world" first introduce gender troubles into liturgical life. The liturgical tradition itself is deeply gendered, and can only be received in this gender-troubled form. Receiving this tradition—rather than seeking to hold a fantasy of purity unmarred by gender—is an act of faithfulness, both to the church's past and to its present. Maybe the path of the incarnation can help to ground such faithfulness: God did not take on human flesh without also submitting to a gendered life. Born of a woman, God became human in the particularity of a male body.[69] Apart from these gendered realities, no real vision of redemption is to be had.

I suggest that this is good news for the very visible struggles around gender issues in ecclesial life today, be they continuing questions about women's ministries, issues surrounding the full ecclesial life of lesbian, gay, bisexual, transgender, and intersex Christians, popular discussions of the need for a more

---

68   Christopher C. Craun has drawn attention to this in his essay "Matronly Monks: Theodoret of Cyrrhus' Sexual Imagery in the *Historia Religiosa*," in *Holiness and Masculinity in the Middle Ages,* ed. P. H. Cullum and Katherine J. Lewis (Toronto: University of Toronto Press, 2005), 43–57, esp. 49–51. See also Carolyn Diskant Muir, "Bride or Bridegroom? Masculine Identity in Mystic Marriages," in *Holiness and Masculinity in the Middle Ages,* 58–78; she points out that in mystic marriages men imagined themselves as either bride or groom depending on whom they wed (e.g., Christ, Wisdom, or Mary).

69   I am not relapsing into essentialism here; neither should my acknowledgment of Jesus' masculinity be taken as a claim about his chromosomal (XY?) make-up. I also do not wish to deny that Jesus, in his own life, subverted gendered categories. Rather, I here simply grant that those around Jesus perceived and understood him to be born male. Jesus' circumcision, the specific period of Mary's postpartum ritual purification (governed by her child being born male rather than female), and Jesus' crucifixion (a form of punishment apparently not practiced on women) are indicators of this understanding and perception.

"muscular" Christianity in an otherwise "impotent" because "feminized" church, reflections on gender in liturgy today, or discussions of "queer worship."[70] Gender is far from being a mark of *past* liturgical practice only. Contemporary struggles have a genealogy in the life of the church and deserve to be seen as part of this larger whole, namely a history of liturgical life and practice that has never been devoid of gender as both a fundamental given and also as deeply contested. This claim does not prejudge the outcome of these various struggles, but embeds them in an ecclesial tradition of ongoing, complex negotiations over gender and liturgical practice. We may be grateful that the liturgical past also contains its own manifold subversions of established gender arrangements. A fascinating task for liturgical history writing would be to uncover how liturgical subversions have genealogies and form a tradition that also can be claimed.[71] I am thinking here, for example, of the rituals of sworn Christian friendship (same-gender) such as the *Ordo ad fratres faciendum*.[72] That, however, is another story than the one told in the present book.

### Finally, "To Be within the Veil"

I wish to conclude with a return to an early Christian liturgical text. Some of the ancient eucharistic liturgies—most importantly the Egyptian version of the Liturgy of Saint Basil, and the Liturgy of Saint James, rite of the church of Jerusalem[73]—contain a prayer called "The Prayer of the Veil." It marks the movement of clergy from the nave into the sanctuary proper, and immediately precedes the anaphora. In the Greek redaction of the Liturgy of Saint James the text reads as follows:

> We thank Thee, O Lord our God, that Thou hast given us boldness for the entrance of Thy holy places, which Thou hast renewed to us as a new and living way through the veil of the flesh of Thy Christ. We therefore, being counted worthy to enter into the place of the tabernacle of Thy glory, and to be within

---

[70]   See, for example, David Plüss, "Liturgische Präsenz und Geschlecht," in *Theologie und Geschlecht: Dialoge querbeet*, ed. Heike Walz and David Plüss, Theologie und Geschlecht 1 (Berlin: LIT Verlag, 2008), 192–203; and Siobhán Garrigan, "Queer Worship," *Theology and Sexuality* 15 (2009): 211–30.

[71]   I owe this insight to Jordan's essay mentioned above.

[72]   Alan Bray published one fourteenth-century Latin version of such an *Ordo ad fratres faciendum* in his *The Friend* (Chicago: University of Chicago Press, 2003), 130–33. John Boswell first drew attention to such rituals in *Same-Sex Unions in Premodern Europe* (New York: Villiard Books, 1994). Both Boswell's and Bray's studies are discussed in detail in Jordan's essay.

[73]   The relationship between these two liturgies and their different versions continues to occupy liturgical scholars; see, most recently, Gabriele Winkler, "Preliminary Observations about the Relationship between the Liturgies of St. Basil and St. James," *Orientalia Christiana Periodica* 76 (2010): 5–55.

the veil, and to behold the Holy of Holies, cast ourselves down before Thy goodness: Lord, have mercy on us: since we are full of fear and trembling, when about to stand at Thy holy altar.[74]

The Prayer of the Veil is noteworthy on a number of counts. Given that it marks the entry "within the veil," the prayer accompanies the move into the very presence of God.[75] The Prayer of the Veil grounds this liturgical movement in the Incarnation, understood here as a form of God's "taking the veil." Drawing on the Letter to the Hebrews (esp. Heb 10:19–20),[76] the text emphasizes that in Christ Jesus God took on the fabric of human flesh, thereby both revealing and concealing the Divine Presence. When approaching the eucharistic altar, human beings are understood to pass through this "veil of the flesh of Christ" to enter into God's Presence, enclosed, revealed, and concealed "within the veil."[77] The ancient prayer weaves together incarnational and eucharistic language (the Johannine "flesh") with tabernacle and temple terminology.[78] The "boldness" of entering into God's presence harkens back not only to a key New Testament term (e.g., Heb 10:19; 2 Cor 3:12–18) but also to baptismal initiation: It is because of their baptism that the faithful dare to stand before God with boldness and "with unveiled faces"

---

[74]    Liturgy of St. James, Prayer of the Veil. Critical edition of the Greek text, with Latin translation, by B. Ch. Mercier, *La Liturgie de Saint Jacques: édition critique du texte grec avec traduction latine*, Patrologia Orientalis 26.2 (Paris: Firmin-Didot, 1946), 121–256, here 194–7. English translation in ANF 7, 537–50, here 543. A more contemporary English translation, by Archimandrite Ephrem Lash, is available online, at http://web.ukonline.co.uk/ephrem/lit-james.htm.

[75]    In terms of liturgical structures, the prayer is comparable to others that accompany the *accessus ad altare*. More on this in Robert Taft, *The Great Entrance: A History of the Transfer of Gifts and Other Preanaphoral Rites of the Liturgy of St. John Chrysostom*, Orientalia Christiana Analecta 200 (Rome: Pontificium Institutum Studiorum Orientalium, 1975), esp. 356–9.

[76]    For the symbolism of the veil in Hebrews, see Harold W. Attridge, *The Epistle to the Hebrews: A Commentary*, Hermeneia (Minneapolis: Fortress Press, 1989), 184f, 285–7. I do, however, see the reference to "the veil of the flesh of Thy Christ" in the Prayer of the Veil as pointing to Christ's Incarnation rather than his sacrifice on the Cross. Mark A. Jennings has recently argued forcefully that this, indeed, is also the meaning in Heb 10:20 itself; see his essay "The Veil and the High Priestly Robes of the Incarnation: Understanding the Context of Heb 10:20," *Perspectives in Religious Studies* 37 (2010): 85–97.

[77]    Even if the Prayer of the Veil is part of the priestly euchology in this liturgy (rather than that of the whole community), entering within the veil—if one takes *Testamentum Domini* 1.23 as an example—was not reserved to the presider alone but to all members of the clergy. In *Testamentum Domini* this included the bishop, presbyters, deacons, canonical widows, subdeacons, deaconesses, readers, and those with spiritual gifts.

[78]    For one possible reading of this connection, see Margaret Barker, *The Great High Priest: The Temple Roots of Christian Liturgy* (New York: T & T Clark, 2003), esp. 201–12.

(2 Cor 3:18).[79] Whether or not the prayer was linked from the beginning to a liturgical practice (e.g., veiling the altar area and/or the eucharistic elements, or even the veiling of baptizands at a prebaptismal exorcism[80]), its theological affirmation is startling indeed, namely, that human beings are able to encounter the Holy One, not only through a veil, but "within the veil."

*Gender Differences and the Making of Liturgical History* has been about much smaller claims and affirmations. Yet the book shares with this ancient prayer not only the image of veiling but also the conviction that human bodies—in all their gendered particularities—matter in the liturgical encounter with Christ's body, veiled in flesh, and given for all. Most importantly though, this ancient prayer, which is still in use, reminds us that liturgical tradition is not to be found in the past alone. At every Eucharist we approach the Holy One through the "veil of the flesh of Christ," and the same Holy Spirit still empowers human beings to enter boldly into God's presence. This movement of the Holy Spirit, which is the heartbeat of liturgical tradition, is as vibrantly alive today as it was in late antique Jerusalem.

Regarding this claim, however, the knowledge protocols of historiography prove insufficient,[81] and the scholarly tools of a historian must yield to other ways of knowing.

---

[79]   More on this in Robert F. Taft, *A History of the Liturgy of St. John Chrysostom V: The Precommunion Rites*, Orientalia Christiana Analecta 261 (Rome: Pontificio Istituto Orientale, 2000), 131–4.

[80]   The latter is implied in Cyril's *Procatechesis* 9; see St. Cyril of Jerusalem's *Lectures on the Christian Sacraments*, 45.

[81]   I agree with the subaltern historian and theorist Dipesh Chakrabarty that modern cultures of scholarship can, at best, make "gods" and faith interesting topics of study. See Chakrabarty's seminal essay, "The Time of History and the Times of Gods," in *The Politics of Culture in the Shadow of Capital*, eds. Lisa Lowe and David Lloyd (Durham, NC: Duke University Press, 1997), 35–59. Cf. Amy Hollywood, "Gender, Agency, and the Divine in Religious Historiography," *The Journal of Religion* 84 (2004): 514–28.

# Bibliography

*Scripture quotations are taken from The Revised Standard Version unless otherwise stated.*

Abdelsayed, John Paul. "Liturgical Exodus in Reverse: A Reevaluation of the Egyptian Elements in the Jerusalem Liturgy." In *Issues in Eucharistic Praying in East and West: Essays in Liturgical and Theological Analysis*. Edited by Maxwell E. Johnson, 139–59. Collegeville: Liturgical Press, 2010.

Abrahamsen, Valerie. "Lydia." In *Women in Scripture: A Dictionary of Named and Unnamed Women in the Hebrew Bible, the Apocryphal/Deuterocanonical Books, and the New Testament*. Edited by Carol Meyers, Toni Craven, and Ross S. Kraemer, 110–11. Boston: Houghton Mifflin, 2000.

Achtemeier, Paul J. *A Commentary on First Peter*. Hermeneia. Minneapolis: Fortress Press, 1996.

Alberti, Johanna. *Gender and the Historian*. New York: Longman, 2002.

Althoff, Gerd. "The Variability of Rituals in the Middle Ages." In *Medieval Concepts of the Past: Ritual, Memory, Historiography*. Edited by Gerd Althoff et al., 71–87. Publications of the German Historical Institute. New York: Cambridge University Press, 2002.

*Anchoress and Abbess in Ninth-Century Saxony: The* Lives *of Liutbirga of Wendhausen and Hathumoda of Gandersheim*. Translated with an introduction by Frederick S. Paxton. Medieval Texts in Translation. Washington, DC: Catholic University of America Press, 2009.

Andrieu, Michel. *Les* Ordines Romani *du haut moyen âge* 4. Spicilegium Sacrum Lovaniense 28. Louvain: Spicilegium Sacrum Lovaniense Administration, 1956.

Angenendt, Arnold. *Liturgik und Historik. Gab es eine organische Liturgie-Entwicklung?* Quaestiones Disputatae 189. Freiburg i.B.: Herder, 2001.

*The Apostolic Church Order: The Greek Text with Introduction, Translation, and Annotations*. Edited and translated by Alistair Stewart-Sykes. Early Christian Studies 10. Strathfield: St. Pauls [sic] Publications, 2006.

*The Apostolic Tradition: A Commentary*. Edited by Paul F. Bradshaw et al. Hermeneia. Minneapolis: Fortress Press, 2002.

Aston, Margaret. "Segregation in Church." In *Women in the Church*. Edited by W. J. Sheils and Diana Wood, 237–94. Studies in Church History 27. Oxford: Basil Blackwell, 1990.

Attridge, Harold W. *The Epistle to the Hebrews: A Commentary*. Hermeneia. Minneapolis: Fortress Press, 1989.

Augustine. *Confessiones.* CCSL 27. English translation, *The Confessions.* Translated by Maria Boulding. Hyde Park, NY: New City Press, 1997.

——. *De civitate Dei.* CCSL 47–8.

——. *Enarrationes in Psalmos.* CCSL 40. English translation, *Expositions of the Psalms.* Translated by Maria Boulding. 6 volumes. The Works of Saint Augustine III:15–20. Hyde Park, NY: New City Press, 2000–2004.

Bailey, Terence. "Ambrosian Processions to the Baptisteries." *Plainsong and Medieval Music* 15 (2006): 29–42.

Balch, David L., and Carolyn Osiek, eds. *Early Christian Families in Context: An Interdisciplinary Dialogue.* Religion, Marriage, and Family. Grand Rapids, MI: Eerdmans, 2003.

Baldovin, John F. "The Uses of Liturgical History." Pp. 158–73 in *Reforming the Liturgy: A Response to the Critics.* Collegeville: Liturgical Press, 2008.

Barclay, John M. G. "The Family as the Bearer of Religion" In *Constructing Early Christian Families: Family as Social Reality and Metaphor.* Edited by Halvor Moxnes, 66–80. New York: Routledge, 1997.

Barker, Margaret. *The Great High Priest: The Temple Roots of Christian Liturgy.* New York: T & T Clark, 2003.

Baumer, Christoph. "Die Schreinmadonna." *Marian Library Studies* 9 (1977): 239–72.

Baumstark, Anton. *Comparative Liturgy* [*Liturgie comparée*, 3d ed.]. Revised by Bernard Botte, translated by F. L. Cross. Westminster, MD: The Newman Press, 1958.

Beckman, Ninna Edgardh. "Mrs Murphy's Arising from the Pew: Ecclesiological Implications." *The Ecumenical Review* 53 (2001): 5–13.

Bede the Venerable. *Ecclesiastical History of the English People.* Edited by Bertram Colgrave and R. A. B. Mynors. Oxford Medieval Texts. Oxford: Clarendon Press, 1991.

Benedict XVI, Pope. Motu Proprio *Summorum Pontificum,* on the "Roman liturgy prior to the reform of 1970." http://www.usccb.org/liturgy/VISEnglishSummPont.pdf._

Berger, Teresa. *Fragments of Real Presence: Liturgical Traditions in the Hands of Women.* New York: Crossroad, 2005.

——. *Liturgie—Spiegel der Kirche. Eine systematisch-theologische Analyse des liturgischen Gedankenguts im Traktarianismus.* Forschungen zur Systematischen und Ökumenischen Theologie 52. Göttingen: Vandenhoeck & Ruprecht, 1986.

——. *"Liturgie und Frauenseele." Die Liturgische Bewegung aus der Sicht der Frauenforschung.* Praktische Theologie Heute 10. Stuttgart: Kohlhammer Verlag, 1993.

——. *Theology in Hymns? A Study of the Relationship of Doxology and Theology according to "A Collection of Hymns for the Use of the People called Methodists" (1780).* Nashville, TN: Abingdon, 1995.

———. "Women in Worship." In *The Oxford History of Christian Worship*. Edited by Geoffrey Wainwright and Karen B. Westerfield Tucker, 755–68. New York: Oxford University Press, 2005.

———. *Women's Ways of Worship: Gender Analysis and Liturgical History*. Collegeville: Liturgical Press, 1999.

Berger, Teresa, and Albert Gerhards, eds. *Liturgie und Frauenfrage. Ein Beitrag zur Frauenforschung aus liturgiewissenschaftlicher Sicht*. Pietas Liturgica 7. St. Ottilien: EOS-Verlag, 1990.

Bernau, Anke. "Virginal Effects: Texts and Identity in *Ancrene Wisse*." In *Gender and Holiness: Men, Women and Saints in Late Medieval Europe*. Edited by Samantha J. E. Riches and Sarah Salih, 36–48. Routledge Studies in Medieval Religion and Culture. New York: Routledge, 2002.

Betz, Johannes. "Die Eucharistie als Gottes Milch in frühchristlicher Sicht." *Zeitschrift für Katholische Theologie* 106 (1984): 1–26, 167–85.

Bird, Phyllis A. "The Place of Women in the Israelite Cultus." Pp. 81–102 in *Missing Persons and Mistaken Identities: Women and Gender in Ancient Israel*. Overtures to Biblical Theology. Minneapolis: Fortress Press, 1997.

Black, Carlene Villaseñor. "The Moralized Breast in Early Modern Spain." In *The Material Culture of Sex, Procreation, and Marriage in Premodern Europe*. Edited by Anne L. McClanan and Karen Rosoff, 191–219. Encarnación. New York: Palgrave, 2002.

Boswell, John. *Same-Sex Unions in Premodern Europe*. New York: Villiard Books, 1994.

Bowes, Kim. *Private Worship, Public Values, and Religious Change in Late Antiquity*. New York: Cambridge University Press, 2008.

Boyarin, Daniel. *Border Lines: The Partition of Judaeo-Christianity*. Divinations: Rereading Late Ancient Religion. Philadelphia: University of Pennsylvania Press, 2004.

———. "Gender." In *Critical Terms for Religious Studies*. Edited by Mark C. Taylor, 117–35. Chicago: University of Chicago Press, 1998.

Boydston, Jeanne. "Gender as a Question of Historical Analysis." *Gender and History* 20 (2008): 558–83.

Bradshaw, Paul F. "Difficulties in Doing Liturgical Theology." *Pacifica* 11 (1998): 181–94.

———. *Eucharistic Origins*. An Alcuin Club Publication. New York: Oxford University Press, 2004.

———. *Liturgical Presidency in the Early Church*. Grove Liturgical Study 36. Bramcote: Grove Books, 1983.

———. *The Search for the Origins of Christian Worship: Sources and Methods for the Study of Early Liturgy*. 2d ed. New York: Oxford University Press, 2002.

Paul F. Bradshaw, ed. *The Canons of Hippolytus*. Translated by Carol Bebawi. Alcuin/GROW Liturgical Study 2; Grove Liturgical Study 50. Nottingham: Grove Books Limited, 1987.

Bradshaw, Paul F., et al., *The Apostolic Tradition: A Commentary*. Hermeneia. Minneapolis: Fortress Press, 2002.

Brakke, David. "The Problematization of Nocturnal Emissions in Early Christian Syria, Egypt, and Gaul." *Journal of Early Christian Studies* 3 (1995): 419–60.

Brakmann, Heinzgerd. "Ἡ ὑπαπαντὴ τοῦ Κυρίου. Christi Lichtmess im frühchristlichen Jerusalem." In *Crossroad of Cultures: Studies in Liturgy and Patristics in Honor of Gabriele Winkler*. Edited by Hans-Jürgen Feulner et al., 151–72. Orientalia Christiana Analecta 260. Rome: Pontificio Istituto Orientale, 2000.

Bray, Alan. *The Friend*. Chicago: University of Chicago Press, 2003.

Brock, Ann Graham. *Mary Magdalene, The First Apostle: The Struggle for Authority*. Harvard Theological Studies 51. Cambridge, MA: Harvard University Press, 2003.

Brock, Sebastian, and Michael Vasey, eds. *The Liturgical Portions of the Didascalia*. Grove Liturgical Study 29. Bramcote: Grove Books, 1982.

Brooten, Bernadette J. "Junia." In *Women in Scripture: A Dictionary of Named and Unnamed Women in the Hebrew Bible, the Apocryphal/Deuterocanonical Books, and the New Testament*. Edited by Carol Meyers, Toni Craven, and Ross Shepard Kraemer, 107. Boston: Houghton Mifflin Company, 2000.

Browe, Peter. *Beiträge zur Sexualethik des Mittelalters*. Breslauer Studien zur historischen Theologie 23. Breslau: Verlag Müller & Seiffert, 1932.

——. *Die Geschichte der Entmannung. Eine religions- und rechtsgeschichtliche Studie*. Breslauer Studien zur historischen Theologie Neue Folge 1. Breslau: Verlag Müller & Seiffert, 1936.

——. "Die Kommunion der Heiligen im Mittelalter." In *Die Eucharistie im Mittelalter. Liturgiehistorische Forschungen in kulturwissenschaftlicher Absicht*. Edited by Hubertus Lutterbach and Thomas Flammer, 199–209. Vergessene Theologen 1. Münster: LIT Verlag, 2003.

Brown, Peter. *The Body and Society: Men, Women and Sexual Renunciation in Early Christianity*. Columbia Classics in Religion. New York: Columbia University Press, 1988; 20th anniversary ed. 2008.

——. *The Cult of the Saints: Its Rise and Function in Latin Christianity*. Chicago: The University of Chicago Press, 1981.

Burrus, Virginia. *"Begotten, Not Made": Conceiving Manhood in Late Antiquity*. Figurae: Reading Medieval Culture. Stanford, CA: Stanford University Press, 2000.

Bynum, Caroline Walker. "'… And Woman His Humanity': Female Imagery in the Religious Writing of the Later Middle Ages." Pp. 151–79 in *Fragmentation and Redemption: Essays on Gender and the Human Body in Medieval Religion*. New York: Zone Books, 1992; 3d ed. 1994.

Bynum, Caroline Walker. "The Body of Christ in the Later Middle Ages." Pp. 79–117 in *Fragmentation and Redemption: Essays on Gender and the Human Body in Medieval Religion*. New York: Zone Books, 1992; 3d ed. 1994.

Bynum, Caroline Walker. "The Female Body and Religious Practice." Pp. 181–
238 in *Fragmentation and Redemption: Essays on Gender and the Human
Body in Medieval Religion*. New York: Zone Books, 1992; 3d ed. 1994.

Bynum, Caroline Walker. *Holy Feast and Holy Fast: The Religious Significance
of Food to Medieval Women*. Berkeley: University of California Press, 1987.

Bynum, Caroline Walker. "Women Mystics and Eucharistic Devotion." Pp. 119–50
in *Fragmentation and Redemption: Essays on Gender and the Human Body in
Medieval Religion*. New York: Zone Books, 1992; 3d ed. 1994.

Bynum, Caroline Walker. *Wonderful Blood: Theology and Practice in Late
Medieval Northern Germany and Beyond.* Philadelphia: University of
Pennsylvania Press, 2007.

*The Canons of Hippolytus*. Edited by Paul F. Bradshaw, translated by Carol Bebawi.
Alcuin/GROW Liturgical Study 2; Grove Liturgical Study 50. Nottingham:
Grove Books Limited, 1987.

Cardile, Paul Y. "Mary as Priest: Mary's Sacerdotal Position in the Visual Arts."
*Arte Cristiana* 72 (1984): 199–208.

Caspers, Charles, and Marc Schneider, eds. *Omnes Circumadstantes: Contributions
toward a History of the Role of the People in the Liturgy* [Festschrift Herman
Wegman]. Kampen: J. H. Kok, 1990.

Castelli, Elizabeth. "'I Will Make Mary Male': Pieties of the Body and Gender
Transformation of Christian Women in Late Antiquity." In *Body Guards: The
Cultural Politics of Gender Ambiguity*. Edited by Julia Epstein and Kristina
Straub, 29–49. New York: Routledge, 1991.

*Catechism of the Catholic Church*. Vatican City: Libreria Editrice Vaticana;
Washington, DC: United States Catholic Conference, 2d rev. edition 2000.

Chakrabarty, Dipesh. "The Time of History and the Times of Gods." In *The
Politics of Culture in the Shadow of Capital*. Edited by Lisa Lowe and David
Lloyd, 35–59. Durham, NC: Duke University Press, 1997.

Clapton, Nicholas. *Moreschi: The Last Castrato*. London: Haus Publishing, 2004.

Clare of Assisi. *Early Documents.* Edited and translated by Regis J. Armstrong.
Mahwah, NJ: Paulist Press, 1988.

Clark, Anne L. "The Priesthood of the Virgin Mary: Gender Trouble in the Twelfth
Century." *Journal of Feminist Studies in Religion* 18 (2002): 5–24.

Clark, Elizabeth A. *History, Theory, Text: Historians and the Linguistic Turn.*
Cambridge, MA: Harvard University Press, 2004.

——. *Jerome, Chrysostom, and Friends: Essays and Translations.* 2d ed. Studies
in Women and Religion 2. New York: The Edwin Mellen Press, 1979, 1982.

——. *Reading Renunciation: Asceticism and Scripture in Early Christianity.*
Princeton, NJ: Princeton University Press, 1999.

——. "Women, Gender, and the Study of Christian History." *Church History* 70:3
(2001): 395–426.

Clement of Alexandria. *Christ the Educator* [*Paedagogos*]. Translated by Simon
P. Wood. The Fathers of the Church 23. New York: Fathers of the Church, Inc.,
1954.

——. *Stromateis*. Translated by John Ferguson. The Fathers of the Church 85. Washington, DC: Catholic University of America Press, 1991.

Coakley, John W. *Women, Men, and Spiritual Power: Female Saints and Their Male Collaborators*. New York: Columbia University Press, 2006.

Cobb, L. Stephanie. *Dying to Be Men: Gender and Language in Early Christian Martyr Texts*. Gender, Theory, and Religion. New York: Columbia University Press, 2008.

Cohen, Shaye. "Menstruants and the Sacred in Judaism and Christianity." In *Women's History and Ancient History*. Edited by Sarah B. Pomeroy, 273–99. Chapel Hill, NC: University of North Carolina Press, 1991.

Coleman, Janet. *Ancient and Medieval Memories: Studies in the Reconstruction of the Past*. New York: Cambridge University Press, 1992.

Congregation for the Doctrine of the Faith. *Inter Insigniores, On the Question of the Admission of Women to the Ministerial Priesthood* (October 15, 1976). In *The Order of Priesthood: Nine Commentaries on the Vatican Decree "Inter insigniores,"* 1–20. Huntingdon, IN: Our Sunday Visitor, 1978.

——. "Letter to the Bishops of the Catholic Church on the Collaboration of Men and Women in the Church and in the World," http://www.vatican.va/roman_curia/congregations/cfaith/documents/rc_con_cfaith_doc_20040731_collaboration_en.html.

Connerton, Paul. *How Societies Remember*. Themes in the Social Sciences. New York: Cambridge University Press, 1989.

*Les Constitutions Apostoliques. Introduction, texte critique, traduction et notes* 3. Edited by Marcel Metzger. Sources chrétiennes 336. Paris: Les Éditions du Cerf, 1987.

*Constitutiones Apostolorum*. English translation, *Constitutions of the Holy Apostles*. Translated by James Donaldson, ANF 7:391–505.

Coon, Lynda L. *Sacred Fictions: Holy Women and Hagiography in Late Antiquity*. The Middle Ages Series. Philadelphia: University of Pennsylvania Press, 1997.

——. "'What is the Word if not Semen?' Priestly Bodies in Carolingian Exegesis." In *Gender in the Early Medieval World: East and West, 300–900*. Edited by Leslie Brubaker and Julia M. H. Smith, 278–300. New York: Cambridge University Press, 2004.

Corley, Kathleen E. *Maranatha: Women's Funerary Rituals and Christian Origins*. Minneapolis: Fortress Press, 2010.

Corrington, Gail Paterson. "The Milk of Salvation: Redemption by the Mother in Late Antiquity and Early Christianity." *Harvard Theological Review* 82 (1989): 393–420.

Craun, Christopher C. "Matronly Monks: Theodoret of Cyrrhus' Sexual Imagery in the *Historia Religiosa*." In *Holiness and Masculinity in the Middle Ages*. Edited by P. H. Cullum and Katherine J. Lewis, 43–57. Toronto: University of Toronto Press, 2005.

Cressy, David. *Birth, Marriage, and Death: Ritual, Religion, and the Life-Cycle in Tudor and Stuart England*. New York: Oxford University Press, 1997.

Culpepper, R. Alan, ed. *Critical Readings of John 6*. Biblical Interpretation Series 22. New York: Brill, 1997.

Cyprian of Carthage. *Ep.* 75 (from Firmilian). English translation in *Ordained Women in the Early Church: A Documentary History*. Edited by Kevin Madigan and Carolyn Osiek, 181–2. Baltimore, MD: The Johns Hopkins University Press, 2005.

Cyril of Jerusalem. *Procatechesis*. PL 33:33–1180. English translation, together with the Greek text, in *St. Cyril of Jerusalem's Lectures on the Christian Sacraments*. Edited by F. L. Cross, 1–11, 40–52. Crestwood, NY: St Vladimir's Seminary Press, 1986.

Dalarun, Jacques. "Ève, Marie ou Madeleine? La dignité du corps féminin (VIe–XIIe siècles." Pp. 3–21 in *"Dieu changea de sexe, pour ainsi dire." La religion faite femme (XIe–XVe siècle)*. Vita regularis 37. Berlin: LIT-Verlag, 2008.

Dalarun, Jacques et al., eds. *The Two Lives of Robert of Arbrissel, Founder of Fontevraud. Legends, Writings, and Testimonies*. Disciplina Monastica 4. Turnhout, Belgium: Brepols, 2006.

Davies, J. G. *The Secular Use of Church Buildings*. New York: The Seabury Press, 1968.

Davis, Stephen J. *The Cult of Saint Thecla: A Tradition of Women's Piety in Late Antiquity*. Oxford Early Christian Studies. New York: Oxford University Press, 2001.

Deißmann, Marie-Luise. "Jugend." In *Antike Medizin—Ein Lexikon*. Edited by Karl-Heinz Leven, 475–76. München: C. H. Beck, 2005.

Denzey, Nicola. *The Bone Gatherers: The Lost Worlds of Early Christian Women*. Boston: Beacon Press, 2007.

Denziger, Heinrich. *Enchiridion Symbolorum: The Sources of Catholic Dogma*. Translated by Roy J. Deferrari. St. Louis: B. Herder Book Co., 1955.

*The Didascalia Apostolorum: An English Version*. Edited and translated by Alistair Stewart-Sykes. Studia Traditionis Theologiae 1. Turnhout, Belgium: Brepols, 2009.

*Didascalia et Constitutiones Apostolorum* 1. Edited by Franz Xaver Funk. Paderborn: Ferdinand Schöningh, 1905.

Dinzelbacher, Peter. "Rollenverweigerung, religiöser Aufbruch und mystisches Erleben mittelalterlicher Frauen." In *Religiöse Frauenbewegung und mystische Frömmigkeit im Mittelalter*. Edited by Peter Dinzelbacher and D. R. Bauer, 1–58. Cologne: Bohlau, 1988.

Dionysius of Alexandria, *Ep. ad Basilidem*. English translation, *The Epistle to Bishop Basilides*. Translated by S. D. F. Salmond. ANF 6:94–6.

Dix, Gregory. *The Shape of the Liturgy*. Reprint of 2d ed. London: Dacre Press, 1970.

Doig, Allan. *Liturgy and Architecture: From the Early Church to the Middle Ages*. Ashgate Liturgy, Worship and Society Series. Burlington, VT: Ashgate, 2008.

Douglas, Mary. *Purity and Danger: An Analysis of Concepts of Pollution and Taboo*. New York: Praeger, 1966.

Downs, Laura Lee. *Writing Gender History.* Writing History. New York: Oxford University Press, 2004.

Driscoll, Michael S. *"Per Sora Nostra Morte Corporale:* The Role of Medieval Women in Death and Burial Practices." *Liturgical Ministry* 10 (2001): 14–22.

Duffy, Eamon. *Faith of Our Fathers: Reflections on Catholic Tradition.* New York: Continuum, 2004.

———. *Marking the Hours: English People and Their Prayers, 1240–1570.* New Haven, CT: Yale University Press, 2006.

Durandus, William. *The Symbolism of Churches and Church Ornaments: A Translation of the First Book of the* Rationale divinorum officiorum . . . by John Mason Neale. Leeds: T. W. Green, 1843.

Egeria. *Itinerarium.* CCSL 175. English translation, *Diary of a Pilgrimage.* Translated and annotated by George E. Gingras. Ancient Christian Writers 38. New York: Newman Press, 1970.

Eisen, Ute E. *Women Officeholders in Early Christianity: Epigraphical and Literary Studies.* Translated by Linda M. Maloney. Collegeville: Liturgical Press, 2000.

Elliott, Dyan. "Pollution, Illusion, and Masculine Disarray: Nocturnal Emissions and the Sexuality of the Clergy." Pp. 14–34 in *Fallen Bodies: Pollution, Sexuality, and Demonology in the Middle Ages.* The Middle Ages Series. Philadelphia: University of Pennsylvania Press, 1999.

———. "Sex in Holy Places: An Exploration of a Medieval Anxiety." Pp. 61–80 in *Fallen Bodies: Pollution, Sexuality, and Demonology in the Middle Ages.* The Middle Ages Series. Philadelphia: University of Pennsylvania Press, 1999.

Engelbrecht, Edward. "God's Milk: An Orthodox Confession of the Eucharist." *Journal of Early Christian Studies* 7 (1999): 509–26.

Fassler, Margot E. *The Virgin of Chartres: Making History through Liturgy and the Arts.* New Haven, CT: Yale University Press, 2010.

Fausto-Sterling, Anne. *Sexing the Body: Gender Politics and the Construction of Sexuality.* New York: Basic Books, 2000.

Fenster, Thelma. "Why Men?" In *Medieval Masculinities: Regarding Men in the Middle Ages.* Edited by Clare A. Lees et al., IX–XIII. Medieval Cultures 7. Minneapolis: University of Minnesota Press, 1994.

Ferguson, Everett. *Baptism in the Early Church: History, Theology, and Liturgy in the First Five Centuries.* Grand Rapids, MI: Eerdmans, 2009.

Fischer, Balthasar. "Gemeinschaftsgebet in den christlichen Gemeinden und in der christlichen Familie in der alten Christenheit." In *Frömmigkeit der Kirche: Gesammelte Studien zur christlichen Spiritualität.* Edited by Albert Gerhards and Andreas Heinz, 1–17. Hereditas 17. Bonn: Borengässer, 2000.

Flanigan, C. Clifford et al. "Liturgy as Social Performance: Expanding the Definitions." In *The Liturgy of the Medieval Church.* Edited by Thomas J. Heffernan and E. Ann Matter, 695–714. Kalamazoo, MI: Medieval Institute Publications, 2001.

Foley, Edward. *From Age to Age: How Christians Have Celebrated the Eucharist*, rev. and expanded ed. Collegeville: Liturgical Press, 2008.

Fonrobert, Charlotte E. "The *Didascalia Apostolorum:* A Mishnah for the Disciples of Jesus." *Journal of Early Christian Studies* 9 (2001): 483–509.

——. "Gender Identity in Jewish Law." In *Jewish Women: A Comprehensive Historical Encyclopedia* (CD-Rom Edition). Edited by Paula Hyman and Dalia Ofer. Philadelphia: Jewish Publication Society, 2007.

——. *Menstrual Purity: Rabbinic and Christian Reconstructions of Biblical Gender.* Contraversions: Jews and Other Differences. Stanford, CA: Stanford University Press, 2000.

Fox, Ruth. "Women in the Bible and the Lectionary." In *Remembering the Women: Women's Stories from Scripture for Sundays and Festivals.* Compiled and annotated by J. Frank Henderson, 359–67. Chicago: LTP, 1999.

Frank, Hieronymus. "Der älteste erhaltene *Ordo defunctorum* der römischen Liturgie und sein Fortleben in Totenageenden des frühen Mittelalters." *Archiv für Liturgiewissenschaft* 7 (1962): 360–415.

Franz, Adolph. *Die kirchlichen Benediktionen im Mittelalter.* 2 vols. Freiburg i.B.: Herder, 1909; reprint Graz: Akademische Druck- und Verlagsanstalt, 1960.

Friedman, Susan Stanford. *Mappings: Feminism and the Cultural Geographies of Encounter.* Princeton, NJ: Princeton University Press, 1998.

Fulkerson, Mary McClintock. *Places of Redemption: Theology for a Worldly Church.* New York: Oxford University Press, 2007.

Funk, Franz Xaver, ed. *Didascalia et Constitutiones Apostolorum* 1. Paderborn: Ferdinand Schöningh, 1905.

Garrigan, Siobhán. "Queer Worship." *Theology and Sexuality* 15 (2009): 211–30.

Gerbino, Giuseppe. "The Quest for the Soprano Voice: Castrati in Renaissance Italy." *Studi Musicali* 33 (2004): 303–57.

Gerhards, Albert, and Benedikt Kranemann. *Einführung in die Liturgiewissenschaft.* Einführung Theologie. Darmstadt: Wissenschaftliche Buchgesellschaft, 2006.

Gilchrist, Roberta. *Gender and Archaeology: Contesting the Past.* New York: Routledge, 1999.

Glancy, Jennifer A. *Corporal Knowledge: Early Christian Bodies.* New York: Oxford University Press, 2010.

Goltz, Eduard von der. *De virginitate: Eine echte Schrift des Athanasius.* Texte und Untersuchungen zur Geschichte der altchristlichen Literatur Neue Folge 14:2a. Leipzig: J. C. Hinrich'sche Buchhandlung, 1905.

Goodall, Jonathan. "Veil." In *The New Westminster Dictionary of Liturgy & Worship.* Edited by Paul Bradshaw, 463–4. Louisville, KY: Westminster John Knox Press, 2002.

Greer, Allan, and Jodi Bilinkoff, eds. *Colonial Saints: Discovering the Holy in the Americas, 1500–1800.* New York: Routledge, 2003.

Gregory of Nyssa, *The Life of Macrina.* In *Macrina the Younger, Philosopher of God.* Edited by Anna M. Silvas, 109–48. Medieval Women: Texts and Contexts 22. Turnhout, Belgium: Brepols, 2008.

Grimes, Ronald L. "Liturgical Supinity, Liturgical Erectitude: On The Embodiment of Ritual Authority." *Studia Liturgica* 23 (1993): 51–69.

Gudorf, Christine E. "The Erosion of Sexual Dimorphism: Challenges to Religion and Religious Ethics." *Journal of the American Academy of Religion* 69 (2001): 863–91.

Gy, Pierre-Marie. *La liturgie dans l'histoire.* Paris: Editions Saint-Paul, 1990.

———. "Die Segnung von Milch und Honig in der Osternacht." In *Paschatis Sollemnia: Studien zur Osterfeier und zur Osterfrömmmigkeit*, Festschrift Josef Andreas Jungmann. Edited by Balthasar Fischer and Johannes Wagner, 206–12. Freiburg i.B.: Herder, 1959.

Hänggi, Anton, and Irmgard Pahl, eds. *Prex eucharistica: Textus e variis liturgiis antiquioribus selecti.* Spicilegium Friburgense 12. Freiburg, Schweiz: Éditions Universitaires Fribourg Suisse, 1968.

Hanssens, Jean Michel. *La Liturgie d'Hippolyte: Documents et Études.* Rome: Libreria Editrice dell'Università Gregoriana, 1970.

Harrill, J. Albert. "Servile Functionaries or Priestly Leaders? Roman Domestic Religion, Narrative Intertextuality, and Pliny's Reference to Slave Christian *Ministrae* (Ep. 10,96,8)." *Zeitschrift für die neutestamentliche Wissenschaft* 97 (2006): 111–30.

Harris, Max. *Aztecs, Moors, and Christians: Festivals of Reconquest in Mexico and Spain.* Austin, TX: University of Texas Press, 2000.

———. *Carnival and Other Christian Festivals: Folk Theology and Folk Performance.* Austin, TX: University of Texas Press, 2003.

Harrison, Verna E. F. "The Care-Banishing Breast of the Father: Feminine Images of the Divine in Clement of Alexandria's *Paedagogus* I." *Studia Patristica* 31 (1997): 401–5.

Harvey, Susan Ashbrook. "Women in Early Byzantine Hagiography: Reversing the Story." In *That Gentle Strength: Historical Perspectives on Women in Christianity.* Edited by Lynda L. Coon, Katherine J. Haldane, and Elisabeth W. Sommer, 36–59. Charlottesville, VA: University Press of Virginia, 1990.

Hayburn, Robert F., ed. *Papal Legislation on Sacred Music: 95 A.D. to 1977 A.D.* Collegeville: Liturgical Press, 1979.

Hayes, Christine. Review of Fonrobert's *Menstrual Purity. Journal of the History of Sexuality* 10:3–4 (2001): 547–53.

Hayes, Dawn Marie. "Earthly Uses of Heavenly Spaces: Non-Liturgical Activities in Sacred Space." Pp. 53–69 in *Body and Sacred Place in Medieval Europe, 1100–1389.* Studies in Medieval History and Culture 18. New York: Routledge, 2003.

Hildegard of Bingen, *Scivias.* Translated by Mother Columba Hart and Jane Bishop. The Classics of Western Spirituality. New York: Paulist Press, 1990.

Hippolytus. *The Canons*. Edited by Paul F. Bradshaw, translated by Carol Bebawi. Alcuin/GROW Liturgical Study 2; Grove Liturgical Study 50. Nottingham: Grove Books Limited, 1987.

———. *Commentary on the Song of Songs*. In *Traité ... sur le Cantique des cantiques ...* Edited and translated by Gérard Garitte. . Corpus scriptorum christianorum orientalium 263–4. Louvain: Secrétariat du Corpus SCO, 1965.

Hoffman, Lawrence A. *Covenant of Blood: Circumcision and Gender in Rabbinic Judaism*. Chicago Studies in the History of Judaism. Chicago: University of Chicago Press, 1996.

Hollywood, Amy. "Gender, Agency, and the Divine in Religious Historiography." *The Journal of Religion* 84 (2004): 514–28.

Ilan, Tal. *Jewish Women in Greco-Roman Palestine*. Peabody, MA: Hendrickson Publishers, 1996.

Intersex Society of North America. http://www.isna.org.

Irenaeus of Lyons. *Irenaeus against Heresies*. Translated by the editors. ANF 1: 315–567.

James, Liz, ed. *Women, Men, and Eunuchs: Gender in Byzantium*. New York: Routledge, 1997.

Jansen, Katherine Ludwig. *The Making of the Magdalen: Preaching and Popular Devotion in the Later Middle Ages*. Princeton, NJ: Princeton University Press, 2000.

———. "Maria Magdalena: *Apostolorum Apostola*." In *Women Preachers and Prophets through Two Millennia of Christianity*. Edited by Beverly Mayne Kienzle and Pamela J. Walker, 57–96. Berkeley: University of California Press, 1998.

Jasper, R. C. D., and G. J. Cuming, eds. *Prayers of the Eucharist: Early and Reformed*. 3d ed., rev. and enlarged. New York: Pueblo Publishing Company, 1987.

Jeanes, Gordon P. *The Day Has Come! Easter and Baptism in Zeno of Verona*. Alcuin Club Collection 73. Collegeville: Liturgical Press, 1995.

Jeffery, Peter. *Translating Tradition: A Chant Historian Reads* Liturgiam Authenticam. Collegeville: Liturgical Press, 2005.

Jennings, Mark A. "The Veil and the High Priestly Robes of the Incarnation: Understanding the Context of Heb 10:20." *Perspectives in Religious Studies* 37 (2010): 85–97.

Jerome. *Adversus Jovinianum*. English translation, *Against Jovinianus*. Translated by W. H. Fremantle. NPNF 2/6:346–416.

———. *Against Vigilantius*. Translated by W. H. Fremantle. NPNF 2/6:417–23.

———. *Dialogue against the Luciferians*. Translated by W. H. Fremantle. NPNF 2/6: 320–34.

———. *Select Letters*. Translated by F. A. Wright. Loeb Classical Library. Cambridge, MA: Harvard University Press, 1975.

John Chrysostom. *Adversus eos qui apud se habent subintroductas virgines*. PG 47:495–514.

——. *Homiliae in Epist. 2 ad Thesalonicenses*. PG 62: 467–500.

——. *Homiliae in Matthaeum*. PG 57–8.

——. *Laus Maximi et quales luxores ducendae*. PG 51:225–42. English translation, "The Kind of Women Who Ought to be Taken as Wives." In *Women in Early Christianity: Translations from Greek Texts*. Edited by Patricia Cox Miller, 270–72. Washington, DC: The Catholic University of America Press, 2005.

——. *Quod regulares feminae viris cohabitare non debeant*. PG 47:513–32.

John Paul II, Pope. *Mulieris Dignitatem, on the Dignity and Vocation of Women*. http://www.vatican.va/holy_father/john_paul_ii/apost_letters/documents/hf_jp-ii_apl_15081988_-mulieris-dignitatem_en.html.

——. *Ordinatio Sacerdotalis, on Reserving Priestly Ordination to Men Alone*. http://www.vatican.va/holy_father/john_paul_ii/apost_letters/documents/hf_jp-ii_apl_22051994_-ordinatio-sacerdotalis_en.html.

Johnson, Maxwell E. "The Apostolic Tradition." In *The Oxford History of Christian Worship*. Edited by Geoffrey Wainwright and Karen B. Westerfield Tucker, 2–75. New York: Oxford University Press, 2006.

Johnson, Trevor. "Gardening for God: Carmelite Deserts and the Sacralisation of Natural Space in Counter-Reformation Spain." In *Sacred Space in Early Modern Europe*. Edited by Will Coster and Andrew Spicer, 193–210. New York: Cambridge University Press, 2005.

Jordan, Mark D. "Arguing Liturgical Genealogies, or the Ghost of Weddings Past." In *Canon, Tradition, and Critique in the Blessing of Same-Sex Unions*. Edited by Mark D. Jordan et al., 102–20. Princeton, NJ: Princeton University Press, 2006.

Julian of Norwich. *Showings*. Translated by Edmund Colledge and James Walsh. New York: Paulist Press, 1978.

Jungmann, Josef Andreas. *The Mass of the Roman Rite*. 2 vols. Translated by Francis A. Brunner from the rev. German ed. of 1949. New York: Benziger Brothers, 1950.

——. "Was ist Liturgie?" *Zeitschrift für Katholische Liturgie* 55 (1931): 83–102.

Justin Martyr, *Dialogue with Trypho, a Jew*. In *Writings of Saint Justin Martyr*. Translated by Thomas B. Falls, 147–366. The Fathers of the Church 6. New York: Christian Heritage, Inc. 1948.

——. *First Apology*, In *Writings of Saint Justin Martyr*. Translated by Thomas B. Falls, 33–111. The Fathers of the Church 6. New York: Christian Heritage, Inc. 1948.

Kannengiesser, Charles. *Handbook of Patristic Exegesis: The Bible in Ancient Christianity* 1. Boston: Brill, 2004.

Kanter, John, and John Marciari, eds. *Italian Paintings from the Richard L. Feigen Collection*. New Haven, CT: Yale University Press, 2010.

Kavanagh, Aidan. *On Liturgical Theology*. New York: Pueblo, 1984.

Kilmartin, Edward J. "The Baptismal Cups: Revisited." In *Eulogema: Studies in Honor of Robert Taft, S.J.* Edited by Ephrem Carr et al., 249–67. Studia

Anselmiana 110; Analecta liturgica 17. Rome: Pontificio Ateneo S. Anselmo, 1993.

King, Karen L. *The Gospel of Mary of Magdala: Jesus and the First Woman Apostle.* Santa Rosa, CA: Polebridge, 2003.

——. "Prophetic Power and Women's Authority." In *Women Preachers and Prophets through Two Millennia of Christianity.* Edited by Beverly Mayne Kienzle and Pamela J. Walker, 21–41. Berkeley: University of California Press, 1998.

Kinzig, Wolfram et al., eds. *Historiographie und Theologie: Kirchen- und Theologiegeschichte im Spannungsfeld von geschichtswissenschaftlicher Methode und theologischem Anspruch.* Arbeiten zur Kirchen- und Theologiegeschichte 15. Leipzig: Evangelische Verlagsanstalt, 2004.

Kohlschein, Franz. "Zur Geschichte der Liturgiewissenschaft im katholischen deutschsprachigen Bereich." In *Liturgiewissenschaft – Studien zur Wissenschaftsgeschichte.* Edited by Franz Kohlschein and Peter Wünsche, 1–12. Liturgiewissenschaftliche Quellen und Forschungen 78. Münster: Aschendorff, 1996.

König, Jacqueline. "Kastration." In *Antike Medizin—Ein Lexikon.* Edited by Karl-Heinz Leven, 484–6. München: C. H. Beck, 2005.

Konrad von Würzburg, *Die Goldene Schmiede.* Edited by Edward Schröder. Göttingen: Vandenhoeck & Ruprecht, 1926.

Krondorfer, Björn, ed. *Men and Masculinities in Christianity and Judaism: A Critical Reader.* London: SCM Press, 2009.

Kuefler, Mathew. *The Manly Eunuch: Masculinity, Gender Ambiguity, and Christian Ideology in Late Antiquity.* The Chicago Series on Sexuality, History, and Society. Chicago: The University of Chicago Press, 2001.

Laeuchli, Samuel. *Power and Sexuality: The Emergence of Canon Law at the Synod of Elvira.* Philadelphia: Temple University Press, 1972.

Lambin, Rosine A. *Le voile des femmes. Un inventaire historique, social et psychologique.* Studia religiosa Helvetica, Series altera 3. Bern: Peter Lang, 1999.

Larbig, Thorsten, and Siegfried Wiedenhofer, eds. *Tradition and Tradition Theories: An International Discussion.* Berlin: LIT Verlag, 2006.

Larin, Vassa. "What is 'Ritual Im/purity' and Why?" *St. Vladimir's Theological Quarterly* 52 (2008): 275–92.

Lathrop, Gordon. *Holy People: A Liturgical Ecclesiology.* Minneapolis: Fortress Press, 1999.

Lattke, Michael, ed. *Odes of Solomon: A Commentary.* Translated by Marianne Erhardt. Hermeneia. Minneapolis: Fortress Press, 2009.

Laurentin, René. *Maria, Ecclesia, Sacerdotium: Essai sur le développement d'une idée religieuse 1.* Paris: Nouvelles Éditions latines, 1952.

Lechner, Gregor Martin. *Maria Gravida: Zum Schwangerschaftsmotiv in der bildenden Kunst.* Münchner kunsthistorische Abhandlungen. München: Verlag Schnell & Steiner, 1981.

——. "Platyteramonstranzen." In *Marienlexikon* 5. Edited by Remigius Bäumer and Leo Scheffcyzk, 253. St. Ottilien: EOS Verlag, 1993.

——. "Priestertum." In *Marienlexikon* 5. Edited by Remigius Bäumer and Leo Scheffcyzk, 314–18. St. Ottilien: EOS Verlag, 1993.

Leclercq, Henri. "Femme." In *Dictionnaire d'archéologie chrétienne et de liturgie*. Edited by Fernand Cabrol, Henri Leclercq et al., 5/1: 1300–1353. Paris: Letouzey et Ané, 1922.

Leclercq, Jean. "Eucharistic Celebrations without Priests in the Middle Ages." *Worship* 55 (1981): 160–68.

*Lectionary for Mass for Use in the Dioceses of the United States of America*. Second Typical Edition. Collegeville: Liturgical Press, 1998.

Leonard, John K. "Rites of Marriage in the Western Middle Ages." In *Medieval Liturgy: A Book of Essays*. Edited by Lizette Larson-Miller, 165–202. Garland Medieval Casebooks 18. New York: Garland Publishing, 1997.

Leyerle, Blake. *Theatrical Shows and Ascetic Lives: John Chrysostom's Attack on Spiritual Marriage*. Berkeley: University of California Press, 2001.

Lies, Lothar. "Zur Eucharistielehre des Johannes Betz (1914–1984)." *Zeitschrift für katholische Theologie* 128 (2006): 53–80.

Lifshitz, Felice. "The Martyr, the Tomb and the Matron: Constructing the (Masculine) Past as a Female Power Base." In *Medieval Concepts of the Past: Ritual, Memory, Historiography*. Edited by P. Geary, G. Althoff, and J. Fried, 311–41. Cambridge: Cambridge University Press, 2002.

Liturgy of St. James. In *La Liturgie de Saint Jacques: édition critique du texte grec avec traduction latine*. Edited by B. Ch. Mercier, 121–256. Patrologia Orientalis 26.2. Paris: Firmin-Didot, 1946. English translation in ANF 7, 537–50.

Lurz, Friedrich. *Erlebte Liturgie. Autobiographische Schriften als liturgiewissenschaftliche Quellen*. Ästhetik Theologie Liturgik 28. Münster: LIT Verlag, 2003.

Lutterbach, Hubertus. *Sexualität im Mittelalter. Eine Kulturstudie anhand von Bußbüchern des 6. bis 12. Jahrhunderts*. Beihefte zum Archiv für Kulturgeschichte 43. Köln: Böhlau Verlag, 1999.

Lyman, Rebecca. "Lex orandi: Heresy, Orthodoxy, and Popular Religion." In *The Making and Remaking of Christian Doctrine*. Edited by Sarah Coakley and David A. Pailin, 131–41. Oxford: Clarendon Press, 1993.

MacDonald, Margaret Y. *Early Christian Women and Pagan Opinion: The Power of the Hysterical Woman*. Cambridge: Cambridge University Press, 1996.

——. "Was Celsus Right? The Role of Women in the Expansion of Early Christianity." In *Early Christian Families in Context: An Interdisciplinary Dialogue*. Edited by David L. Balch and Carolyn Osiek. Religion, Marriage, and Family, 157–84. Grand Rapids, MI: Eerdmans, 2003.

McDowell, Linda. *Gender, Identity and Place: Understanding Feminist Geographies*. Minneapolis: University of Minnesota Press, 1999.

McGinn, Bernard. *The Doctors of the Church: Thirty-Three Men and Women Who Shaped Christianity*. New York: Crossroad, 1999.

McGowan, Andrew. *Ascetic Eucharists: Food and Drink in Early Christian Ritual Meals*. Oxford Early Christian Studies. Oxford: Clarendon Press, 1999.

McKee, Elsie Anne. "Katharina Schütz Zell and the 'Our Father'." In *Oratio. Das Gebet in patristischer und reformatorischer Sicht*. Edited by Emidio Campi et al., 239–47. Forschungen zur Kirchen- und Dogmengeschichte 76. Göttingen: Vandenhoeck & Ruprecht, 1999.

MacMullen, Ramsay. *Christianizing the Roman Empire (A.D. 100–400)*. New Haven, CT: Yale University Press, 1984.

——. *The Second Church: Popular Christianity A.D. 200–400*. SBL Writings from the Greco-Roman World Supplement Series 1. Atlanta: Society of Biblical Literature, 2009.

Macy, Gary. "The Future of the Past: What Can the [sic] History Say about Symbol and Ritual?" In *Practicing Catholic: Ritual, Body, and Contestation in Catholic Faith*. Edited by Bruce T. Morrill, 29–41. Gordonsville, VA: Palgrave Macmillan, 2006.

——. *The Hidden History of Women's Ordination: Female Clergy in the Medieval West*. New York: Oxford University Press, 2008.

——. *Treasures from the Storeroom: Medieval Religion and the Eucharist*. Collegeville: Liturgical Press, 1999.

Madigan, Kevin, and Carolyn Osiek, eds. and trans. *Ordained Women in the Early Church: A Documentary History*. Baltimore: The Johns Hopkins University Press, 2005.

Maguire, Eunice Dauterman et al. *Art and Holy Powers in the Early Christian House*. Illinois Byzantine Studies 2. Urbana and Chicago: Krannert Art Museum and University of Illinois Press, 1989.

Maier, Christl M. *Daughter Zion, Mother Zion: Gender, Space, and the Sacred in Ancient Israel*. Minneapolis: Fortress Press, 2008.

Maier, Harry O. "Heresy, Households, and the Disciplining of Diversity." In *Late Ancient Christianity*. Edited by Virginia Burrus, 213–33. A People's History of Christianity 2. Minneapolis: Fortress Press, 2005.

Marinis, Vasileos, ed. and trans. "The Life of St. Anna/Euphemianos." *Journal of Modern Hellenism* 27 (2009/2010): 53–69.

Marshall, Paul V. "Reconsidering 'Liturgical Theology': Is There a *Lex Orandi* for All Christians?" *Studia Liturgica* 25 (1995): 129–51.

Mathews, Thomas F. "An Early Roman Chancel Arrangement and its Liturgical Functions." *Rivista di Archeologia Cristiana* 38 (1962): 73–95.

Mattila, Sharon Lea. "Where Women Sat in Ancient Synagogues: The Archaeological Evidence in Context." In *Voluntary Associations in the Graeco-Roman World*. Edited by John S. Kloppenborg and Stephen G. Wilson, 266–86. New York: Routledge, 1996.

Maxwell, Jaclyn. "Lay Piety in the Sermons of John Chrysostom." In *Byzantine Christianity*. Edited by Derek Krueger, 19–38. A People's History of Christianity 3. Minneapolis: Fortress Press, 2006.

Mayer, Wendy. "The Dynamics of Liturgical Space: Aspects of the Interaction between St John Chrysostom and his Audiences." *Ephemerides Liturgicae* 111 (1997): 104–15.

———. "Female Participation and the Late Fourth-Century Preacher's Audience." *Augustinianum* 39 (1999): 139–47.

Mayer, Wendy, and Pauline Allen. *John Chrysostom*. The Early Church Fathers. New York: Routledge, 2000.

Meens, Rob. "Ritual Purity and the Influence of Gregory the Great in the Early Middle Ages." In *Unity and Diversity in the Church*. Edited by R. N. Swanson, 31–43. Studies in Church History 32. Cambridge, MA: Blackwell, 1996.

Messner, Reinhard. "Zur Eucharistie in den Thomasakten: Zugleich ein Beitrag zur Frühgeschichte der eucharistischen Epiklese." In *Crossroad of Cultures: Studies in Liturgy and Patristics in Honor of Gabriele Winkler*. Edited by Hans-Jürgen Feulner et al. Orientalia Christiana Analecta 260, 493–513. Rome: Pontificio Istituto Orientale, 2000.

———. "Grundlinien der Entwicklung des eucharistischen Gebets in der frühen Kirche." In *Prex Eucharistica* 3/1. Edited by Albert Gerhards et al., 3–40. Spicilegium Friburgense 42. Freiburg, Schweiz: Academic Press Fribourg, 2005.

———. "Über einige Aufgaben der Erforschung der Liturgiegeschichte der frühen Kirche." *Archiv für Liturgiewissenschaft* 50 (2008): 207–30.

———. "Die vielen gottesdienstlichen Überlieferungen und die eine liturgische Tradition." In *Liturgische Theologie: Aufgaben systematischer Liturgiewissenschaft*. Edited by Helmut Hoping and Birgit Jeggle-Merz, 33–56. Paderborn: Schöningh, 2004.

Methuen, Charlotte. "'For Pagans Laugh to Hear Women Teach': Gender Stereotypes in the *Didascalia Apostolorum*." *Studies in Church History* 34 (1998): 23–35.

Metzger, Marcel, ed. *Les Constitutions Apostoliques. Introduction, texte critique, traduction et notes* 3. Sources chrétiennes 336. Paris: Les Éditions du Cerf, 1987.

———. "Pages féminines des *Constitutions Apostoliques*." In *Crossroad of Cultures: Studies in Liturgy and Patristics in Honor of Gabriele Winkler*. Edited by Hans-Jürgen Feulner et al., 515–41. Orientalia Christiana Analecta 260. Rome: Pontificio Istituto Orientale, 2000.

Meyers, Carol. "Having Their Space and Eating There Too: Bread Production and Female Power in Ancient Israelite Households." *Nashim: A Journal of Jewish Women's Studies and Gender Issues* 5 (2002): 14–44.

———. *Households and Holiness: The Religious Culture of Israelite Women*. Minneapolis: Fortress Press, 2005.

Meyers, Eric M. "The Problems of Gendered Space in Syro-Palestinian Domestic Architecture: The Case of Roman-Period Galilee." In *Early Christian Families in Context: An Interdisciplinary Dialogue*. Edited by David L. Balch and

Carolyn Osiek, 44–69. Religion, Marriage, and Family series. Grand Rapids, MI: Eerdmans, 2003.

Milavec, Aaron, ed. *The Didache: Text, Translation, Analysis, and Commentary.* Collegeville: Liturgical Press, 2003.

Miles, Margaret R. *A Complex Delight: The Secularization of the Breast 1350–1750.* Berkeley: University of California Press, 2008.

——. "Infancy, Parenting, and Nourishment in Augustine's *Confessions.*" *The Journal of the American Academy of Religion* 50 (1982): 349–64.

Miller, Patricia Cox, ed. *Women in Early Christianity: Translations from Greek Texts.* Washington, DC: Catholic University of America Press, 2005.

Miller, Patrick D. "Things Too Wonderful: Prayers of Women in the Old Testament." In *Biblische Theologie und gesellschaftlicher Wandel.* Edited by Georg Braulik et al., 237–51. Freiburg i.B.: Herder, 1993.

Miller, Vincent. *Consuming Religion: Christian Faith and Practice in a Consumer Culture.* New York: Continuum, 2005.

Mockridge, Diane L. "Marital Imagery in Six Late Twelfth- and Early Thirteenth-Century Vitae of Female Saints." In *That Gentle Strength: Historical Perspectives on Women in Christianity.* Edited by Lynda L. Coon, Katherine J. Haldane, and Elisabeth W. Sommer, 60–78. Charlottesville, VA: University Press of Virginia, 1990.

Mooney, Catherine M. "Voice, Gender, and the Portrayal of Sanctity." In *Gendered Voices: Medieval Saints and Their Interpreters.* Edited by Catherine M. Mooney, 1–15. The Middle Ages Series. Philadelphia: University of Pennsylvania Press, 1999.

Moran, Neil. "Byzantine Castrati." *Plainsong and Medieval Music* 11 (2002): 99–112.

More, Thomas. *Thomas More's Prayer Book: A Facsimile Reproduction of the Annotated Pages.* Edited by Louis L. Martz and Richard S. Sylvester. The Elizabethan Club Series 4. New Haven, CT: Yale University Press, for the Elizabethan Club, 1969.

Morgan, Sue, ed. *The Feminist History Reader.* New York: Routledge, 2006.

Morrill, Bruce T., ed. *Bodies of Worship: Explorations in Theory and Practice.* Collegeville: Liturgical Press, 1999.

Moxnes, Halvor, ed. *Constructing Early Christian Families: Family as Social Reality and Metaphor.* New York: Routledge, 1997.

Muessig, Carolyn. "Paradigms of Sanctity for Thirteenth-Century Women." In *Models of Holiness in Medieval Sermons: Proceedings of the International Symposium (Kalamazoo, 4–7 May 1995).* Edited by Beverly Mayne Kienzle et al., 85–102. Textes et études du Moyen Age 5. Louvain-la-Neuve: Fédération internationale des instituts d'études médiévales, 1996.

Muir, Carolyn Diskant. "Bride or Bridegroom? Masculine Identity in Mystic Marriages." In *Holiness and Masculinity in the Middle Ages.* Edited by P. H. Cullum and Katherine J. Lewis, 58–78. Toronto: University of Toronto Press, 2005.

Mulder-Bakker, Anneke B., and Jocelyn Wogan-Browne, eds. *Household, Women, and Christianities in Late Antiquity and the Middle Ages.* Medieval Women: Texts and Contexts 14. Turnhout, Belgium: Brepols, 2005.

Murray, Jacqueline. "Masculinizing Religious Life: Sexual Prowess, the Battle for Chastity and Monastic Identity." In *Holiness and Masculinity in the Middle Ages.* Edited by P. H. Cullum and Katherine J. Lewis, 24–42. Toronto: University of Toronto Press, 2004.

Muschiol, Gisela. *Famula Dei. Zur Liturgie in merowingischen Frauenklöstern.* Beiträge zur Geschichte des alten Mönchtums und des Benediktinerordens 41. Münster: Aschendorff, 1994.

——. "Liturgie und Klausur. Zu den liturgischen Voraussetzungen von Nonnenemporen." In *Studien zum Kanonissenstift.* Edited by Irene Crusius, 129–48. Studien zur Germania Sacra 24. Göttingen: Vandenhoeck & Ruprecht, 2001.

——. "Men, Women and Liturgical Practice in the Early Medieval West." In *Gender in the Early Medieval World: East and West, 300–900.* Edited by Leslie Brubaker and Julia M. H. Smith, 198–216. New York: Cambridge University Press, 2004.

——. "Time and Space: Liturgy and Rite in Female Monasteries of the Middle Ages." In *Crown and Veil: Female Monasticism from the Fifth to the Fifteenth Centuries.* Edited by Jeffrey F. Hamburger and Susan Marti; translated by Dietlinde Hamburger, 191–206. New York: Columbia University Press, 2008.

——. "Wer braucht den Drachentöter noch? Heiligenlegenden nach der Revision des römischen Kalenders." *Diakonia* 31 (2000): 127–31.

Muth, Robert. "Kastration." In *Reallexikon für Antike und Christentum* 20. Edited by Georg Schöllgen et al., 285–342. Stuttgart: Anton Hiersemann, 2004.

Myers, Susan E. *Spirit Epicleses in the* Acts of Thomas. Wissenschaftliche Untersuchungen zum Neuen Testament II, 281. Tübingen: Mohr Siebeck, 2010.

Neureiter, Livia. "John Chrysostom's Treatises on Spiritual Marriage." *Studia Patristica* 41 (2006): 457–62.

Newman, John Henry. *Hymni Ecclesiae e Breviario Parisiensi.* Oxford: Parker, 1838.

Nye, Robert A. "Sexuality." In *A Companion to Gender History.* Edited by Teresa A. Meade and Merry E. Wiesner-Hanks, 11–25. Blackwell Companions to History. Malden, MA: Blackwell Publishing, 2004.

Økland, Jorunn. *Women in Their Place: Paul and the Corinthian Discourse of Gender and Sanctuary Space.* JSNTSup 269. New York: T&T Clark, 2004.

Opitz, Claudia. *Um-Ordnungen der Geschlechter: Einführung in die Geschlechtergeschichte.* Historische Einführungen 10. Tübingen: Edition Diskord, 2005.

Origen. *Fragmenta e catenis in Epistulam primam ad Corinthios.* Edited by Claude Jenkins. *Journal of Theological Studies* 9 (1908): 500–514, and 10 (1909): 29–51.

——. *Homilies on Leviticus, 1–16*. Translated by Gary Wayne Barkley. The Fathers of the Church: A New Translation 83. Washington, DC: The Catholic University of America Press, 1990.

——. *Homilies on Numbers*. Edited by Christopher A. Hall; translated by Thomas P. Scheck. Ancient Christian Texts. Downers Grove, IL: IVP Academic, 2009.

Orsi, Robert A. *Thank You, St. Jude: Women's Devotion to the Patron Saint of Hopeless Causes*. New Haven, CT: Yale University Press, 1996.

Osiek, Carolyn, and Margaret Y. MacDonald, with Janet H. Tulloch. "Women Leaders of Households and Christian Assemblies." Pp. 144–63 in *A Woman's Place: House Churches in Earliest Christianity*. Minneapolis: Fortress, 2006.

Pacik, Rudolf. "Josef Andreas Jungmann: Liturgiegeschichtliche Forschung als Mittel religiöser Reform." *Liturgisches Jahrbuch* 43 (1993): 62–84.

Pahl, Irmgard. "'Eine starke Frau, wer wird sie finden?' Aspekte des Frauenbildes in den Meßformularen der Heiligenfeste." In *Liturgie und Frauenfrage: Ein Beitrag zur Frauenforschung aus liturgiewissenschaftlicher Sicht*. Edited by Teresa Berger and Albert Gerhards, 433–52. Pietas Liturgica 7. St. Ottilien: EOS-Verlag, 1990.

Palmer, William. *Origines Liturgicae, or, Antiquities of the English Ritual: And a Dissertation on Primitive Liturgies*. Oxford: At the University Press, 1832.

Payer, Pierre J. *Sex and the Penitentials: The Development of a Sexual Code 550–1150*. Toronto: University of Toronto Press, 1984.

Percival, Henry R., ed. *The Seven Ecumenical Councils of the Undivided Church, Their Canons and Dogmatic Decrees, Together with the Canons of All the Local Synods Which Have Received Ecumenical Acceptance*. NPNF 2.14.

Pierce, Joanne M. "'Green Women' and Blood Pollution: Some Medieval Rituals for the Churching of Women after Childbirth." *Studia Liturgica* 29 (1999): 191–215.

Pius X, Pope. *Tra le Sollecitudini*. English translation in Robert F. Hayburn, *Papal Legislation on Sacred Music: 95 A.D. to 1977 A.D.*, 223–31. Collegeville: Liturgical Press, 1979.

Plüss, David. "Liturgische Präsenz und Geschlecht." In *Theologie und Geschlecht: Dialoge querbeet*. Edited by Heike Walz and David Plüss, 192–203. Theologie und Geschlecht 1. Berlin: LIT Verlag, 2008.

Pock, Johannes. "Der Priester als 'Mann Gottes'. Die Bedeutung des Geschlechts für das katholische Priesterverständnis." In *Geschlecht quer gedacht. Widerstandspotentiale und Gestaltungsmöglich-keiten in kirchlicher Praxis*. Edited by M. E. Aigner and J. Pock, 227–40. Werkstatt Theologie 13. Vienna: LIT, 2009.

Procter-Smith, Marjorie. *In Her Own Rite: Constructing Feminist Liturgical Tradition*. Nashville: Abingdon Press, 1990.

——. *Women in Shaker Community and Worship: A Feminist Analysis of the Uses of Religious Symbolism*. Lewiston, NY: E. Mellen Press, 1985.

*Protoevangelium of James*. English translation in *The Infancy Gospels of James and Thomas*. Edited by Ronald F. Hock, 31–77. The Scholars Bible 2. Santa Rosa, CA: Polebridge Press, 1995.

[Ps-]Epiphanius. "Homilia V in Laudes Sanctae Mariae Deiparae." PG 43:485–502.

Rahner, Hugo. *Symbole der Kirche: Die Ekklesiologie der Väter*. Salzburg: Otto Müller Verlag, 1964.

Riches, Samantha J. E. "St. George as a Male Virgin Martyr." In *Gender and Holiness: Men, Women, and Saints in Late Medieval Europe*. Edited by Samantha J. E. Riches and Sarah Salih, 65–85. Routledge Studies in Medieval Religion and Culture 1. New York: Routledge, 2002.

Riches, Samantha J. E., and Sarah Salih, eds. *Gender and Holiness: Men, Women and Saints in Late Medieval Europe*. Routledge Studies in Medieval Religion and Culture. New York: Routledge, 2002.

Ricoeur, Paul. *Freud and Philosophy: An Essay on Interpretation*. New Haven, CT: Yale University Press, 1970.

Rieder, Paula. *On the Purification of Women: Churching in Northern France, 1100–1500*. The New Middle Ages. New York: Palgrave Macmillan, 2006.

Ringrose, Kathryn M. *The Perfect Servant: Eunuchs and the Social Construction of Gender in Byzantium*. Chicago: The University of Chicago Press, 2003.

*RitualSong: A Hymnal and Service Book for Roman Catholics*. Chicago: GIA Publications, 1996.

Rivard, Derek A. *Blessing the World: Ritual and Lay Piety in Medieval Religion*. Washington, DC: The Catholic University of America Press, 2009.

Roll, Susan. "The Churching of Women after Childbirth: An Old Rite Raising New Issues." *Questions Liturgiques* 76 (1995): 206–29.

Rouwhorst, Gerard. "Leviticus 12–15 in Early Christianity." In *Purity and Holiness: The Heritage of Leviticus*. Edited by M. J. H. M. Poorthuis and J. Schwartz, 181–93. Jewish and Christian Perspectives Series. Boston: Brill, 2000.

Rubin, Miri. *Corpus Christi: The Eucharist in Late Medieval Culture*. New York: Cambridge University Press, 1991.

Rupert of Deutz. *Liber de divinis officiis*. Edited by Helmut and Ilse Deutz. Fontes Christiani: Zweisprachige Neuausgabe christlicher Quellentexte 33:1–4. Freiburg i.B.: Herder, 1999.

Ruschmann, Susanne. *Maria von Magdala im Johannesevangelium: Jüngerin— Zeugin—Lebensbotin*. Neutestamentliche Abhandlungen n.F. 40. Münster: Aschendorff, 2002.

Salih, Sarah. "Staging Conversion: The Digby Saint Plays and *The Book of Margery Kempe*." In *Gender and Holiness: Men, Women, and Saints in Late Medieval Europe*. Edited by Samantha J. E. Riches and Sarah Salih, 121–34. Routledge Studies in Medieval Religion and Culture 1. New York: Routledge, 2002.

Saller, Richard. "Women, Slaves, and the Economy of the Roman Household." In *Early Christian Families in Context: An Interdisciplinary Dialogue*. Edited by

David L. Balch and Carolyn Osiek, 185–204. Religion, Marriage, and Family. Grand Rapids, MI: Eerdmans, 2003.

Schäfer, Daniel. "Geburt." In *Antike Medizin—Ein Lexikon*. Edited by Karl-Heinz Leven, 327–9. München: C. H. Beck, 2005.

Schleif, Corine. "Men on the Right—Women on the Left: (A)Symmetrical Spaces and Gendered Places." In *Women's Space: Patronage, Place, and Gender in the Medieval Church*. Edited by Virginia Chieffo Raguin and Sarah Stanbury, 207–49. SUNY Series in Medieval Studies. Albany, NY: State University of New York Press, 2005.

Schmidt, Hans-Joachim."Geschichte und Prophetie: Rezeption der Texte Hildegards von Bingen im 13. Jahrhundert." In *Hildegard von Bingen in ihrem historischen Umfeld*. Edited by Alfred Haverkamp, 489–517. Mainz: Verlag Philipp von Zabern, 2000.

Schulenburg, Jane Tibbetts. "Gender, Celibacy, and Proscriptions of Sacred Space: Symbol and Practice." In *Women's Space. Patronage, Place, and Gender in the Medieval Church*. Edited by Virginia Chieffo Raguin and Sarah Stanbury, 185–205. SUNY Series in Medieval Studies. Albany, NY: State University of New York Press, 2005.

———. "Women's Monasteries and Sacred Space: The Promotion of Saints' Cults and Miracles." In *Gender and Christianity in Medieval Europe: New Perspectives*. Edited by Lisa M. Bitel and Felice Lifshitz, 68–86. The Middle Ages Series. Philadelphia: University of Pennsylvania Press, 2008.

Schwiebert, Jonathan. *Knowledge and the Coming Kingdom: The* Didache's *Meal Ritual and its Place in Early Christianity*. Library of New Testament Studies 373. London: T & T Clark, 2008.

Scott, Joan Wallach. "Gender: A Useful Category of Historical Analysis." *American Historical Review* 91 (1986): 1053–75.

Selhorst, Heinrich. *Die Platzordnung im Gläubigenraum der altchristlichen Kirche*. Münster: Aschendorff, 1931.

Senn, Frank C. *The People's Work: A Social History of the Liturgy*. Minneapolis: Fortress Press, 2006.

*The Seven Ecumenical Councils of the Undivided Church, Their Canons and Dogmatic Decrees, Together with the Canons of All the Local Synods Which Have Received Ecumenical Acceptance*. Edited by Henry R. Percival. NPNF 2.14.

Shail, Andrew, and Gillian Howie, eds. *Menstruation: A Cultural History*. New York: Palgrave Macmillan, 2005.

Shaw, Teresa M., translator. "Pseudo-Athanasius: *Discourse on Salvation to a Virgin*." In *Religions of Late Antiquity in Practice*. Edited by Richard Valantasis, 82–99. Princeton Readings in Religion. Princeton, NJ: Princeton University Press, 2000.

Signori, Gabriela. *Räume, Gesten, Andachtsformen: Geschlecht, Konflikt und religiöse Kultur im Mittelalter*. Ostfildern: Jan Thorbecke Verlag, 2005.

Silvas, Anna M., ed. *Macrina the Younger, Philosopher of God.* Medieval Women: Texts and Contexts 22. Turnhout, Belgium: Brepols, 2008.

Sivan. Hagith. "Holy Land Pilgrimage and Western Audiences: Some Reflections on Egeria and her Circle." *Classical Quarterly* 38 (1988): 528–35.

———. "Who was Egeria? Piety and Pilgrimage in the Age of Gratian." *Harvard Theological Review* 81 (1988): 59–72.

Smith, Bonnie G. *The Gender of History: Men, Women, and Historical Practice.* Cambridge, MA: Harvard University Press, 1998.

Smith, Julia M. H. *Europe after Rome: A New Cultural History, 500-1000.* New York: Oxford University Press, 2005.

———. "Women at the Tomb: Access to Relic Shrines in the Early Middle Ages." In *The World of Gregory of Tours.* Edited by Kathleen Mitchell and Ian Wood, 161–80. Cultures, Beliefs and Traditions: Medieval and Early Modern Peoples 8. Boston: Brill, 2002.

Spieser, Jean-Michel. "Ambrose's Foundations at Milan and the Question of Martyria." Chap. 7 in *Urban and Religious Spaces in Late Antiquity and Early Byzantium.* Variorum Collected Studies Series. Burlington, VT: Ashgate, 2001.

*The St. Albans Psalter.* Studies of the Warburg Institute 25. Leiden: E. J. Brill, 1960.

Stevenson, Walter. "Eunuchs and Early Christianity." In *Eunuchs in Antiquity and Beyond.* Edited by Shaun Tougher, 123–42. London: The Classical Press of Wales and Duckworth, 2002.

Stewart-Sykes, Alistair, ed. and trans. *The Apostolic Church Order: The Greek Text with Introduction, Translation, and Annotations.* Early Christian Studies 10. Strathfield: St. Pauls [sic] Publications, 2006.

———. *The Didascalia Apostolorum: An English Version.* Studia Traditionis Theologiae 1. Turnhout, Belgium: Brepols, 2009.

Stringer, Martin D. *A Sociological History of Christian Worship.* New York: Cambridge University Press, 2005.

Strocchia, Sharon T. "When the Bishop Married the Abbess: Masculinity and Power in Florentine Episcopal Entry Rites, 1300–1600." *Gender & History* 19 (2007): 346–68.

Strotmann, Angelika. "Die göttliche Weisheit als Nahrungsspenderin, Gastgeberin und sich selbst anbietende Speise." In *"Eine gewöhnliche und harmlose Speise?" Von den Entwicklungen frühchristlicher Abendmahlstraditionen.* Edited by Judith Hartenstein et al., 131–56. Gütersloh: Gütersloher Verlagshaus, 2008.

Swancutt, Diana. "Hungers Assuaged by the Bread from Heaven. 'Eating Jesus' as Isaian Call to Belief: The Confluence of Isaiah 55 and Psalm 78(77) in John 6.22–71." In *Early Christian Interpretation of the Scriptures of Israel: Investigations and Proposals.* Edited by Craig A. Evans and James A. Sanders, 218–51. Journal for the Study of the New Testament, Supplement series 148. Sheffield: Sheffield Academic Press, 1997.

Taft, Robert F. *Beyond East and West: Problems in Liturgical Understanding.* 2d ed. Rome: Edizioni Orientalia Christiana, Pontifical Oriental Institute, 2001.

——. *The Great Entrance: A History of the Transfer of Gifts and other Preanaphoral Rites of the Liturgy of St. John Chrysostom.* Orientalia Christiana Analecta 200. Rome: Pontificium Institutum Studiorum Orientalium, 1975.

——. *A History of the Liturgy of St. John Chrysostom V: The Precommunion Rites.* Orientalia Christiana Analecta 261. Rome: Pontificio Istituto Orientale, 2000.

——. "Home-Communion in the Late Antique East." In *Ars Liturgiae: Worship, Aesthetics and Praxis.* Festschrift Nathan D. Mitchell. Edited by Clare V. Johnson, 1–25. Chicago: Liturgy Training Publications, 2003.

——. *The Liturgy of the Hours in East and West: The Origins of the Divine Office and Its Meaning for Today.* Collegeville: Liturgical Press, 1986; 2d rev. ed. 1993.

——. "St. John Chrysostom, Preacher Committed to the Seriousness of Worship." In *The Serious Business of Worship: Essays in Honour of Bryan D. Spinks.* Edited by Melanie Ross and Simon Jones, 13–21. New York: Continuum, 2010.

——. *Through Their Own Eyes: Liturgy as the Byzantines Saw It.* Berkeley, CA: InterOrthodox Press, 2006.

——. "Women at Church in Byzantium: Glimpses of a Lost World." *Bollettino della Badia Greca di Grottaferrata series* 3/6 (2009): 255–86.

——. "Women at Church in Byzantium: Where, When—and Why?" *Dumbarton Oaks Papers* 52 (1998): 27–87. Reprinted as chapter 1 in *Divine Liturgies – Human Problems in Byzantium, Armenia, Syria, and Palestine.* Collected Studies 716. Burlington, VT: Ashgate, 2001.

Taft, Robert F., and Gabriele Winkler, eds. *Comparative Liturgy Fifty Years after Anton Baumstark (1872–1948).* Orientalia Christiana Analecta 265. Rome: Pontificio Istituto Orientale, 2001.

Tanner, Kathryn. *Theories of Culture: A New Agenda for Theology.* Guides to Theological Inquiry Series. Minneapolis: Fortress Press, 1997.

Taschl-Erber, Andrea. *Maria von Magdala—Erste Apostolin? Joh 20,1–18: Tradition und Relecture.* Herder's Biblical Studies 51. New York: Herder, 2007.

Teresa of Avila. "Meditations on the Song of Songs". In *The Collected Works of St. Teresa of Avila* 2. Translated by Kieran Kavanaugh and Otilio Rodriguez, 244f. Washington, DC: Institute of Carmelite Studies, 1980.

——. "Nada te turbe." In *The Collected Works of St. Teresa of Avila* 3. Translated by Kieran Kavanaugh and Otilio Rodriguez, 386. Washington, DC: Institute of Carmelite Studies, 1985.

Tertullian, *De Exhortatione castitatis.* English translation in *Treatises on Marriage and Remarriage.* Translated by William P. Le Saint, 42–64. Ancient Christian Writers 13. Westminster, MD: Newman Press, 1951.

Thibodeaux, Jennifer D. "Man of the Church, or Man of the Village? Gender and the Parish Clergy in Medieval Normandy." *Gender & History* 18 (2006): 380–99.

Tilley, Terrence W. *History, Theology, and Faith: Dissolving the Modern Problematic.* Maryknoll, NY: Orbis Books, 2004.

———. *Inventing Catholic Tradition.* Maryknoll, NY: Orbis Books, 2000.

Timothy of Alexandria, *Canonical Answers.* Greek text (with French translation) in *Discipline Générale Antique* 2. Edited by Périclès-Pierre Joannou, 240–58. Fonti 9. Grottaferrata: Tipografia Italo-Orientale S. Nilo, 1963.

Torjesen, Karen Jo. *When Women Were Priests: Women's Leadership in the Early Church and the Scandal of their Subordination in the Rise of Christianity.* San Francisco, CA: HarperCollins, 1993.

Tougher, Shaun, ed. *Eunuchs in Antiquity and Beyond.* London: The Classical Press of Wales and Duckworth, 2002.

"Holy Eunuchs! Masculinity and Eunuch Saints in Byzantium" In *Holiness and Masculinity in the Middle Ages.* Edited by P. H. Cullum and Katherine J. Lewis, 93–108. Toronto: University of Toronto Press, 2005.

Tougher, Shaun, ed. *Eunuchs in Antiquity and Beyond.* London: The Classical Press of Wales and Duckworth, 2002.

Tulloch, Janet H. "Women Leaders in Family Funerary Banquets." In *A Woman's Place: House Churches in Earliest Christianity.* Edited by Carolyn Osiek and Margaret Y. MacDonald, with Janet H. Tulloch, 164–93. Minneapolis: Fortress, 2006.

Wallis Budge, E. A., trans. *The Book of the Cave of Treasures.* English translation of the Syriac *Spelunca Thesaurorum.* London: The Religious Tract Society, 1927.

Webb, Diana. "Domestic Space and Devotion." In *Defining the Holy: Sacred Space in Medieval and Early Modern Europe.* Edited by Andrew Spicer and Sarah Hamilton, 27–47. Burlington, VT: Ashgate, 2005.

Webster, Jane S. *Ingesting Jesus: Eating and Drinking in the Gospel of John.* Academia Biblica 6. Atlanta: Society of Biblical Literature, 2003.

Wendebourg, Dorothea. "Die alttestamentlichen Reinheitsgesetze in der frühen Kirche." *Zeitschrift für Kirchengeschichte* 95 (1984): 149–69.

West, Fritz. *The Comparative Liturgy of Anton Baumstark.* Alcuin Club and Group for Renewal of Worship Joint Liturgical Studies 31. Bramcote: Grove Books, 1995.

Whalen, Michael D. "In the Company of Women? The Politics of Memory in the Liturgical Commemoration of Saints—Male and Female." *Worship* 73 (1999): 482–504.

Whitaker, E. C. *Documents of the Baptismal Liturgy.* Rev. and expanded ed. Edited by Maxwell E. Johnson. London: SPCK, 2003.

White, L. Michael. *The Social Origins of Christian Architecture* 2. Harvard Theological Studies 42. Valley Forge, PA: Trinity Press International, 1997.

White, Susan J. *A History of Women in Christian Worship*. Cleveland: Pilgrim Press, 2003.

Williams, Rowan. *Why Study the Past? The Quest for the Historical Church*. Sarum Theological Lectures. London: Darton, Longman and Todd, 2005.

Winkler, Gabriel. "Preliminary Observations about the Relationship between the Liturgies of St. Basil and St. James." *Orientalia Christiana Periodica* 76 (2010): 5–55.

Wogan-Browne, Jocelyn. *Saints' Lives and Women's Literary Culture, c. 1150–1300: Virginity and its Authorizations*. New York: Oxford University Press, 2001.

Wright, J. Robert, ed. *Ancient Christian Commentary on Scripture: Old Testament* 9. Downers Grove, IL: InterVarsity Press, 2005.

Zeno of Verona. *Baptismal Homilies*. In Gordon P. Jeanes, *The Day Has Come! Easter and Baptism in Zeno of Verona*. Alcuin Club Collection 73, 54–99. Collegeville: Liturgical Press, 1995.

Zomer, Hiltje F. H. "The so-called Women's Gallery in the Medieval Church: An Import from Byzantium." In *The Empress Theophano: Byzantium and the West at the Turn of the First Millennium*. Edited by Adelbert Davids, 290–306. New York: Cambridge University Press, 1995.

# Scripture Index

# General Index

Abdelsayed, John Paul, 102n
Abelard, 157n
Abrahamsen, Valerie, 49n
Achtemeier, Paul J., 74n
*Acta Sanctorum*, 10
*Acts of Thecla*, 37–8
*Acts of Thomas*, 68n
Aelred of Rievaulx, 86
*agape*, 69, 90
Albert the Great, 149
Alberti, Johanna, 24n
Allen, Pauline, 22n, 57
Althoff, Gerd, 9n, 63n
Ambrose of Milan, 63–4, 145
*anamnesis*, 12, 33, 166
Andreas of Fontevraud, 3
Andrieu, Michel, 40n
Angenendt, Arnold, 8n, 13
Anna, mother of Mary, 100, 121–2
*Annales* school, 13, 15
Antony the Great, 111
*Apostolic Church Order*, 139–40, 141–2
*Apostolic Constitutions,* 54n, 109
    and bodily flows, 106–7, 110, 117, 123
    and the eucharistic liturgy, 89–91
    and eunuchs, 134, 146
    and gender, 57–60
*Apostolic Tradition,* xv, 80n, 91n, 134, 145
    and bodily flows, 98, 117–18, 123–4
    and gender separation, 54–5, 58, 59
    and milk and honey cup, 81–3
    and veils, xiv n
ascetic cohabitation, 21–2
ascetic life, 109, 141
ascetic men, 21–2
ascetic women, 22, 61, 88, 92–3
Aston, Margaret, 56n
Athanasius, 111–12
Athanasius, pseudo-, 88, 92
Attridge, Harold W., 181n

Augustine of Canterbury, 107–8, 113,
    119n, 124–5
Augustine of Hippo, 57n, 58, 64, 78–9,
    112, 148
authorizing claims, xv, 4–7, 129, 155, 160,
    165, 167–70
*Ave Verum Corpus,* 154

Bailey, Terence, 58n
Baldovin, John F., 161–2
baptism, 50, 58, 65, 73, 81, 83, 181
    of eunuchs, 61
    as new birth, 73–4, 76, 85
    of women, and men, 54, 100–102,
    103–5, 162
Barclay, John M. G., 47n
Barker, Margaret, 181n
Basil of Ancyra, 145
Basilides, Bishop, 102–3, 110–11
Batiffol, Pierre, 92n
Baumer, Christoph, 153n
Baumstark, Anton, 9, 13–14
Beckman, Ninna Edgardh, 169n
Bede the Venerable, 107n, 113n, 119n,
    125n
Bell, John L., 166
Benedict XVI, 160
Benvenuta, 152
Bernard of Clairvaux, 157n
Bernau, Anke, 30n
Berquist, Jon L., 2
Betz, Johannes, 73–4, 76n, 79, 80–81
Bible, 45–7, 71–2, 99–100, 104, 114, 121,
    166, 173
Bieritz, Karl-Heinrich, 18
Bird, Phyllis A., 45n
birth-giving, 76, 80, 83, 97, 99, 121–5,
    161, 162, 164
bishops, 52, 102, 132, 142–3, 171, 176
Black, Carlene Villaseñor, 86n

Congregation for the Doctrine of the Faith, 25n, 129n
Connerton, Paul, 170
continence, 116, 138, 141–5, 147
convents, 9, 23, 56
Coon, Lynda L., 151n, 178n
Cooper, Kate, 49n
Corley, Kathleen E., 63n
Corpus Christi, feast of, 2, 13n, 153
Corrington, Gail Paterson, 73n
Council of Carthage, 84n
Council of Constantinople, 102
Council of Elvira, 142–3
Council of Gangra, 92n, 117, 163
Council of Nicaea, 143n, 145–6
Council of Trent, 65
Craun, Christopher C., 147n, 179n
Cyprian of Carthage, 131
Cyril of Alexandria, 145
Cyril of Jerusalem, xiii n, 58–60, 162, 182n

daily prayers, 44, 88
Dalarun, Jacques, 1n, 4n
Darwin, Charles, 14
Davies, J. G., 44n
Davis, Stephen J., 37n, 38n, 51–2
*De virginitate*, 88–92, 98
deaconesses, 37–9, 55, 59, 181
Deir Balyzeh fragments, 91
Deißmann, Marie-Luise, 133n
Denzey, Nicola, 63n
Derrida, Jacques, 27
Dhuoda, 18
*Didache,* 53, 59, 72, 89–91, 130–31
*Didascalia Apostolorum,* xiv n, 52–5, 58, 59, 103–7, 110, 114, 117, 123, 133
"difference," 25
Dinzelbacher, Peter, 153n
Dionysius of Alexandria, 102–3, 105, 108, 100–111, 116
Dioscorus, 111
*Discourse on Salvation to a Virgin*, see *De virginitate*
Dix, Gregory, 9, 14, 90
*doctores ecclesiae*, 176
Doig, Allan, 50n
Dorotheus, 137
Douglas, Mary, 98n

Downs, Laura Lee, 24n
Driscoll, Michael S., 41n
Duffy, Eamon, 5n, 95n, 170
Dura-Europos, 50, 64
Durandus of Mende, 10n

Egeria, 18, 37–40, 51, 52
Egypt
    liturgy, 91, 102, 112, 180
    monasticism, 111–12
Eisen, Ute E., 129n, 131n, 132nn
Elizabeth of Schönau, 152
Elizabeth of Thuringia, xiv
Elliott, Dyan, 114n
emissions of semen, xv, 35, 97, 101n, 105, 109–14, 125, 141
Engelbrecht, Edward, 73n, 76n, 85n
Epiphanius of Salamis, 145, 148
episcopacy, *see* bishops
*Epistle of Barnabas,* 73, 79n
Ethiopian eunuch, 29, 61, 135–6
Eucharist, 6, 46, 50, 55, 65, 90–93, 147–50, 153, 154, 182
    ascetic, 89
    and baptism, 31, 73, 76, 80–85, 88, 101n
    and bodily flows, 102–8, 111–13, 119, 141
    and gender, 11, 55, 68–80, 131, 139–40
    as God's milk, 31, 72–9, 86–7
    practice, 1, 4, 12, 70
    reception, 11–12
Eugene III, 149
eunuchs, xiii, xv, 5, 22, 29, 31, 61–2, 64, 126, 133–8, 171, 177
    by forced castration, 146
    liturgical presence, 133–8, 141, 143n, 145–61, 171
    by nature, 134–5, 136, 137, 146–7
    religious (*galli*), 136
    as title of honor, 138
    by voluntary castration, 135, 145–6
Eusebius, 137, 145n
Eustathius of Sebaste, 117
Evagrius of Ponticus, 111
exorcisms, xiii, 65, 162
Eyck, Jan van, 152
Ezekiel, 100